ROUTLEDGE LIBRARY EDITIONS: INEQUALITY

Volume 2

THE INHERITANCE OF INEQUALITY

THE INHERITANCE OF INEQUALITY

LEONARD BROOM,
F. L. JONES,
PATRICK McDONNELL
and TREVOR WILLIAMS

Routledge
Taylor & Francis Group

LONDON AND NEW YORK

First published in 1980 by Routledge & Kegan Paul Ltd

This edition first published in 2023
by Routledge
4 Park Square, Milton Park, Abingdon, Oxon OX14 4RN

and by Routledge
605 Third Avenue, New York, NY 10158

Routledge is an imprint of the Taylor & Francis Group, an informa business

British Library Cataloguing in Publication Data
A catalogue record for this book is available from the British Library

ISBN: 978-1-032-43329-5 (Set)
ISBN: 978-1-032-43378-3 (Volume 2) (hbk)
ISBN: 978-1-032-43380-6 (Volume 2) (pbk)
ISBN: 978-1-003-36704-8 (Volume 2) (ebk)

DOI: 10.4324/9781003367048

Publisher's Note
The publisher has gone to great lengths to ensure the quality of this reprint but points out that some imperfections in the original copies may be apparent.

Disclaimer
The publisher has made every effort to trace copyright holders and would welcome correspondence from those they have been unable to trace.

The inheritance of inequality

Leonard Broom
F. L. Jones
Patrick McDonnell
Trevor Williams

Routledge & Kegan Paul
London, Boston and Henley

First published in 1980
by Routledge & Kegan Paul Ltd
39 Store Street, London WC1E 7DD,
Broadway House, Newtown Road,
Henley-on-Thames, Oxon RG9 1EN and
9 Park Street, Boston, Mass. 02108, USA
Photoset in 10 on 11pt Times by
Kelly Typesetting Ltd, Bradford-on-Avon, Wiltshire
and printed in Great Britain by
Redwood Burn Ltd,
Trowbridge and Esher

British Library Cataloguing in Publication Data

The inheritance of inequality. – (International
library of sociology).
1. Social structure – Australia
2. Australia – Social conditions
I. Broom, Leonard II. Series
301.4'00994   HN843.5   79–41296

ISBN 0 7100 0345 5

Contents

Foreword

The great American sociologist Charles Horton Cooley, in his book *Social Process* published in 1918, devoted a chapter to the topic 'Opportunity and Class' which opens with the sentence: 'All societies are more or less stratified into classes, based on differences in wealth, occupation and enlightenment, which tend to be passed on from parents to children; and this stratification creates and perpetuates difference in opportunity' (p. 78). It is to the further examination of this proposition that research of the genre reported in this book is devoted.

Although Cooley and several of his sociological contemporaries wrote perceptively about social stratification, the development of systematic research on this subject may be said to have received its greatest impetus from the publication of Pitirim Sorokin's great classic, *Social Mobility*, in 1928. In this book Sorokin not only developed a systematic theory of social mobility but also examined the evidence on the transmission of occupation from fathers to sons using whatever data he could find for western societies, including an empirical study he and his students made in Minneapolis. He concluded from this analysis that, although all of the data indicated that there was a good deal of occupational inheritance, there was evidence also of considerable occupational mobility in all of the samples studied.

Sorokin went on to examine the data, particularly from the Minneapolis study, to discern trends in the transmission of occupations across generations, the nature and the extent of upward and downward occupational mobility, and several related questions. He arrived at a number of tentative conclusions that he believed should be tested on larger and more representative samples. We need not be concerned here with the details of Sorokin's analysis or his findings, other than to say that he mapped the course that the systematic study of social mobility was to follow for the next half century.

The landmark studies in the Sorokin tradition would include at least the following monographs: Natalie Rogoff, *Recent Trends in Occupational Mobility* (1953); D. V. Glass, *Social Mobility in Britain* (1954); Gosta Carlsson, *Social Mobility and Class Structure* (1958); Kaare Svalastoga, *Prestige, Class, and Mobility* (1959); Peter M. Blau and Otis Dudley Duncan, *American Occupational Structure* (1967); and David L. Featherman and Robert M. Hauser, *Opportunity and Change* (1978). Of all of these the most influential was certainly the Blau and Duncan volume; first, because it was by far the most thorough examination of father-son occupational transmission ever attempted on a large and well-designed national sample; and, second, because it introduced a new and imaginative way of examining social mobility as a process of status attainment.

Blau and Duncan viewed status attainment as a process that develops over the life cycle of the individual and is dependent not only on one's social origins but also on one's own characteristics and experiences that intervene between origin and destination statuses. Using data from a 1962 sample survey of employed males in the United States, they estimated a causal model of status attainment beginning with the educational and occupational status of the father, followed by the son's education, the son's first job, and ending with the son's current occupation. This model provided a quantitative assessment of the antecedent conditions of socio-economic achievement and of the relative importance of social origins and educational attainment for later socioeconomic achievements. It is not necessary to summarize here the many findings resulting from their application of this basic model to various age cohorts and subpopulations. Actually these may be less important than the approach and methodology that lie behind the basic model.

The publication of the *American Occupational Structure* stimulated renewed interest in the study of social mobility throughout the world. The Blau–Duncan basic model has been employed in numerous studies in the United States and in other nations. Many of these studies have focused on the replication of the basic model, using other cross-sectional findings, especially where comparable measurements have been employed. Still others have modified the basic model by incorporating other variables believed to be important in the status attainment process and by extending the model to include other socioeconomic outcomes (Duncan, Featherman and Duncan 1972; Sewell *et al.*, 1969, 1970; Sewell and Hauser, 1972, 1975).

The Inheritance of Inequality is the most extensive study of stratification and social mobility in the status attainment tradition thus far reported for any national population other than the United States. The analysis reported in this volume is based on data collected in a national survey, conducted in 1973, in Australia. Although data were obtained for both men and women, the results reported in this particular book are only for male respondents.

The analysis begins with the Blau–Duncan model expanded to include additional family origin variables, a broader conceptualization of education, occupations at the beginning, middle and current stages of the working career, and current earnings. Having established the explanatory power of this model for their sample, the authors then test for group differences to detect variations in the status attainment process of language and nationality groups, occupational categories, rural and urban residents and migrant and non-migrant groups. They then examine the specific links in the chain of status transmission, including the link between education and first occupation, the dynamics of occupational careers, the occupational and economic rewards to early attainment, and finally, inheritance of inequality over three generations: grandfathers, sons, and grandsons and daughters.

All of this analysis is carefully done and well integrated with current theoretical developments in the field of social stratification. This book is important not only because it contributes greatly to knowledge about social stratification and mobility in Australia but also because it adds significantly to our general knowledge concerning the status attainment process.

Madison
March 1979

William H. Sewell
Vilas Research Professor
University of Wisconsin

Preface

The discipline of sociology was late to arrive in Australian universities. The first two departments were established only in 1959 and 1961, first at the University of New South Wales and later in the Research School of Social Sciences at the Australian National University. It is, therefore, hardly surprising that in the mid-1960s there was a dearth of systematic analysis of Australia's social structure. In 1965 we began, with the collaboration of Jerzy Zubrzycki, a long-term program of research into the social stratification of Australia, beginning with a nationwide sample survey.

The findings from that survey along with related research were published between 1968 and 1976 in a series of papers and in a book listed in the references to the present work. The first survey (1965) had slender financial support, but since we were convinced of the merits of a national sample, we opted for brief interviews and for the male workforce as the target population. In 1973 we were able to expand both our aims and our budget, and to include women as primary respondents and subjects, in a more ambitious national sample survey (1973) which is the basis of the present study.

The place of our research in the growing body of knowledge about stratification in Australia and in some comparable nations is outlined in the first chapters of both this book and an earlier monograph (Broom *et al.*, 1977a). The present monograph is largely restricted to men. Parallel reports on women, the retirement process and other findings from the survey are planned for separate publication. Our larger sample and more detailed information on social background and occupational careers open up a wider range of issues and alternative analytic strategies compared with our earlier work.

Inevitably social changes have already overtaken the historical context within which the ANU 1973 survey was conducted. We do not believe it is the task of sociology to issue the latest news flashes but it should be noted that interviewing was conducted just before major changes in Australian social history. If the survey had taken place a few years later we would have encountered a different Australia, with higher unemployment and higher inflation, and an Australia that had experienced an unprecedented constitutional crisis with the dismissal in November 1975 of the Whitlam Government. These events, and others, limit the currency of the analysis presented here in ways that we and our readers can only guess at.

The principal investigators in the 1973 survey were Paul Duncan-Jones, Patrick J. McDonnell, Trevor Williams and ourselves. McDonnell participated in all aspects of the research from July 1972 until October 1978 as did Duncan-Jones from July 1972 until December 1975. Williams was engaged in the project from February 1976 until May 1978. All of us were involved in other research while working on this study.

Ms Betty Gamble prepared the tabular materials for publications. Throughout the research she contributed far more than her meticulous secretarial services. Ms Vivien Read prepared the text for automated printing. The following research workers were associated with the project for extended periods: Ms Michele Robertson, Ms Judy Dillon, Ms Bevis King, Ms Beverley Delly, Mr Patrick Keogh and Mr David Carrick. To all these, to others who worked for briefer periods, to our interviewers, and to our respondents, we express our appreciation.

Canberra   Leonard Broom
February 1979   F. L. Jones

1 Introduction

This volume is part of a long-term program of research, which began in the mid-1960s, into the social differentiation and stratification of Australian society. A summary volume (Broom and Jones, 1976) reports many of the findings from the first stages of this program, which was based in part on a brief national sample survey conducted in 1965. Subsequently the studies were extended and diversified. In 1973 a second and more ambitious national survey on social mobility and social stratification was undertaken.[1] This book deals exclusively with selected findings from that survey and is the first of several intended reports. Background and technical papers on the survey may be found in Broom *et al.* (1977a, b, c; 1978a, b).

The ANU 1973 survey had three major objectives: first, to replicate the 1965 baseline study of Australian stratification and mobility and further to redress the slender body of information on the topics in this country; second, to broaden understanding of social mobility and social stratification in Australia beyond the restricted findings of the 1965 baseline, not only by including more details on family background, education and class images, but also by including women as respondents in their own right; and third, to enhance the opportunities for comparison with national surveys in other countries.

Similar research on a national scale has been actively pursued since 1949 (e.g., Glass, 1954; Carlsson, 1958; Svalastoga, 1959) and has developed rapidly in scope and method. The earlier studies culminated in 1962 with a large survey of the United States (Blau and Duncan, 1967), and are sometimes referred to as the 'first generation' of national mobility studies. The ANU 1965 survey belongs in this category and was concerned in part to assess the degree of openness of Australian society. The 1973 survey is one of a growing number of second-generation studies (Broom and

1

McDonnell, 1974/7), which attempt to measure the role of family inheritance versus the role of individual achievement.

The first-generation studies described openness as the relative chances that men from different social strata had to move into another social stratum over the course of their working lives. The standard analytic approach was the outflow mobility table, showing how far or how little sons had moved from their social origins (as measured by father's occupation) during their own occupational careers. The central methodological problem in most of these studies was to determine how to measure the degree of openness in the society as a whole, and how to compare the relative rigidity of different social strata or occupational groupings.

Family inheritance or individual achievement?

A concern with equality of opportunity and societal openness or rigidity still remains an important issue for most contemporary research, but the current method and analytic style are more individualistic. Among the typical questions now asked are the following: How far do social origins, favourable or unfavourable, affect the educational and occupational careers of men and women? To what extent are social inequalities inherited from one generation to the next? How far does the educational system reproduce existing inequalities and how far does it provide an avenue for individual mobility? These questions are usually answered in terms of a methodology that estimates the relative impact of social origins and early achievement on status attainment over the socioeconomic life-cycle, and also the relative importance of ascription versus achievement in the process of stratification from generation to generation. There is now fair consensus among investigators in this field of research about how to go about answering such questions, although, as we shall see, interpretations of empirical findings differ substantially.

The twin concepts of family inheritance versus personal achievement are more easily distinguished in principle than in practice. The basic opposition between them revolves around the notion of choice: persons cannot choose their family of origin but can exercise some choice over the paths they follow later in life. If inheritance, broadly defined to include not merely material inheritance but also mental, physical and social skills, were the sole basis for allocating social roles across generations, social inequalities would be routinely reproduced from one period to the next. We evaluate such a hypothetical model with empirical data in our last chapter.

A particular society might attempt to break the nexus between generations by eliminating the inheritance of wealth and providing compensatory environments designed to equalize the unearned fortune, or misfortune, of membership in a particular family. A broad contrast can be drawn between a society where outcomes are largely given at the start (the unfolding of a predetermined social pattern) and a society where who gets what is emergent and contingent on individual abilities and performance that are conditioned by opportunity and realized through experience (cf. Brittain, 1977, pp. 2–5). Societies embody the principles of inheritance and individual achievement to varying degrees, and how a particular society should be characterized in terms of their relative strength is a matter of heated debate. It is instructive that for the United States, the best documented of Western societies, all the logically possible combinations of inheritance and achievement have been advanced over the last decade as correct portrayals of its stratification regime.

Blau and Duncan, for example, found less evidence of ascription than achievement. They judged that family background had a smaller influence on occupational achievement than did formal education and concluded that in general the United States approached a type of society that 'perpetuates a structure of differentiated positions but not their inheritance' (1967, p. 441). That interpretation has not gone unchallenged, but paradoxically it has been criticized on mutually contradictory grounds by scholars claiming to espouse a socialist or Marxist perspective. Thus, Jencks and his colleagues argued that status attainment models contributed little to explaining inequalities in schooling, social status or income (1972, p. 253), and that *neither* inheritance *nor* achievement much influenced who got what. To them, the workings of American society seemed to approximate a giant lottery where chance factors largely determined who became rich and who became poor. They therefore urged a direct attack to reduce inequalities in social and economic institutions: 'This is what other countries usually call socialism' (1972, p. 265).

Bowles (1972), on the other hand, asserted that conventional models of status attainment grossly understated the real extent of social inheritance, and exaggerated the role of achievement in the transmission of inequality from generation to generation for two main reasons. First, the analytic models most commonly used did not take adequate account of important aspects of social background such as family income, parental wealth and the position of parents in the hierarchy of work relations. Therefore the influence of family background on a child's schooling was understated. Second, Bowles argued that there were more serious errors in the retrospective, proxy reports given by children about their family origins than in current or recent reports of the respondent's own status, and that these greater errors also led to understating both the impact of social origins on schooling and later achievement and the rigidity of stratification (1972, p. 223). In short, unlike Blau and Duncan, Bowles saw inheritance as considerably more important than achievement.

On the one hand, Jencks argues that inequalities, and especially inequalities in earned income, cannot be adequately explained by the conventional models used by sociologists: 'Economic success seems to depend on varieties of luck and on-the-job competence that are only moderately related to family background, schooling or scores on standardized tests' (1972, p. 8). On the other hand, Bowles (1972) claims that in a capitalist society the transmission of inequality from generation to generation is much more highly structured than conventional analyses suggests. In a later study he and Gintis conclude that the educational system does not reduce inequality but serves fundamentally to legitimate 'economic inequality and the smooth staffing of unequal work roles' (1976, p. 108) and to reproduce 'the prevailing class structure of society' (1976, p. 126). In short, achievement is largely disguised inheritance.

In yet another interpretation, Brittain (1977) adopts a broad definition of inheritance which includes all those characteristics (genetic, social, environmental and material) that the children in a particular family share. According to his account, based mainly on a small sample of brothers in an American city, 'the overall degree of inheritance of economic status [is] very substantial'. If there are elements of Jencks's lottery in the allocation of economic rewards, 'it is as though the lottery gave discounts to participants with privileged socioeconomic backgrounds' (Brittain, 1977, p. 17). Both advantage and disadvantage tend to be inherited. But there are other factors at work as well, and educational achievement is not simply a function of inheritance. Brittain's findings 'indicate a strong influence of socioeconomic background on the economic status of men and women, *and* a substantial effect of educational attainment that is independent of background' (1977, p. 3). In the analyses that follow, we incline to an interpretation that is closer to Brittain than to any of the other three positions identified.

Stratification versus class analysis

In national studies of social inequality there is opposition between what may be broadly described as the liberal-democratic stratification perspective on the one hand and a neo-Marxist class perspective on the other (for an Australian example of the latter, see Connell, 1977, pp. 26, 183). These two stances are distinguishable on several counts. First, they stem from different substantive literatures with little agreement about what is to be explained or how explanation should proceed. They employ different terminology and different methods. Becker, for example, in his opening remarks on Bowles's 1972 paper referred to above, expresses this generalized antithesis when he rejects the term social class in favour of the more neutral term family background: 'its meaning [social class] is obscure and . . . its recent use in economics has impeded clear thinking' (Becker, 1972, p. S252).

Another general, although not universal, difference between the two approaches is that most Marxist writing tends to be historical and conceptual, in the sense of devoting more attention to elaborating distinctions than to establishing their empirical cash value. Stratification research on the other hand tends to be empirical and quantitative, to use mass survey data, both cross-sectional and longitudinal, and to employ concepts that can be fairly readily operationalized to test competing theoretical interpretations.

Finally, the rhetoric and postures adopted are quite different. As might be expected, Marxist authors tend to call for total reconstruction and a new society. Stratification theorists, when they turn from social analysis to social criticism, tend to be meliorist in tone. There is nothing in Blau and Duncan, for example, to compare with Bowles's and Gintis's conclusion to their first chapter (1976, p. 17):

A revolutionary transformation of social life will not simply happen through piecemeal change. Rather, we believe it will occur only as a result of a prolonged struggle based on hope and a total vision of a qualitatively new society, waged by those social classes and groups who stand to benefit from the new era.

Blau and Duncan do at points express a concern with the policy implications of their research but they offer no program for change. Their approach to change is one of piecemeal adaptation rather than a radical transformation of society. Their very general suggestions about the need to break the 'vicious cycle' of disadvantage that affects black Americans would hardly satisfy radical or many other commentators, nor would their general conclusion: 'the American occupational structure is largely governed by universalistic criteria of performance and achievement, with the notable exception of the influence of race' (Blau and Duncan, 1967, p. 241). Brittain, however, who is also meliorist, devotes more attention to social policies that might serve to reduce the extent of both inheritance and inequality (1977, pp. 28–34).

It is not our purpose to review here the fields of stratification research or class analysis, either in Australia or elsewhere. We have touched on some of these issues in the volume dealing with the mid-1960s (Broom and Jones, 1976), and a more comprehensive overview awaits the completion of our present research. In this book we accept the main elements of the status attainment approach as a set of research and interpretive strategies, without endorsing every viewpoint or proposition espoused by those who identify themselves with that perspective. By the same token, we do not reject outright the insights of Marxist writers, let alone concede to them a monopoly of concern with the human condition. The implications of a choice between revolutionary change and piecemeal reform are not exhausted merely by announcing the need for new social arrangements without specifying how such changes are to be achieved. We do not aim to write either a non-Marxist manifesto or a capitalist apologia. Our selective comments on other writers serve simply to identify our position in relation to other macro-sociological approaches. There are, of course, points where our analysis and findings engage specific issues that separate different schools of thought, such as the question dealt with in the final chapter of whether and in what sense contemporary Australia can be said to approximate a class society.

Our findings on the inheritance of inequality are susceptible to a variety of policy interpretations, but in this book we set ourselves the limited but necessary task of improving the evidential basis for wider debate, not that of raising the temperature of people and views before the evidence is in. We turn now to developing the conceptual basis of our approach and to specifying the range of topics with which this volume is concerned. We have no illusions that either our findings or our strategy will satisfy anyone committed to an entrenched view. Nevertheless, what *is* can be distinguished from what *might be*, and from what *should be*. For the present we confine ourselves to a descriptive and explanatory account of processes of status attainment in contemporary Australia.

Stratification and inequality

There have been numerous attempts to specify the central concepts and issues involved in status attainment research, and what follows draws together common threads in discussions by Duncan (1968), Haller (1970), Haller and Portes (1973) and Jones (1975). Although terminology varies, the general conceptual orientations are similar.

A first distinction needs to be made between social differentiation, social inequality and social stratification. All human societies are functionally differentiated in the sense that they have a division of labour in which some members perform different tasks from those carried out by others. It is conceivable that in such a differentiated society all roles might be equally regarded and equally rewarded, but in all known societies some different roles are unequally regarded and unequally rewarded in symbolic or material terms. Whether such inequality is inescapable has been a matter of heated debate, especially as it has sometimes been supposed that to assert that institutionalized inequality is functionally necessary is to endorse all its historical forms and to garb existing inequalities in a cloak of legitimacy. We shall not rehearse a debate which has been going on for over three decades (for a summary, see Wesolowski, 1979; Broom and Cushing, 1977), but simply state that the fact of social organization implies an inequality of power. To live humanly is to live collectively, and to live collectively is to live according to an irreducible commonality of social rules. The existence of such rules, however derived and however legitimated, implies some minimal acceptance of their moral force and authority if society is to persist. But inequality of legitimate power as a necessary condition for social order does not imply that extravagant inequalities in rewards and life chances are either necessary or justifiable.

If the search for absolute equality is a chimera, the need to confront existing inequalities is not. Empirical research is indispensable to informed debate on the extent of institutionalized inequalities: about how just or unjust, how fair or unfair they may be; how far they reinforce one another during individual careers; and how rigidly they are transmitted from one generation to the next. An adequate conceptual framework should allow the identification and assessment of the main kinds of structured inequality, including how far the several forms of inequality reinforce one another and how rigid and persistent those inequalities are. All of these topics are analytic ones open to empirical investigation, although they invite normative evaluation as well. As we have emphasized, we intend our main contribution to be an analysis of how inequalities of different kinds and degrees are transmitted over time across families.

The explanaton of how a specific division of labour is produced, together with its attendant inequalities, requires a kind of analysis that cannot be developed in this study (see Thurow, 1975, for one such attempt). Researchers working from the status attainment perspective do not usually consider how a specific structure of inequalities originally arose or reached its present form. Instead they try to examine, within the context of an existing structure of inequalities, the most important factors influencing who gets what. Two related questions are uppermost: what social roles determine access to particular kinds of rewards, and what factors determine access to those roles. There have been numerous attempts to list the most important rewards, or dimensions of inequality, of which

Weber's triad of class, status and party is perhaps the best known (cf. Haller, 1970, p. 471). Svalastoga (1973) adds informational status or amount of education and knowledge as a fourth factor, while Duncan (1968) lists seven basic dimensions of inequality in life-chances: economic production status, economic consumption status, social status, informational status, cultural status, political status and civic status.

For various reasons, sometimes pragmatic but often theoretical and methodological, different researchers have stressed some of these dimensions over others. For example, differences in life-style are more readily conceptualized and understood at the level of small communities or neighbourhoods, whereas the distribution of income and political rights often demands a national frame of reference. Our general strategy has been to give primary attention to filling in the broad outline and to analysing the general structure of social inequalities in Australian society. Because we are interested in the dynamics of socioeconomic life-cycles, we have adopted a cross-sectional approach that includes men and women from all walks of life and social backgrounds. This emphasis differs from studies of elites or ruling classes. Even if elites are by definition more powerful economically and politically than the masses, the range and extent of social inequalities experienced by a cross-section of the whole population needs to be thoroughly understood. Such an analysis is important in its own right but also because in a liberal democracy the experience of the population at large ultimately determines the fate of elites, unless one takes the extreme view that elites are able to manipulate the masses at will. In a liberal democracy even the elite is obliged periodically to marshal mass support. It cannot simply command acquiescence.

These observations should make it clear that this book does not pretend to offer a comprehensive or exhaustive account of the causes of social and economic inequalities in Australia. Rather, it examines a range of important inequalities in order to assess how, and how far, they are transmitted within families and over careers. Little will be said here about the distribution of power or wealth, not because we judge them unimportant – quite the opposite – but because they require a different approach from the mass survey. Political and economic elites are by definition small and their analysis requires more focused approaches like those adopted by our colleagues Higley (Higley *et al.*, 1979) and Rubinstein (1979). While the unequal distribution of private wealth is of central importance in a capitalist economy, in many treatises its ideological significance seems to outweigh its material impact. It is not, however, the major contributing factor to income inequality. According to one estimate, removing property income from the distribution of personal income would reduce the degree of inequality in the United States by only about 20 per cent (Brittain, 1977, p. 5). In Australia at the time of our survey, property income accounted for 11 per cent of total household income (Samuelson *et al.*, 1973, p. 200). By far the largest component of income inequality is in wages and salaries.

Assumptions of the attainment model

There can be no doubt that the primary mechanisms for distributing unequal shares in Australia are the family, the school and the workplace. Families provide a set of resources – genetic, material, psychological, cultural – that influence the achievements of their children. The general contour of this generational cycle is the main concern of the present investigation.

Analytic models of any kind require a number of simplifying assumptions about how the world works. Such models evolve through stages – observing behaviour, noting interconnections or regularities of different kinds, speculating about the causes of those regularities, testing speculations and their implications against new information, refining the initial 'theories' and making further observations. In some fields there is fair agreement among scholars working on similar problems about what requires explanation and what counts as evidence for or against particular explanations of those problems. In other areas of investigation there is relatively little agreement, and two or three schools of thought compete for dominance. For instance in the study of social inequality the tension between status attainment research and Marxist analysis and their differing problematics has already been indicated. The concern of this book is not to be preoccupied with the presumed merits of underlying ideologies but to be clear about the problematic adopted and faithful to the analytic specification required by it.

As already mentioned, a major goal of status attainment research is to specify and analyse processes whereby inequalities are transmitted over the socioeconomic life-cycle and between generations. At the most general level such processes can be grouped into three broad classes, initial factors, intervening contingencies and outcomes. *Initial factors* include family background, innate aptitudes and abilities, mother tongue, country of birth, region of birth and the like; *intervening contingencies* are such variables as socialization, schooling, career expectations and migration; and the *outcomes* of participation in the world of work include the social statuses of jobs, the money income they yield and attitudes and life-styles associated with them.

How many of these processes and variables are actually included

9

in a given analysis varies from one study to another. Some researchers place particular emphasis on the years of adolescence and on how educational and occupational aspirations, the peer group, mental ability and academic performance in school interact with home background to influence how long students stay in school and the kinds of jobs they enter (cf. Haller and Portes, 1973, p. 59). Data relevant to such concerns usually require longitudinal studies in which a cohort of students is followed from school into the workplace (cf. Sewell and Hauser, 1975).

The ANU 1973 survey has a different strategy. It pays greater attention to extending the range of measures of family background, to widening the concept of education to include post-school training and its influence on individual careers, and to comparing status attainment patterns among women as well as men. However, this first monograph from the survey is confined to male respondents, except for the last chapter in which the status attainment of sons and daughters of male respondents is compared. The processes of status attainment among women will be analysed in detail in a separate report.

Status attainment research is cast in terms of quantitative causal models relating background, education and careers. Typical questions are the following: What is the effect of a difference in family background (for example, the number of children in the family of orientation) on how long a child stays on in school? What is the effect of age at leaving school on the status of a person's first job? To answer such questions it is necessary to estimate the *relative* importance of different causes, and to operationalize concepts so that they are amenable to quantification. The degree to which such attempts are successful does not admit of a conclusive answer and, as mentioned above, the major studies so far published disagree, not merely in points of detail but also about so broad a problem as the relative importance of inheritance versus achievement.

Because any analysis involves selection from the flux of ongoing behaviour, there is always the possibility that what has been excluded is precisely that which from another viewpoint merits scrutiny. What one researcher regards as an irrelevant complication, another sees as crucial. Irrelevance and centrality can be defined only in relation to a specific theoretical position. In our view, status attainment models have achieved a coherent theoretical focus and significant success in identifying the main processes of social stratification in industrial societies. Their explanatory power can be readily assessed (a property not shared by some other approaches), and deficiencies in the model can be specified and corrected. Status attainment models can be, and have been, modified in the light of new information and, as research over the last decade testifies, they can be constructively criticized. Moreover, the implications of formal models are more open to critical assessment than less testable theories whose proponents sometimes seem more concerned to preserve the theory than to confront contradictory evidence (cf. Lakatos, 1970).

Most variables used in status attainment models have relatively unambiguous meanings. For example, measures of family size, type of community and country of birth can be agreed upon even if the underlying processes which they are later called upon to represent remain to be specified (Leibowitz, 1977, p. 29). Similarly schooling and education can be measured in a number of ways such as years of education, sector (state, private, or church), or by levels and certificates to form a credentialism scale. In this monograph we use a variety of such measures for different purposes. However, the concept of occupational status, which is central to the analysis presented here, requires a fuller description. But before proceeding to that discussion, something needs to be said about our treatment of historical and life-cycle time.

History, social structure and event analysis

Because survey research in general and status attainment research in particular involve aggregated information on a cross-section of individuals, they tend not to give direct attention to unique historical episodes. Broad secular trends such as increasing urbanization and industrialization impinge on individual life-cycles, but an emphasis on average trends and standardized stages in the life-cycle may be taken to imply that relatively stable structural features of a society combine with choices made by individual actors to determine their careers. Indeed, this study, like other status attainment studies, tends to view the process of career development as a sort of contest in which the individual strives to make the most of his prior circumstances to find a niche in the social order.

No matter how robust the generalizations stemming from status attainment research may be, persons work out their careers in given historical contexts. They are not carried through the life-cycle on a steady, undisturbed or homogeneous current of time. Whole generations are exposed to waves and cross-currents of history that drastically alter, for better or worse, the expectations implied in prior commitments, individual preparation and family decisions.

From the standpoint of the processual model of occupational mobility, unique individual experiences and personal incidents can be regarded as career contingencies (Duncan, Featherman and Duncan, 1972, chapter 9). For example, personal decisions about whether, when, or whom to marry, about the timing and spacing of children, about migration from country to town or from one country to another can readily be incorporated into the life-cycle framework provided there are enough such people to form analysable groups (cf. Broom *et al.*, 1977a, p. 7). Similarly, major structural features of a society such as language or ethnic divisions, regional differences, or urban/rural residence can be taken into account by defining specific sub-groups. But often historical time is left out of account as if only life-cycle 'time' mattered.

The type of research in which we are engaged here deals with groups of individuals confronted not just by common structural constraints and opportunities but also by different historical conditions. We think it is desirable to open analysis to such influences and have done so in a variety of ways. The simplest is to use birth cohorts rather than age cohorts. Although in strict operational terms the two are the same (that is, in 1973, the year of the survey, men born between 1924 and 1933 are the same men as those in the age cohort of 40 to 49 years), birth cohorts direct attention to historical time whereas age cohorts direct attention to life-cycle time. Also, at various points we define cohorts in terms of the period when the men in the sample embarked on crucial steps in their individual careers – most commonly when they first started work. Chapters 4 and 6 pay special attention to the historical periods in which individual careers were played out.

Finally, throughout the analysis major societal episodes have been incorporated into the status attainment model, an analytic strategy for which we have coined the term 'event analysis'.[2] Examples of such episodic events are starting work in the depression (chapters 2 and 4), volunteering for service in the Australian Armed Services (chapter 4), or being a member of a particularly small birth cohort (chapter 6). In all such cases we are interested in establishing how such events affect the careers of particular cohorts, and how long such historical influences persist over the career.

Occupational status

A working assumption of status attainment research, and for that matter most social science research, is that human behaviour is directed towards goals or ends. In the sphere of occupational behaviour this assumption implies that people develop individual occupational aspirations as a result of socialization in the home, in the peer group and at school. There is a wealth of evidence for Australia and other societies that those aspirations are disproportionately directed towards jobs that are highly regarded in the society. For example, a 1969 survey of adolescents in Sydney showed that between half and three-quarters of girls and boys between the ages of eleven and eighteen expected to enter professional or technical jobs when they first left school, whereas only one in six or seven teenagers in an out-of-school sample actually entered such jobs (Connell *et al.*, 1975, pp. 223–4). From opinions reported in the same study, it is clear that this bias towards high-status jobs would have been even more marked if the comparison had been between the jobs school-leavers aspired to ('wanted' rather than 'expected') and the jobs they actually entered.

Obviously occupational aspirations depend on family background, school experience and actual or perceived ability, but it is also clear that the high occupational aspirations and expectations of Australian youth reflect prevailing norms about what is good and desirable in work roles. A cumulative body of social science data extending over thirty years shows that people in Western industrial societies rate the general social standing, or general desirability, of jobs in a highly consistent manner (Treiman, 1977). Consistency does not mean complete agreement but simply that most people tend to agree about the relative goodness of one job compared with another. This general agreement reflects a basic stability in how the occupational hierarchy is perceived by the members of many industrial societies.

Goldthorpe and Hope (1972, pp. 19–79) conducted an interesting experiment in grading occupations using a four-factor, completely crossed analysis of variance design (40 occupations, 10 respondents, 2 occasions, 4 dimensions). They showed that two non-normative dimensions, Prestige in the Community and Standard of Living, closely approximated to the traditional results obtained by asking people to rate the general social standing of jobs. However, their normative dimension, Value to Society, stood somewhat apart from these two dimensions and was characterized by lower consensus (pp. 53–8). Even so, it was positively correlated with the other dimensions.

These results suggest three conclusions. First, considerable agreement exists about the symbolic and material rewards that go with different jobs. Second, there is less agreement about whether the distribution of rewards is just or legitimate. Third, and by extension, individuals may be motivated differently in the face of those inequalities. To put the last point another way, because greater disagreement exists about the legitimacy than the fact of unequal rewards associated with jobs, individual occupational aspirations will be influenced both by existent inequalities and also by a personal evaluation of that reality. The value system is not universally endorsed nor is it reacted to in the same way by different people.

Status attainment models imply that, other things equal, people seek more desirable jobs. Yet there is no universal calculus of desirability for all persons, despite wide agreement about the general social standing of jobs. Other factors than desirability enter into the occupational choices that people actually make. Thus, a scale of occupational goodness, or desirability, abstracts only one generalized aspect, albeit a central and important one, of occupational behaviour. There can be no serious disagreement that occupational status scales capture a major structural feature of industrial societies, although some relativistic nihilists have not been deterred from asserting quite the contrary.

The ANU 2 scale

The scale of occupational status used in this study has been fully described elsewhere (Broom *et al.*, 1977a, pp. 58–111; 1977b). It is based on personal ratings made by four groups of professionals on the social standing of 198 jobs (Broom *et al.*, 1977a, p. 66) and on the relationship of those ratings to characteristics of occupants in those jobs as recorded in the 1971 census. The scale is designed for use with the occupational classification of the Australian Bureau of Statistics. The validity of the scale is discussed in the earlier publication, and it is validated further here through internal analysis of survey findings, first in terms of levels of satisfaction expressed by men in jobs with different status, and second from responses to an open-ended question: 'Looking back over your working life, what would you say is the best job you've ever had?' It seems reasonable to assume that people in jobs with high social standing should be more satisfied than those in jobs with lower social standing. Table 1.1 presents some results for men in the top octile, the middle quartile, and the bottom octile of the ANU 2 status scale.

These data show a consistent tendency for respondents to report greater satisfaction if they have jobs with higher status. However, reports of satisfaction are relatively high at all levels of status because once people have jobs they tend to adjust their expectations to their experience (cf. Emery and Phillips, 1976, pp. 8–18). In the bottom eighth of the status hierarchy 49 per cent think they have a good job compared with other men living near by. This is a high figure, even allowing for residential segregation and the tendency for the status range to be narrower in specific neighbourhoods than it is across the nation as a whole. Of course, the estimation is not as high as it is among men in the top octile. Levels of job satisfaction are similarly high. Two in every three men in low-status jobs enjoy their work and find it a source of great satisfaction. Among men in high-status jobs the figure is nine out of ten.

TABLE 1.1 *Satisfaction with job by social status groups*

Question	Status groups		
	Bottom eighth	Middle quarter	Top eighth
Q.197 – Considering your present job in comparison with the jobs of other men who live around here, would you say you had a *good job*, an *average job*, or *not too good a job*?			
% saying a 'good job'	49·2	59·5	81·1
Q.199 – Some people really enjoy their work and find it a source of great satisfaction; others look on their work as something they have to do in order to make a living. Which way do you feel?			
% who enjoy work	69·3	76·9	93·2
Q.200 – Considering the job you have now, how satisfied would you say you are with your:			
% very satisfied with:			
Earnings	14·2	12·0	26·4
Kind of work	16·6	24·3	43·7
Promotion chances	9·7	14·3	30·7
Work as a whole	26·2	26·9	46·3
% very dissatisfied with:			
Earnings	3·7	2·9	1·0
Kind of work	2·9	1·1	0·7
Promotion chances	10·9	6·6	1·8
Work as a whole	2·9	0·6	0·3

Respondents were also asked how satisfied they were on a four-point scale (very satisfied, satisfied, dissatisfied, very dissatisfied) with their earnings, the kind of work they did, their boss, chances of promotion, the people they worked with and their work taken overall. Table 1.1 presents further data on the four areas most relevant to the validity of the status scale. 'Very satisfied' responses are two to three times more frequent in the top than the bottom 12 per cent, and extreme dissatisfaction is generally low except among men in low-status jobs who express strong dissatisfaction about their chances for promotion. These findings also confirm that the scale reflects relevant and important aspects of the world of work.

A final check on the scale's validity is provided by answers to the following question, which was asked of every respondent who had held more than one job: 'Looking back over your working life, what would you say is the best job you have ever had?' If the status scale accurately captures individual judgments about the desirability of different jobs, most men should nominate as their best job their highest-status job. The interview asked for information on the respondent's first job, job at ten, twenty, thirty and forty years after first job, and job at time of interview (last job, if retired). Eighty-seven per cent of the men in the sample answered this question (almost all the others had been in the same job throughout their careers). Of the men who answered the question, 77 per cent answered in terms of a job described somewhere else in the questionnaire. Because all these jobs were coded twice to ensure maximum reliability, the following analysis is restricted to the 2,119 men who answered the 'best job' question in terms of a first or a later job recorded elsewhere in the questionnaire.

A strong tendency exists for men to nominate their current job as their 'best job': about 70 per cent answered that the job held at the time of interview was the best they had ever had. Nevertheless, in all except the oldest career cohort, a clear majority nominated as the best job they had ever had their highest-status job as measured by the ANU 2 scale. For men with between 10 and 20 years of work experience, 60 per cent nominated their highest-status job; for men with between 20 and 30 years' work experience, the figure was 56 per cent; and for men with 30 to 40 years work experience, 45 per cent. In the sample as a whole 55 per cent chose their highest-status job as measured on the ANU 2 scale. Of those who chose a job with a lower status score a large proportion chose a job with a very similar status. Across the sample as a whole, three out of four men chose either their highest-status job as their best job, or a job within half a standard deviation (50 status points on a scale with an effective range of between 331 and 896) of their highest-status job. Given these findings we believe that the ANU 2 status scale is a valid and reliable measure of the general desirability of jobs in terms both of the objective social characteristics of job-holders and of their views about those jobs.

The plan of this book

The analysis that follows takes as its expository paradigm an extension of the basic model of status attainment introduced by Blau and Duncan (1967). In its simplest form this model examines how far the socioeconomic status of a family is converted into marketable resources for children, which later influence their own careers. The list of family resources that might be included in such a model is very wide, ranging from conventional indicators such as father's job and education to wealth, income, parental encouragement, health, and social psychological dispositions such as aversion to risk, need for achievement and so on (Sahota, 1978, pp. 3–7). Similarly, the means by which these resources are converted into attainments by the next generation vary widely: formal education, informal peer-group pressures, availability of significant role models, migration to areas offering greater opportunity, and even more general social conditions such as the rate of economic growth. However, the social outcomes of the processes that have been subjected to serious scrutiny are more limited in scope and are largely confined to occupational and economic 'success', defined in terms of job status and earnings.

Success so defined is a relatively narrow concept. It does not explicitly address the questions of how far people seek to maximize status and income or at what point they may trade status and income for increased leisure, to give only one example. That such trade-offs are made cannot be doubted. However, the fact that status attainment models explain significant amounts of the variation in the social statuses of our sample supports the overall plausibility of our assumptions.

The next chapter is based on the 1967 Blau–Duncan model but embodies four main departures from it. First, in order to take account of Bowles's (1972) criticisms, a wider range of family origin characteristics is examined. Second, in order to give due consideration to human capital theory, the concept of education is extended to include not just full-time schooling but on-the-job training and post-school courses.[3] Third, career mobility is not restricted to the conventional span between first and current job but is extended to encompass early, middle and late career mobility, and the effects of post-school training on occupational careers. Finally, both earnings and status are included in the explanatory model, an extension of the Blau–Duncan model that has been made by other researchers, including Duncan and his co-workers (1972).

In addition to analysis of the extended status attainment model for the whole sample of men, we also test for group differences to see how far processes of status attainment differ by language groups, occupational groups, town and country dwellers, and other groups where previous research suggests achievement may take a different course. Successive chapters then examine specific links in the chain of status transmission: the link between education and career beginnings (chapter 3), the dynamics of occupational careers (chapter 4), status and income returns to early attainment (chapter 5), and a three-generational analysis of the inheritance of inequality (chapter 6).

Before proceeding to these analyses, the treatment of errors of measurement should be mentioned. Partly in response to criticisms such as those made by Bowles (1972) but also as a result of wider methodological and substantive concerns, the decade since Blau and Duncan's seminal work has seen a burgeoning literature on measurement error in status attainment models. However, that work has not in general supported the intuitively plausible idea put forward by Bowles, that retrospective reports about family members other than the respondent himself (or herself) are substantially less reliable than reports on the respondent's own characteristics. In an important investigation of this issue Bielby *et al.* (1977) established that ignoring response errors led to an underestimation of the effects of social background on the later achievement of nonblack American men, but the effect of education on job status was also underestimated to much the same extent (1977, p. 1276):

> We think there is persuasive evidence that reports of social background and achievement variables by nonblacks are subject only to random response error. Moreover, we find no evidence that social background variables are measured substantially less reliably than are contemporaneous achievement variables among nonblack men.

However, while these authors believe that their findings do not offer conclusive support to either of two extreme positions (response errors are trivial versus response errors are substantial), they seem to adopt a revisionist stance relative to Blau and Duncan in their admission that ignoring measurement error underestimates the role of social background on inheritance by about the same amount as it overestimates personal achievement, or meritocracy (1977, p. 1277). These and other findings on measurement error have been taken into account in our substantive interpretation but not in our formal analysis. A re-measurement program was not attempted in this study, although we did essay an internal replication of the basic model across three generations. That replication (Broom *et al.*, 1978a, b) produced results that counsel against making cast-iron interpretations of what look to be 'exact' results. An example of the measurement error problem is given in the next chapter where the basic model is re-estimated using what we judge to be plausible reliabilities.

While results are presented quantitatively and data are analysed with realistic but hopefully not dogmatic rigour, our interpretations rest more on relative orders of magnitude than on slavish adherence to decimal differences. The analyses reported are based on far more detailed examination of data than can be presented in this book, and our interpretations are informed by a critical awareness of the promises and pitfalls of quantitative models of social processes. Their promise continues to be enhanced by the growing body of comparable studies in other industrial societies, both capitalist and socialist. We will rest content if our findings and interpretations are taken into account in this wider scholarly exchange.

2 The socioeconomic career: a basic model

This chapter develops the basic status attainment model that is the major analytic theme of this work. The social backgrounds of a sample of economically active men are related to their schooling, career beginnings, further education, present job and income. The model's structure can be thought of as a causal chain: the advantages or disadvantages of being born into a given family are converted by various social processes into individual attributes and trained capacities such as education and qualifications, which in turn are exchanged in the market place for job status and income.

As noted in chapter 1, this analytic scheme can be expanded by generalizing the content of each broad stage in the socioeconomic career, by specifying intervening social processes that link its several stages, and by establishing how far the processes represented by the model hold good for different social groups. This last point can be illustrated by the concept of the 'cycle of poverty'. If a cycle of poverty exists, children from poor families would experience multiple handicaps over their socioeconomic careers. This possibility is evaluated in the latter part of this chapter where the experience of men from disadvantaged origins is compared with that of the remainder of the sample, in order to see whether they have significantly different patterns of status attainment.

First, however, it is necessary to detail how Blau's and Duncan's initial model of status attainment has been extended. In measuring education we differentiate between education undertaken before and after beginning full-time work. The conception of social background is also broadened to include not merely father's job and father's education, but also mother's education, a measure of the economic resources in the parental home and family size. Opinion is divided over how far education (and therefore later achievement) is determined by social background. Thus it is necessary to establish to what extent education serves to certify social status and to what extent it facilitates social mobility between the generations.

Variables in the basic attainment model

Since we are interested in how socioeconomic careers develop, attention is limited here to the 2,715 economically active males who reported their 1973 income. In fact, only 84 respondents declined to disclose their income. When weighted and adjusted to compensate for unequal probability of selection and non-response (Broom *et al.*, 1977a, pp. 39–43) effective sample size (equivalent to a non-weighted sample) is reduced to 2,560. The variables in the model will now be briefly described.

Occupation

In order to speak concisely about the great diversity of occupations they have been assigned status scores, which are designed to reflect the characteristics of jobs and workers in the Australian economy. The development of these scores is fully reported in Broom *et al.* (1977a, pp. 58–111; 1977b). The scores have been scaled to have a mean of 500 and a standard deviation of 100. All occupations were coded to the three-digit level of the 1971 Australian Bureau of Statistics occupational classification (ABS, 1971a) and scores were then assigned to each occupation category.

Two comments about the scores should be made. First, they are based on the relationship of forty-five social characteristics of members of the Australian workforce to perceptions of the general social standing of jobs in Australia. Because they reflect a wider variety of occupational characteristics, they are not strictly speaking a socioeconomic index in the sense intended by Duncan (1961, pp. 109–38). Second, scores for farmers fall near the middle of the range, rather than, as with Duncan's scores, near the bottom. We believe the ANU 2 scale accurately represents the social and economic status of Australian farmers during the period covered by the ANU survey.

Information on father's occupation (DADJOB)[1] was in response to the questions: 'When you were fourteen years old, what kind of work did your father do?' Detailed responses were collected by interviewers and like other occupational information reported here were coded twice into the ABS classification. Discrepancies between first and second coding were resolved in a third coding.

The respondent's first occupation (JOB1) is defined somewhat differently in this survey from the practice in some mobility surveys in which first occupation is taken as the first full-time job after finishing all full-time education. In the ANU 1973 survey first occupation is defined as the first regular job held in the first year or more out of school, regardless of whether the respondent subsequently undertook further full-time education. While fewer than 5 per cent of men in the sample did undertake further full-time education, this treatment of first job facilitates an analysis of the influence of further education on careers. Respondent's current occupation (JOBN) is the one held at time of interview.

Education

Father's and mother's education (DADED, MOMED) are represented in terms of years of education, by subtracting six (the compulsory age for entering school) from the age at which the father or mother finished full-time education. Respondent's education is measured by two variables, BASED and ADDED. The first includes any schooling, education or training experienced before beginning work, as well as any training commenced during the same year that the respondent held his first job. The reason for including such courses in BASED is that the ABS occupational classification does not in general take notice of statuses such as apprentice, trainee, or probationer. Such beginners are clearly identified in only about three categories. Although many people undertake some training as part of their first job, apprentices and master tradesmen are coded to the same occupation category and thus have the same status score. In other words, early job-related training by definition has no effect on job status, because it is built into the coding system. We therefore combined such training into BASED.

Because education and training received after schooling is often part-time, the model presented here assigns such training a full-time equivalent before it is incorporated into BASED or ADDED. Information was secured on the length of courses undertaken after leaving school. We experimented with a variety of weights for part-time education (cf. Müller, 1973; Sewell and Hauser, 1975, p. 20) and five variously defined education variables (weighting part-time courses as 0·1, 0·2, 0·3, 0·5 and 1·0 to obtain a full-time equivalent) and, after comparing a number of regression analyses, chose to weight each year of part-time education as the equivalent of three-tenths of a year of full-time education. In fact the analyses with weights of up to 0·3 gave indistinguishable results. As noted, the first component of basic education, the number of years of education or training, was inferred from age left school. More than twenty years of education were truncated to twenty. As already mentioned, further education which began in the same year as the respondent left school was coded into BASED.

Respondent's additional education (ADDED) is defined in a manner similar to basic education but it includes only education begun in a year later than first job. In fact 44 per cent of the sample had no such further education or training; the rest ranged from 0·3 of a year to 9·4 years. Part-time courses lasting less than one year were excluded from both education variables.

Family size

Family size (FAMSZ) is simply the sum of the number of brothers, the number of sisters, plus the respondent. Respondents with more than eight brothers (or sisters) were coded as eight, so that maximum family size is seventeen.

Income

Information on the respondent's current income (INCOME) was secured in response to the question: 'Can you tell me the letter on this card which comes closest to your personal income, before any deductions like tax, rent or superannuation?' The card had sixteen categories with weekly and yearly equivalents. The first category was under $20 a week. Categories increased by $10 a week up to $120, by $20 for the next two and by $40 for the next two. The highest category is over $240 per week. Dollar amounts representing the mid-point of each range were subsequently assigned to these categories. The first and last categories were assigned the average dollar amounts reported by men in those ranges ($9 and $330 per week, respectively) in a government survey of income for the year 1973–4 (ABS, 1976). The use of income categories introduces little imprecision in estimates of dollar returns to education. The mean weekly income of respondents was $129, compared with $131 in the government survey for male income recipients aged 25 to 64 years of age (ABS, 1976, Table 13). This is a reassuringly close fit.

Parental income

As mentioned in chapter 1, the lack of any measure of the economic status of a person's family of origin may understate the effect of social background on later attainment. Since we could not expect a valid response to a question about parental income when the respondent was growing up, questions about parental home ownership and consumer durables were asked. A proxy for parental income (WLTH) was constructed as an index derived from the principal component of five such items: home-ownership, and possession of a car, telephone, refrigerator and inside toilet. As shown below, this composite variable contributes significantly to explaining differences in later attainment.

Relative effects of background and early attainment

The development and estimation of causal models in sociology unites two traditions: the structural equation models of econometricians such as Fisher, Koopmans and Wold, and the causal (path) models developed in population genetics, notably by Sewall Wright. Since their introduction into sociology in the 1960s, the use of structural equation models to represent theories about social processes has seen rapid growth, particularly in the application of path analysis to simple recursive models which assume independent disturbance terms and variables measured without error.[2]

The system of hypothetical cause-effect relationships shown in Table 2.2 incorporates the following assumptions: (a) it can be described by a series of five simple structural equations; (b) in each equation the variance of the effect is completely determined by specified causes and the disturbance term; (c) causation is one-way (i.e. there are no feedback loops); (d) all disturbance terms are assumed to be independent of each other and of causally prior variables; (e) all variables are assumed to be measured without error; and (f) the relationships among the five exogenous (social origin) variables are taken as initial conditions for the development of a man's socioeconomic life-cycle. Actual estimation of relative effects is carried out by regressing each of the five endogenous variables in the model on all causally prior variables. Both standardized and unstandardized regression coefficients are shown in Table 2.2.

Although the present analysis treats all variables as if they are measured without error, this is obviously untrue, even for self-reported data. However, the resources available for the survey did not allow for multiple indicators or a remeasurement program. Therefore treatment of measurement error can be only informal, since there is no direct way to estimate the nature and degree of bias. We also need to consider whether the model is correctly specified in the sense that it includes the most important variables and identifies correctly the direction of causation. Unfortunately no measure is available of respondent's mental ability, possibly an important determinant of occupational status and income. To the extent that ability directly affects occupational status and income independently of education, our model is mis-specified, the estimates of the effects of other causal variables are higher than their true values, and so the status and economic returns to education may be overestimated. However, if the effect of ability on occupation and income is largely indirect through educational attainment, the estimates will be little affected.

Evidence for the United States points to a substantial effect of mental ability on educational attainment and thereby on occupational attainment and income (Duncan, 1968; Jencks *et al.*, 1972; Sewell and Hauser, 1975; Alexander *et al.*, 1975). Evidence in favour of a direct influence on occupation and income is equivocal. A direct effect implies that among men with the same formal schooling more intelligent individuals attain higher status and earn more. Duncan (1968, p. 6), Jencks *et al.* (1972, p. 339) and Sewell and Hauser (1975, chapter 3) demonstrate small direct effects on occupation and earnings. However, Alexander, Eckland and Griffin (1975, pp. 330–1, 334–5) find an anomalous negative effect for earnings only, while Griliches and Mason (1973, pp. 285–316) suggest that any effect on earnings is marginal. Ability cannot easily be measured in the sort of sample survey from which our data were secured, and no attempt has been made to assess directly the extent of possible bias. The evidence surveyed above suggests a minor bias towards overestimating the returns to education.

The omission of any measure of parental financial status from the respondent's socioeconomic background has been thought to be a serious mis-specification affecting estimates of the economic returns to education. Griffin (1976; see also Bowles, 1972) demonstrates such a bias in several United States samples, especially those limited to men in early career. As mentioned the ANU survey avoids this deficiency by providing a surrogate measure of parental income indexed by household possessions (WLTH).

The pattern of relationships among the status variables is shown in Table 2.1, along with some other basic statistics. The regression coefficients are shown in Table 2.2, together with the squared multiple correlation coefficient, which indicates how much of the variance in the dependent variable is explained by the causally prior statuses included in the model. In Table 2.3 the correlations among variables are decomposed into direct effects, indirect effects and causally unanalysed components. These terms are explained in the following discussion.

Table 2.1 gives an overview of the data. Respondents have more years of education than their parents, and there is a tendency for spouses to have similar educational levels: the correlation between MOMED and DADED is 0·486. Occupational status is highest for JOBN and lowest for JOB1, which also has less variation because men start off in a relatively narrow range of jobs and move to a variety of other jobs during their careers (see chapter 4).

TABLE 2.1 : *Measures of association and distribution for status model variables*

Status variable	Zero order correlations										INCOME X̄	SD	CV	No. of cases
	DADED	DADJOB	MOMED	WLTH	FAMSZ	BASED	JOB1	ADDED	JOBN	INCOME				
DADED	1·000										8·45	2·98	0·353	2,032
DADJOB	0·1351	1·000									515·27	111·54	0·216	2,316
MOMED	0·486	0·193	1·000								8·21	2·02	0·246	2,196
WLTH	0·237	0·321	0·271	1·000							0·00	1·02	a	2,444
FAMSZ	−0·1170	−0·099	−0·161	−0·182	1·000						4·62	2·58	0·558	2,547
BASED	04·361	0·218	0·372	0·345	−0·269	1·000					9·57	2·28	0·238	2,560
JOB1	0·205	0·312	0·221	0·270	−0·147	0·507	1·000				486·36	90·07	0·185	2,558
ADDED	0·093	0·005	0·064	0·051	−0·110	−0·054	−0·054	1·000			0·50	0·90	1·800	2,560
JOBN	0·242	0·259	0·245	0·327	−0·232	0·481	0·495	0·254	1·000		525·11	116·65	0·222	2,560
INCOME	0·181	−0·171	0·171	0·286	−0·187	0·363	0·359	0·162	0·526	1·000	128·54	70·17	0·546	2,560

[a] Not calculated because the indicators forming this variable are in standardized form.

The three variables with the greatest relative variation are ADDED, FAMSZ and INCOME, all of which are skewed towards high values. Most men have little further education, but a few undertake numerous courses. Similarly, family size is more likely to deviate from the average towards a fairly high upper limit, and the same tendency affects the distribution of income, especially in Australia where minimum wage legislation prevents employed people from falling too far below the national average.

The inheritance of social statuses leads to the expected result that, except for FAMSZ, all the status variables show a pattern of positive association. The more affluent have smaller families than the less affluent, and the larger is the size of a man's family of origin, the lower are his later achievements. Coming from a large family constitutes a barrier to later attainment, as Table 2.3 shows. Note also that the relationship between education and jobs seems stronger among respondents than among fathers. Cohort analysis indicates that BASED is a more important determinant of career beginnings among younger men: the correlation between BASED and JOB1 is 0·598 for men aged 30 to 39 years in 1973, compared with 0·504 for those aged 40 to 49, and 0·358 for those aged 50 to 59. Especially in chapters 3 and 6, we provide other evidence relating to the strength of meritocratic processes in Australian society.

Two other features of Table 2.1 should be noted. First, looking across the first five rows, one can see that on balance the social origin variables are more closely related to the respondent's early statuses (BASED and JOB1) than to his later statuses (JOBN and INCOME). Second, except for ADDED, the highest correlations tend to be clustered in the bottom right-hand corner of the table where the statuses of the respondent rather than his family of origin are represented. We now submit these impressions to more formal scrutiny.

Determinants of income

The explanatory model for income is the structural equation shown at the bottom of Table 2.2, which specifies current income as a function of social origins, education, career beginnings, additional education and present job. All but one of the social origin variables has insignificant effects, and only WLTH shows a significant and positive effect on current income. There are two possible explanations for this effect: either more affluent parents make direct monetary contributions to their sons, including transfers of wealth which generate income, or better-off parents guide their sons into particular kinds of occupational niches where they receive higher incomes independently of other factors such as years of education.

TABLE 2.2 Path coefficients and path regressions for status attainment model[a]

Dependent variables	Independent variables									R sq. (Intercept)
	DADED	DADJOB	MOMED	WLTH	FAMSZ	BASED	JOB1	ADDED	JOBN	
BASED	0·176 (0·134)	0·035 (0·001)	0·197 (0·222)	0·208 (0·474)	−0·166 (−0·147)					0·261 (5·595)
JOB1	−0·059 (−1·777)	0·213 (0·172)	0·026 (1·152)	0·052 (4·676)	−0·000 (−0·015)	0·454 (17·949)				0·302 (224·788)
ADDED	0·083 (0·025)	−0·052 (−0·000)	0·012 (0·005)	0·024 (0·022)	−0·095 (−0·033)	−0·024 (−0·009)	−0·042 (0·000)			0·021 (0·467)
JOBN	0·004 (0·159)	0·065 (0·068)	0·021 (1·210)	0·114 (13·305)	−0·071 (−3·194)	0·238 (12·165)	0·296 (0·384)	0·210 (27·022)		0·388 (169·645)
INCOME	0·018 (0·420)	−0·018 (−0·011)	−0·019 (−0·645)	0·102 (7·124)	−0·038 (−1·043)	0·084 (2·587)	0·094 (0·073)	0·047 (3·338)	0·390 (0·235)	0·306 (−40·676)

[a] Path coefficients (standardized partial regression coefficients) uppermost in each pair. Path regressions (unstandardized partial regression coefficients) in parentheses. Underlined coefficients do not exceed twice their standard error.

In this connection we should point out that, although we use a very detailed job classification, residual internal variation in earnings within occupational categories remains: for example, the category for medical doctor ranges from self-employed specialists to salaried medical officers. Similarly, there is internal variation in the education measures, since BASED and ADDED distinguish amount but not kind of schooling.

Table 2.2 shows that five variables explain 31 per cent of the variation in income, a figure somewhat higher than that usually reported for age-comparable samples (cf. Jencks *et al.*, 1972, p. 339), and much higher than that from studies of men in their early career (Alexander *et al.*, 1975, p. 330). In order of importance the main determinants of respondent's personal income are JOBN (0·390), WLTH (0·102), JOB1 (0·094), BASED (0·084) and ADDED (0·047). If WLTH is omitted, the effects of socioeconomic background on income appear as entirely indirect and mediated through BASED, JOB1, JOBN and, to some extent, ADDED. Including WLTH reduces the apparent direct effect of BASED on INCOME. Even so, in this Australian sample, as in comparable samples from the United States, income is predominantly a function of current occupational status.

Other effects operate mainly through intervening variables. The decomposition of the simple correlations in the last panel of Table 2.3 shows that WLTH has a small direct effect on INCOME, with slightly higher indirect effects through BASED and to a lesser degree JOBN. Similarly the indirect effects of BASED on INCOME are double the size of the direct effects. In chapter 5 more complex models of the determinants of earnings explain considerably greater amounts of income variation.

Determinants of current occupational status

Nearly 40 per cent of the variance in occupational status at time of interview can be explained by six variables. The 40 per cent figure is comparable to those reported by others (Blau and Duncan, 1967, p. 170; Jencks *et al.*, 1972, p. 339; Alexander *et al.*, 1975, pp. 339–5; Sewell and Hauser, 1975, p. 100). In terms of relative importance the determinants of current job status are: JOB1 (0·296), BASED (0·238), ADDED (0·210), WLTH (0·114) and DADJOB (0·065). As one would expect, a man's first regular job has the strongest impact on his current status.

The strong effect on occupational attainment of continuing investments in education, independently of basic education, social background and first job, supports the general arguments of human capital theorists. Against this meritocratic process we need also to

TABLE 2.3   Decomposition of effects for status attainment model[a]

Dependent variable	Predetermined variable	Zero-order correlation	Total causal effect	Total direct effect	Total indirect effect	Indirect effects via BASED	Indirect effects via JOB1	ADDED	JOBN	Causally unanalysed component
BASED	DADED	0·361	0·176	0·176						0·185
	DADJOB	0·218	0·035	0·035						0·183
	MOMED	0·372	0·197	0·197						0·175
	WLTH	0·345	0·208	0·208						0·137
	FAMSZ	−0·269	−0·166	−0·166						−0·103
JOB1	DADED	0·205	0·021	−0·059	0·080	0·080				0·184
	DADJOB	0·312	0·228	0·213	0·015	0·015				0·085
	MOMED	0·221	0·115	0·026	0·089	0·089				0·106
	WLTH	0·270	0·147	0·052	0·095	0·095				0·123
	FAMSZ	−0·147	−0·076	−0·000	−0·076	−0·076				−0·071
	BASED	0·507	0·454	0·454						0·053
ADDED	DADED	0·093	0·080	0·083	−0·003	−0·001	−0·002			0·013
	DADJOB	0·005	−0·043	−0·052	0·009	0·000	0·009			0·048
	MOMED	0·064	0·012	0·012	0·000	0·000	0·000			0·052
	WLTH	0·051	0·025	0·024	0·001	−0·001	0·002			0·026
	FAMSZ	−0·110	−0·094	−0·095	0·001	0·000	0·000			−0·016
	BASED	0·054	−0·005	−0·024	0·019	0·001	0·019			0·059
	JOB1	0·054	0·042	0·042						

TABLE 2.3 *continued*

Dependent variable	Predetermined variable	Zero-order correlation	Total causal effect	Total direct effect	Total indirect effect	Indirect effects via				Causally unanalysed component
						BASED	JOB1	ADDED	JOBN	
JOBN	DADED	0·242	0·069	0·004	0·065	0·065	−0·017	0·017		0·173
	DADJOB	0·259	0·132	0·065	0·067	0·013	0·065	−0·011		0·127
	MOMED	0·245	0·104	0·021	0·083	0·073	0·008	0·002		0·141
	WLTH	0·327	0·213	0·114	0·099	0·078	0·016	0·005		0·114
	FAMSZ	−0·232	−0·152	−0·071	−0·081	−0·061	−0·001	−0·019		0·080
	BASED	0·481	0·371	0·238	0·133		0·138	−0·005		0·110
	JOB1	0·495	0·305	0·296	0·009			0·009		0·190
	ADDED	0·254	0·210	0·210						0·044
INCOME	DADED	0·181	0·065	0·018	0·047	0·048	−0·013	−0·011	0·001	0·116
	DADJOB	0·171	0·056	−0·018	0·074	0·009	0·046	−0·007	0·026	0·115
	MOMED	0·171	0·050	−0·019	0·069	0·053	−0·006	−0·001	−0·009	0·121
	WLTH	0·286	0·217	0·102	0·115	0·057	0·011	−0·003	0·044	0·069
	FAMSZ	−0·187	−0·123	−0·038	−0·085	−0·045	0·000	−0·012	−0·028	−0·064
	BASED	0·363	0·271	0·084	0·187		0·097	−0·003	−0·093	0·092
	JOB1	0·359	0·215	0·094	0·121			0·005	0·116	0·144
	ADDED	0·162	0·125	0·043	0·082				0·082	0·037
	JOBN	0·526	0·390	0·390						0·136

a Only standardized coefficients are shown. Underlined coefficients do not exceed twice their standard error.

balance the evidence for occupational 'inheritance' across generations represented by the effects of DADJOB and WLTH. There is
also indirect evidence of career mobility in the almost equal effects
of BASED (0·238) and JOB1 (0·296) on JOBN. Education gained
prior to entering the workforce affects not only initial placement
within the occupational structure but also later occupational mobility (cf. Blau and Duncan, 1967, p. 174; Müller, 1973, pp. 233–55).

Further Education

The R sq. for this variable is very low and the model tells us almost
nothing about what differentiates men who undertook further
education training after workforce entry from those who did not.
Three determinants with statistically significant effects – FAMSZ
(−0·095), DADED (0·083) and DADJOB (−0·052) – explain a
trivial 2 per cent of the variance when other variables are taken into
account. Respondents from backgrounds where the father had
more schooling tend to undertake further education after they start
work, but those from families with higher average occupational
status and larger families tend not to. The plausible notion that
low-status individuals advance their initial occupational attainments through further education is not supported here, though it
has been shown for West Germany (Müller, 1973, p. 234).
However, the West German study counted apprenticeships as
further education, and as noted above the Australian census
classification of occupations precludes a similar result in our data,
because apprenticeships begun immediately after leaving school are
included in BASED.

Career beginnings

BASED (0·454) has by far the strongest effect on first job status. It
is more than double the direct effect of DADJOB (0·213), an effect
which represents both occupational inheritance strictly interpreted
but also family effects on motivations, aspirations and the like. The
anomalous but small negative effect of DADED (−0·059) means
that among respondents in this sample with similar educational
levels and occupational backgrounds, those whose fathers had more
education tend to have first jobs with marginally lower status.
WLTH has a small positive effect on first job, while FAMSZ and
MOMED have no significant impact.

Basic education

Social background explains about a quarter of the variance in

BASED, a figure comparable to USA samples (Blau and Duncan, 1967, p. 170; Jencks *et al.*, 1972, p. 33). However, because a larger set of origin variables was used, we expected to explain more of the variation in respondents' schooling. The fact that we do not is probably because in Australia a minimum school-leaving age was legally defined throughout the period under study, and even most low-income families were able to keep their children in school up to that age. In terms of specific aspects of the family background, it is interesting that the educational and economic aspects of home environment rather than father's job status *per se* have the strongest influence on son's basic education. Family size has the expected negative effect on years of education.

Direct and indirect effects

So far little has been said about indirect effects. In simple recursive models such as the one presented here, the correlation between any two variables (DADED and JOBN, for example) can be broken down into three parts: the direct influence of DADED on JOBN; the indirect effect of DADED on JOBN through prior causal variables such as BASED; and a causally unanalysed part (joint effect) due to the unanalysed exogenous correlation of DADED with other social background variables (Alwin and Hauser, 1975). The first two components, direct and indirect effects, are termed the *total causal effect*.

Table 2.3 provides a breakdown of the simple correlations. To use the same example as before, the correlation between DADED and JOBN (0·242) can be decomposed into an unanalysed component (0·173), an insignificant direct effect (0·004) and a total indirect effect of 0·065 mediated by BASED (0·065), JOB1 (−0·017) and ADDED (0·017). The unanalysed component for this and some other correlations is large because there are five background variables whose causal relationships are not explored and therefore share a common causal influence.

For JOB1 there are small indirect effects of social background. Except for DADJOB these indirect effects exceed their direct effects. The direct effect of DADJOB can be interpreted as a generalized tendency towards status, and perhaps job, inheritance. No discussion of ADDED is warranted because the model does not discriminate effectively those who get more further education from those who get less. For JOBN the influence of DADED is largely indirect through BASED (0·065), whereas the indirect influence of DADJOB is mainly through JOB1. The total indirect effect of BASED (roughly half the size of the direct effect at 0·133) is also through JOB1, while that of JOB1 is negligible (0·009). Since no

33

variables intervene between ADDED and JOBN, there can be no indirect effect in this case.

Social origins contribute to current job status largely through their effect on educational attainment and career beginnings. They exert slightly less influence on current job than basic education, further education and first job: the five social origin variables together explain a maximum of 18·1 per cent of the variance in current job, or nearly half the total variance explained by all the causes specified in the model.

The influence of social origins on INCOME is lower than for JOBN, accounting for 11·5 per cent of the variance, or 38 per cent of the total variance explained when BASED, ADDED, JOB1 and JOBN are also included. As with current job status, the effect of social origins are largely transmitted by intervening variables. WLTH, however, has a direct effect comparable to its indirect effect, reflecting not simply transfers of wealth generating additional income but also such factors as the propensity to take risks, entrepreneurship and self-employment (cf. Sahota, 1978, p. 16). The indirect effect of BASED (0·187) is about double its direct effect (0·084) and operates mainly through career beginnings and current job. The indirect effect of ADDED (0·082) is, of necessity, via JOBN.

In most respects the basic model resembles the broad results from USA samples. Social and economic attainments reflect social background because the advantages and disadvantages associated with membership in a family are converted into educational advantages and disadvantages. Education and social origins significantly affect career beginnings and later occupational attainment. However, the level at which a man enters the occupational status system does not fix his subsequent attainments. Education exerts a continuing impact on occupational and economic status over the career, and education and training obtained after starting work yield status returns not much below those contributed by earlier schooling.

The social and economic impact of education

The model described here can be used to calculate the increases in current status and income that result from schooling secured before and after beginning work. The relevant statistics are the standardized coefficients and unstandardized coefficients for BASED and ADDED in Table 2.2. In substantive terms, among men with comparable social origins and career beginnings, a one-standard deviation change in BASED or ADDED produces a P standard deviation change in the outcome, where P is a standardized (path) coefficient. Similarly, a one-*unit* change in BASED or ADDED produces an R unit change in the outcome, where R is a regression coefficient. This second type of coefficient is often termed 'metric' because the original metric of both variables is preserved.

Consider first the occupational status gains from basic education. Using the standard deviation values shown in Table 2.1, the standardized coefficients in Table 2.3, and controlling for social background, a one-standard deviation change in BASED produces a 0·371 standard deviation change in JOBN (total causal effect, Table 2.3). An extra year of basic education, independently of differences in social origins, increases current occupational status by 19 status points $[(0·371)*(116·65)/(1)*(2·28)]$ on a scale ranging from a low of 331 to a high of 880. Such a change approximates the status difference between a lawyer and an electrical engineer, or a coalminer and a factory labourer. Of the 19 status points, 14 represent the direct effect of BASED on JOBN and the remainder indirect effects, largely through JOB1 (see Table 2.3). Similarly, one year of additional education (ADDED) adds 27 status points net of other causes of JOBN status $[(0·21)*(116·65)/(1)*(0·90)]$. Put another way, individuals alike in all other respects specified by the model will differ in JOBN status by a factor of nineteen times their difference in years of basic education. For a high school graduate compared with a man with a bachelor's degree, such a difference amounts to 60 to 70 status points. And individuals alike in all respects, including level of basic education, but differing in their investment in additional education, will differ by twenty-seven times the difference in that investment in years of further education and training.

The economic gains from education can be calculated in similar fashion. Each extra year of BASED, net of social background effects, returns a little more than $8 per week $[(0·271)*(70·17)/(1)*(2·28)]$ in additional income, or about $430 a year. Of this $430, about one-third is due to the direct influence of BASED on INCOME net of other attainments, and the remainder to indirect effects through occupational attainments over the career. Similarly, a year of additional education returns about $10 per week $[(0·125)*(70·17)/(1)*(0·90)]$, or around $510 a year, one-third through the direct effect of ADDED on INCOME and the remaining two-thirds due to an indirect effect on the status of JOBN. In other words, individuals differing by one year in BASED will differ by about $430 a year in current income, while those alike in all respects including BASED but differing only in their investment in ADDED will differ in income by a factor of $510 times the difference in years of further education.

We should also note that, if one had the choice, coming from an affluent background is almost as good an 'investment' as basic education. The WLTH variable contributes about equally to current status and to current income, both directly and indirectly through BASED. Its direct effect on income is about $360 a year $[(0\cdot102)*(70\cdot17)/(1)*(1\cdot02)]$, not much less than the figure estimated for a year of basic education. Affluent families provide double insurance for their sons: they can afford to keep them at school longer but they also make contributions to their current income either by cash transfers or by influencing aspects of education and jobs not explicitly considered by this model.

Inheritance and achievement reconsidered

The basic model of status attainment assumes and substantiates the central mediating role played by schooling. Education converts the advantages or disadvantages of social origins into later attainments that express both the ascriptive influence of families and the personal efforts of individuals. The relative importance of these two general factors can be more readily evaluated by combining the five indicators of family background into a single measure. In Table 2.4 the individual correlations of Table 2.1 are replaced with the multiple correlation coefficients between the five social origin variables and later statuses. This summarizing device eliminates the unanalysed causal components shown in Table 2.3 and clarifies the influence of social background on attainment.

TABLE 2.4   *Observed and corrected correlations between social background and later attainment* [a]

Status variable	Correlation coefficients					
	SOCBAK	BASED	JOB1	ADDED	JOBN	INCOME
SOCBAK	1·000	0·511	0·390	0·140	0·426	0·339
BASED	0·601	1·000	0·507	0·054	0·481	0·363
JOB1	0·459	0·579	1·000	0·054	0·495	0·359
ADDED	0·165	0·062	0·062	1·000	0·254	0·162
JOBN	0·501	0·550	0·566	0·290	1·000	0·526
INCOME	0·399	0·415	0·410	0·185	0·601	1·000

[a] Observed coefficients are shown above the diagonal, corrected coefficients below. Social background coefficients are multiple correlations between the five social background variables shown in Table 2.1 and the attainment of respondents.

The upper triangle of coefficients shown in Table 2.4 is taken from Table 2.1, except for the first line in which multiple correlation coefficients between the five indicators of social background

(SOCBAK) and the remaining variables are shown. The lower triangle of coefficients has been adjusted to allow for possible measurement error. A number of alternative adjustments were carried out, including one with reliabilities reported by Bielby *et al.* (1977). But their reliabilities are probably not appropriate for these data.

Since most reported estimates of reliability lie in the range of 0·800 to 0·900, we arbitrarily selected a figure of 0·875 for 'own' statuses, and the somewhat lower figure of 0·825 for the statuses of 'others'. If reliabilities of 0·900 and 0·800 had been used, the adjusted coefficients would be changed by no more than 0·001. The only way to obtain dramatically different results would be to assume drastically different reliabilities. Clearly one can magnify the effects of ascription merely by assuming a very low reliability for social background (say, 0·700) and very high reliability for achieved statuses (say, 0·950). But there is no warrant for such assumptions. In fact, the most thorough study so far published suggests that our assumption of somewhat greater unreliability for social background measures may be unwarranted (Bielby *et al.*, 1977). But we have tried not to understate the overall effect of ascriptive processes.

TABLE 2.5   *Added-variance analysis of effects[a] in the basic model corrected for measurement error*

Dependent variable	Independent variables					R sq.
	SOCBAK	BASED	JOB1	ADDED	JOBN	
BASED	0·601					0·361
JOB1	0·459					0·211
	0·174	0·475				0·355
ADDED	0·165					0·027
	0·200	−0·058				0·029
	0·199	−0·062	0·006			0·029
JOBN	0·501					0·251
	0·267	0·390				0·348
	0·208	0·229	0·338			0·422
	0·163	0·243	0·336	0·227		0·472
INCOME	0·399					0·159
	0·234	0·274				0·207
	0·195	0·169	0·223			0·239
	0·169	0·177	0·222	0·132		0·256
	0·090	0·059	0·059	0·023	0·483	0·379

[a] Causes are entered serially from the earliest to the latest. The decline in the size of a coefficient (standardized regression coefficient) indicates how much of the total effect of an earlier cause is mediated through an intervening, later variable.

Table 2.5 presents a stepwise analysis of effects, in which the total effect of social background is shown first, with intervening variables added later to see how initial effects are mediated. The first R sq. is considerably higher than in Table 2.2, a difference resulting from our assumptions about measurement error. It is perhaps more instructive to take career beginnings (JOB1) as an expository example, because the relative importance of SOCBAK can be compared with BASED, the first achieved status in the model.

Career beginnings

So far as career beginnings are concerned, the total effect of social background (0·459) is almost as great as the direct effect of education (0·475). However, when BASED is introduced as an intervening variable, the coefficient for SOCBAK is reduced substantially, indicating that the larger part of its effect (about three-fifths) is mediated by schooling. If we attribute the indirect as well as the direct effect of background *wholly* to ascriptive forces (an arguable decision for reasons discussed below), the effect of schooling not attributable to background is less than the total effect of social origins: the R sq. for JOB1 status increases from 0·211 to 0·355 when BASED is included as an intervening cause of JOB1 status, thereby contributing 40 per cent to the final R sq. compared with 60 per cent for SOCBAK.

Further education and current job

The model explains very little of the variation in post-school training (ADDED) for reasons which become clearer in the next chapter. The only significant effect is social background, as would be expected from Table 2.2. For current job status the total effect of background is about as important as all other variables combined, almost doubling the R sq. from 0·251 to 0·472. About half the effect of social background on current status is mediated by BASED, about one-eighth by JOB1, and one-tenth by ADDED. Somewhat surprisingly, there is no appreciable diminution in the direct effect of social background on job status over the career. The direct effects of SOCBAK on JOB1 and JOBN are of the same order, 0·174 and 0·163 respectively.

Income

For income, however, the effects of ascription, again measured generously in terms of the total effect of social background, however mediated, are less important. Social background contributes less to an explanation of the income distribution than any other outcome in the status attainment process, although it still contributes up to 40 per cent of the total variance explained.

It is important to emphasize that by identifying the *total* effect of social background with ascriptive forces we have biased interpretation in favour of ascription versus achievement. In fact not all the influences of the family represent direct inheritance of inequality because family members display social, cultural and psychological similarities merely by being exposed to more similar environments than non-family members. None the less, identifying total effects with ascription establishes the upper limit for the influence of forces stemming from inequalities in family background. In general we find that such forces decline in importance over the socioeconomic career to the point where by mid-career (the average age of men in this analysis is forty-four) achieved statuses influence later attainment at least as much as ascription. This general conclusion is reinforced by the analysis over three generations described in chapter 6, and by analysis of the relative achievements of brothers (Sweetser and McDonnell, 1978). Like Brittain, we conclude that processes of ascription and achievement are equally important influences on the socioeconomic life-cycle.

The chapters that follow examine specific links in the chain that transmits social inequality from one generation to the next. Before proceeding to those analyses we should consider whether the general model describing the average experience of the men in the sample applies equally to specific groups.

Technical notes on group differences

The basic status attainment model reviewed above is a summary statement that does not take into account the varying experiences of different groups in the population. For example, formal education may have been more or less important for men whose careers spanned different periods. Similarly immigrants whose careers bridged two societies, and whose later careers may have been hampered by limited competence in English, may not have gained the same occupational returns for their schooling. Analogous considerations suggest separate analysis of the experience of men from different socioeconomic origins, with employee versus employer status, or with different residential histories affecting access to schooling and jobs.

In addition to these specific considerations, inequality of opportunity, discrimination, differences in values and life-styles and changes in educational and occupational structures may impinge with different weight on different groups. If, for example, the members of a particular group cannot convert their educational attainments into occupational and economic attainments as effectively as other groups, discriminatory job practices may be at work. Variations in cause-effect relationships might also result from age differences or broad historical trends such as the increasing differentiation and specialization of occupations, as well as increased credentialism in the labour market.

Much of the existing evidence for intergroup differences is based on North American studies, which have found significant variation in status attainment processes for groups defined by race and gender. There is substantial evidence that the process of status attainment for American blacks, the most thoroughly studied minority, is not the same as for whites. Even when blacks get as much education as whites they are unable to convert their educational attainments into equivalent occupational and economic rewards.[3] The observed occupational and income differences between ethnic groups in Australia could also result from discrimination (Australian Population and Immigration Council, 1976).

It has also been claimed, although with less supporting evidence, that processes of status attainment are affected by differences in social backgrounds. The fact that mobility is less than perfect because 'the occupational distributions of sons born of fathers in different strata do not match' (Eckland, 1967, p. 189) is often interpreted as evidence of inequality of opportunity and as support for the existence of a culture of poverty (Lewis, 1968). The so-called radical school-reform critics (e.g. Katz, 1971; Rist, 1973; Carnoy, 1974) have found such arguments attractive because if there is a culture of poverty, different kinds of schooling for socially disadvantaged groups may be required, not just more of the same kind of education that the population at large receives.

To explore such questions, we grouped respondents both according to the social status of their father's job (broadly defined as higher or lower white-collar, and higher or lower blue-collar) and according to the employment status of their fathers: owners of businesses (self-employed and employers), employees and an intermediate group of managers and supervisors (cf. Wright and Perrone, 1977). If the socioeconomic life-cycles of men differ markedly according to social background, such differences should appear when groups are separately analysed.

We also compare the experience of men who grew up in rural or farm areas with that of men from urban backgrounds. Apart from cultural and attitudinal differences that may distinguish rural and urban environments (cf. Blau and Duncan, 1967, p. 61), people from rural origins contended with increasingly restricted opportunities for rural employment (Broom and Jones, 1976, p. 35). As a consequence many confronted the problem of converting their rural experience and educational resources into occupational and economic attainments in urban settings. Since the turn of the century, increasing industrialization and urbanization, the shift from an agricultural to an extraction-based export economy, two world wars, the great depression of the 1930s and substantial postwar immigration have transformed the Australian occupational and social structure (Broom and Jones, 1976, pp. 33–7). That changing job opportunities and economic fluctuations affected the process of status attainment among cohorts of men exposed to these historical currents at different stages in their careers has been documented both for the United States (Blau and Duncan, 1967; Lane, 1975; Winsborough, 1975; Featherman and Hauser, 1976a) and for Australia (Broom and Jones, 1976, p. 102). We present further evidence on this issue below. However, as the demonstration of these effects requires a somewhat technical exposition, readers interested primarily in substantive conclusions may wish to turn to the summary at the end of this chapter.

Statistical comparisons of group effects

The substantive identification of group differences in status attainment processes translates into a statistical problem of comparing basic model effects estimated separately for different groups. To assess, for example, whether BASED is a more important influence on JOB1 in one group than another involves an analysis of covariance in which group membership is the covariate. Alternatively, the problem can be conceived as an instance of statistical interaction in which group membership modifies the effects represented in the basic model. In either case the partial regression coefficients across groups must be compared to determine whether group membership makes a difference to the impact of one variable on another. If the effects are reliably different, it can be inferred that the causal processes they represent are also different.

Questions like these can be answered by using dummy variables to represent group membership (see Bottenberg and Ward, 1963; Gujarati, 1970; Stolzenberg, 1974; and Specht and Warren, 1976 for details of method). The technique is similar to the conventional use of product terms in regression equations to test for interactions among continuous variables (see, for example, Digman, 1966; Ezekiel and Fox, 1967), except that categories of group membership are coded as dummy variables and product terms are formed between these dummies and the independent variables in a particular equation (Gujarati, 1970, p. 20). The dependent variable is then regressed on the independent variables, on all but one of the dummy variables, and on the product terms defined by the included dummies (Gujarati, 1970, p. 22). Partial regression coefficients for the product terms and the dummy variables are then interpreted by reference to the omitted category of group membership, as follows: a significant coefficient for a particular dummy variable represents an additive group 'treatment' effect because knowing which group a man belongs to adds to the amount of variance explained in the dependent variable. Significant coefficients for the product terms indicate that group membership affects the size of the partial relationship between the dependent and independent variable in one group compared with another. Both kinds of additional terms may improve the power of the explanatory model compared with the simpler additive one. If they do so to a statistically significant degree, and in theoretically meaningful ways, this more complex representation of social processes is to be preferred.

This technique has been used in sociological research (Jackson and Burke, 1965; Lane, 1968; Sewell and Hauser, 1975, p. 121; Spaeth, 1977), and a recent exposition is given by Specht and Warren (1976). However, it does present problems. Glass (1954) notes interpretive ambiguities associated with product terms in regression equations, and Althauser (1971) raises the same point in relation to multicollinearity among product-term coefficients. Nevertheless, the ambiguities pertain largely to the substantive interpretation of product-term coefficients and not to their statistical significance (Allison, 1977). In most cases we are concerned with statistical significance as an *indication* of group differences in effects. Substantive interpretation rests, not on those coefficients, but on within-group analyses conducted as a second step in which the basic model is estimated separately for specific groups.

For technical reasons, only respondents with complete data on all the variables in question can be retained for analysis with this technique, resulting in the loss of 760 cases and yielding a final (weighted) sample size of 1,800 men. However, a comparison of basic model coefficients estimated from these data with those estimated from correlations based on the maximum number of cases for each pair of variables (see Table 2.1) showed only minor differences in the coefficients. In terms of substantive interpretation the results from either sample are indistinguishable. This finding is reinforced by analyses duplicating those reported below, in which average values for each variable were assigned to non-respondents. Since the substantive interpretation is unchanged, we are satisfied that results are not biased by the exclusion of non-respondents.

Immigrants and status attainment

The status attainment process is now explored for three groups defined broadly by birthplace and mother-tongue: respondents born in Australia, respondents born in another English-speaking country and respondents born in a country where the language is not English. This grouping represents two important aspects of social differentiation: immigrant status and language.

The results reported in Table 2.6 are discussed in some detail because they form the pattern of interpretation followed in Tables 2.7 to 2.10, which are appended to the end of this chapter. The body of the table contains partial regression coefficients for each of the three groups, equation by equation, along with the values of the intercepts, R sq. for the basic model for each group (the column headed R sq.), R sqs for the basic model for the sample as a whole (Rsqr, the restricted model), R sqs based on the model incorporating dummy variables and product terms (R sqf, the full model), the increment to explained variance added by the full model (column headed f–r%), and finally the weighted sample size for each group (column headed N).

In each panel of three lines, coefficients for the foreign-born, non-English-speaking group is uppermost ($N = 273$), foreign-born, English-speaking men come next ($N = 238$); and the Australian-born comparison group is listed last ($N = 1,289$). The coefficients are unstandardized and therefore can be compared within each panel for the same variable, and across variables where the measurement scales are the same. Coefficients not shown in the table do not exceed twice their standard error, and asterisked coefficients are significantly different at the 5 per cent level from those for the Australian-born comparison group. Means and standard deviations for each group are given at the base of the table (the values for INCOME appear under the column headed Intercept). The coefficients shown derive from separate analyses of each group. Mention of an omitted comparison group refers to supporting analyses in which between-group differences are directly tested. These latter analyses provide the basis for establishing group differences, but for the reasons given above substantive interpretation depends on within-group analyses.

Because analysis does not follow the strict deductive pattern of hypothesis-testing but is exploratory, some statistical differences may emerge merely by chance. Not every statistically significant difference is substantively meaningful, and the problem arises of which coefficients to interpret and which to ignore. One general rule is to take consistent differences seriously, whether across groups for a particular variable (for example, the coefficients for

43

TABLE 2.6 National origins:[a] basic model coefficients and tests for group differences[b]

Dependent variables	Independent variables									Intercept	R sq.	R sqr / R sqf	f-r%	N
	DADED	DADJOB	MOMED	WLTH	FAMSZ	BASED	JOB1	ADDED	JOBN					
BASED	0-242*		0-251	—	-0-148					5-719*	0-340	0-266	2-1	273
	—		0-234	0-731	-0-178					7-469	0-321	0-287		238
	0-101		0-198	0-453						7-480	0-247			1,289
JOB1	—*	0-152	5-855		—*	7-944*				328-534	0-172*	0-331	3-7	
	—					19-577*				247-782	0-391*	0-368		
	0-183					25-602				147-812	0-404			
ADDED	0-041			0-245*		—	—			0-816	0-091	0-020	1-9	
	—			—	—*	—	—			0-546	0-013	0-039		
	0-041			—	-0-050	—	—			0-547	0-027			
JOBN	—*		—		—	11-026	0-298*	39-498*		262-733*	0-460	0-422	3-0	
		0-148				8-039	0-529	22-535		130-067	0-436	0-452		
			—		-2-600	12-372	0-454	23-683		102-698	0-436			
INCOME	—			—	-2-884	4-374	—*	—*	0-241	-40-766	0-302	0-282	1-1	
	—			—	—	2-903	—	—	0-223	-57-095	0-377	0-293		
	—			5-809	—	—	0-121	—	0-211	-55-895	0-269			
Means	8-988	535-346	8-063	-0-339	4-758	9-884	493-604	0-381	496-332	115-807				
	8-499	492-638	8-381	-0-281	4-408	10-023	484-564	0-493	510-016	124-498				
	8-278	510-315	8-195	0-223	4-405	9-605	489-851	0-572	541-604	138-107				
Standard deviations	3-952	111-986	2-903	0-800	2-546	3-045	93-001	0-853	103-335	55-990				
	2-648	109-842	1-785	0-971	2-508	2-252	83-537	0-862	106-119	61-554				
	2-292	107-480	1-675	1-029	2-435	2-017	93-991	0-977	117-519	74-533				

[a] National origin groups were defined in terms of respondent's birthplace as follows: respondents born in Australia (N = 1,289); respondents born in another English-speaking nation (N = 238); respondents born in a non-English-speaking nation (N = 273). An asterisked coefficient differs significantly from that for the Australian-born group.

[b] Tests for group differences are by comparison with Australian-born group. R sqr = proportion of variance explained by basic model; R sqf = proportion of variance explained by basic model plus dummy variables plus product terms. f-r = Rsqf–R sqr, additional variance explained by group membership variables.

* An asterisked coefficient differs significantly from that for the Australian-born group.

BASED in the equation for JOB1), or across variables within groups (e.g., the equation for JOBN in Table 2.6). But what is to be done with an isolated but significant coefficient like ADDED in the INCOME equation? One would not want to assign much meaning to the fact that of two coefficients, both of which are not reliably different from zero, one achieves statistical significance by comparison with the Australian-born. In cases like this an interpretation is offered only if there are plausible theoretical reasons or if the effect is relatively large. By focusing on substantial, consistent and theoretically relevant differences, a real but small and idiosyncratic group difference may be ignored, but such a risk seems justified.

Table 2.6 shows that the influence of BASED on JOB1 is a recurring point of difference across groups. Other things being equal, both immigrant groups are significantly less successful in converting years of basic education into first job status than the Australian-born group. An analysis not reported here shows the difference between the two foreign-born groups to be significant as well. Thus, other things being equal, Australian-born respondents convert one year of basic education into 26 points of first job status, respondents from other English-speaking nations gain 20 status points for each year, and respondents from non-English-speaking nations gain only 8 status points for each year of their basic education.

Two plausible explanations for these differences can be offered: first, there may be job discrimination against migrant groups, particularly those from non-English-speaking countries; second, employers may be unwilling or unable to evaluate educational qualifications gained outside Australia, especially from non-English-speaking nations. A governmental survey conducted at about the same time as the ANU 1973 survey found systematic differences in the recognition of qualifications gained in different countries. The survey also documented the importance of English-language competence for finding more highly skilled jobs (Australian Population and Immigration Council, 1976, p. 51). However, because only a minority of either foreign-born group actually started work in Australia, such interpretations should be accepted with reservation, at least so far as they bear on the status of the first job. Four in five of the English-speaking foreign-born group and five in six of the non-English-speaking group held their first job in an overseas country. In other words, the varying influence of BASED on first job status represents a complex mix of social processes, not simply or even primarily job discrimination by Australian employers.

Three other findings are worth mention. First, current job status for the foreign non-English group is less strongly tied to first job, suggesting that migration was much more of a disruption to their careers. Such an interpretation fits the report of the Australian Population and Immigration Council (1976, p. 19) about the importance of language skills in job placement and the greater difficulty such immigrants have in maintaining their occupational careers because their qualifications are less likely to be recognized in Australia. Moreover, many men in this group moved from farm to factory work. Second, the two immigrant groups have lower average current occupational status and income than the Australian-born group, with foreign-born men from English-speaking backgrounds outranking those from non-English-speaking countries. However, there are no group differences in the INCOME equation, implying that immigrant status as such does not appear directly to modify the processes of economic attainment as represented in this model. To the extent that discrimination exists, it does not affect income so much as the range of jobs immigrants are able to enter. Given the official machinery for arbitration and wage-setting in Australia, this finding is not surprising.

So far two main points have been documented. First, the attainments of immigrants do not match those of Australian-born respondents, and foreign-born men from English-speaking backgrounds have more favourable occupational experiences than those from non-English-speaking nations. Second, processes of status attainment may be somewhat different in the three groups, principally because immigrants gain lower returns from education, and first job status is a less important influence on current status for men from non-English-speaking countries. But as we have pointed out, the difference in status returns to basic education involves more than job discrimination, language difficulties or an unwillingness on the part of employers to recognize non-Australian qualifications.

It needs to be emphasized that these minor differences in *processes* of status attainment are quite consistent with major concentrations of migrants from specific countries in particular kinds of jobs, or in jobs with low status. The reason is that immigrants from different countries have different backgrounds and schooling. When differences in social background between migrants and non-migrants are taken into account, the processes of status allocation are found to be much the same. Put another way, because their social inputs are different, the same processes produce different social outputs for each group.

Socioeconomic origins and status attainment

In Table 2.7 parallel analyses are reported for men grouped

according to the social status of their father's job when respondents were fourteen years old. The four groups, upper and lower white-collar and upper and lower blue-collar, derive from the six-point ANU 1 scale (Broom and Jones, 1969b, p. 651). The farm population is discussed later.

In these comparisons a basic model variable, DADJOB, is used to define the groups. Differences in coefficients for this variable across groups should therefore be ignored, as should differences in R sq., but the remaining coefficients are comparable. For purposes of statistical testing, the lower blue-collar group is the comparison group.

So far as the determinants of BASED are concerned, the negative coefficient for FAMSZ in both nonmanual groups is significantly greater than for the manual comparison group and is the only interpretable group difference. However, the direction of the difference is contrary to what one might expect. Under a traditional resource allocation explanation, family size should make the greatest difference among families with least resources. But according to these results the negative effect of having an additional sibling on years of basic education was greater in white-collar than in blue-collar families. The higher coefficients for MOMED suggest a possible interaction between mother's education and family size. Women with large families and nonmanual husbands may have relatively low educational achievements and may hold lower educational aspirations for their sons.

For JOB1 the most important difference is that sons of upper white-collar fathers are highly successful in converting their educational attainments into first job status. The net effect of one year of basic education is 30 status points for sons in this group, but only about 20 points for those from other social backgrounds. This result confirms assumptions about access to resources. Sons from higher-status backgrounds apparently have resources that gain them early advantage in the status attainment process. While we cannot directly identify specific mechanisms, social contacts (Meade, 1973) or private education (Williams et al., 1977) are likely candidates.

For ADDED, again no substantive comment is warranted. Of the 28 coefficients 22 are not reliably different from zero and the remainder show no discernible pattern. For JOBN, there is only one significant difference: the greater impact of career beginnings in the upper manual group, which probably reflects the high degree of career immobility in the skilled trades (see chapter 4). On the surface one might expect a similar effect in the upper nonmanual group, because professionals also show high career immobility. But this group also includes managers, and few of them start out in that category. Thus, the high career mobility of managers counter-balances the low mobility among professionals.

Among the influences on income, JOBN has a significantly smaller effect in the lower manual than in the other groups: 10 status points are worth $3·20 a week to upper nonmanual workers but only $1·30 to lower manual workers. Other things being equal, individuals from high-status backgrounds get paid more for the same kind of job. This difference probably results from socio-economic group differences in access to contacts or information, and even differences in interpersonal skills that link background to earning capacity. Although the evidence for a direct effect of ability on earnings is somewhat equivocal (cf. Griliches and Mason, 1973), group differences in individual ability may also be at work (cf. Duncan, 1968).

All in all, the similarities in status attainment processes between socioeconomic groups are more evident than are the differences. However, analogously to the comparisons of non-migrants and migrants, there is evidence that higher-status groups convert their resources and advantages more successfully than do lower-status groups, especially in the translation of education attainments into first job status. Higher-status groups simply command more resources that enable them to exploit their educational advantages: information, informal contacts and interpersonal skills, all of which facilitate socioeconomic success.

Worker categories and status attainment

We now explore whether there are differences in processes of status attainment for three groups defined in terms of the father's employment status: *owners*, who were self-employed or employed others; *managers*, who were not employers or self-employed but held positions of authority; and *workers*, who neither owned businesses nor supervised the work of others but simply sold their labour. These three categories are operationally defined by two variables: whether the respondent's father had his own business when the respondent was fourteen years of age; and whether he supervised the work of others. Table 2.8 gives the results of estimating the basic model separately for each origin grouping and indicates where effects differ significantly between groups. Workers are the comparison group.

There are no consistent differences across these three groups. Most of the significant differences point to the advantage enjoyed by men whose father was an owner or manager. Family wealth is a more important influence on current job status for the sons of owners and managers, although among the latter the effect does not reach statistical significance because of small sample size. Almost all (95 per cent) of employers and self-employed men in the father's generation are best described as petit bourgeois, being small businessmen in establishments with fewer than twenty-five employees. We would hardly expect them to pass on to their sons social advantages beyond a higher average level of family resources and perhaps the inheritance of a family business.

Farm, rural and urban origins and status attainment

Three categories of residence were defined to represent differences in schooling and job opportunities when the respondent was growing up: men who lived on a farm, in a village or country town or in a middle-sized or large city. For the farm group, and to some degree for the rural group, this classification amounts to controlling on DADJOB, at least for farmers and farm workers. Note the smaller standard deviations for DADJOB in the first group. Therefore, as in the analyses of socioeconomic groups, we do not attempt to interpret the DADJOB coefficients for the farm group, or any differences from the rural and urban groups for this variable.

Inasmuch as the only significant differences in the influence of social background on BASED involve DADJOB, we conclude that in each group the resources of social background are converted into educational attainments in much the same way. However, in the conversion of educational attainment into initial occupational status, both rural groups are disadvantaged. A year of education yields them about 10 status points less than it does for the urban group. Since there is no comparable difference in the influence of background on BASED, we interpret this reduced effect as evidence of more restricted occupational opportunities in the rural job market. The fact that the basic model fits the experience of the urban group much better also indicates that its meritocratic and universalistic assumptions fit the urban environment better than the rural or farm sector.

The pattern of effects for JOBN offers further support of restricted occupational opportunities in smaller localities. For both rural groups, but particularly for the farm group, the direct effects of BASED on JOBN exceed by about half as much again the effect in the urban group, though the difference does not quite achieve statistical significance. This reversal of educational effects – higher on first job for the urban group but higher on current job for the two rural groups – is consistent with a less meritocratic opportunity structure in rural areas. Restricted opportunities in rural markets result in two 'career beginnings' for some men from rural origins, especially sons of farmers. First they start work in rural areas in jobs determined more by the narrow range of job available than their educational attainment.[4] But in a second career beginning after leaving rural areas, educational attainment is converted once again into an occupational attainment influenced less by their earlier rural job status than by their formal schooling. Men from villages or country towns occupy an intermediate position between the farm and urban groups. Patterns of rural-urban migration further support this interpretation: 80 per cent of respondents with farm or rural origins reported a first job in a rural area, but ten years later only 64 per cent worked in a rural area.

Cohorts and status attainment

A comparison of age cohorts rests on an assumption that social and economic conditions influence status attainment. Four broad periods are distinguished: (a) the years up to and including 1928, when unemployment was around 6 to 9 per cent, migration was adding as many as 50,000 new settlers each year, and the workforce and gross domestic product (GDP) were both increasing; (b) the years 1929 to 1939, spanning the great depression, when male unemployment ranged from 10 to 30 per cent, there was net emigration up to 1935 followed by only a small net intake of immigrants, GDP fluctuated within a small range from year to year, and the total workforce climbed from just over two and a half million at the beginning of the period to three million at the end; (c) the years 1940 to 1948 spanning World War II and the beginnings of postwar reconstruction, during which GDP almost doubled, unemployment fell to around 2 per cent of the male workforce, and net immigration began to accelerate; and (d) the period 1949 to 1970 in which the size of the workforce increased by over two million, GDP increased five-fold, there was essentially full employment, and immigration added between 50,000 and 150,000 settlers each year.

There can be little doubt that such gross shifts in the economic and social climate affect educational and occupational opportunity. In Table 2.10 the most recent cohort is taken as a baseline because it seems sensible both to compare how things were with how they are and to contrast a more expansionary economic period with less expansionary ones. Because cohorts are defined in terms of year of entry into the labour force, labour force experience is partly controlled.

It turns out that there are no significant differences among the three older cohorts. Apart from small, and probably unreliable, differences in the effects of DADJOB in the equation for BASED, the most striking cohort differences relate to the effects of BASED on career beginnings for the youngest cohort. The effect of each completed year of basic education on initial job status in the youngest cohort is double that in the oldest: a year of basic education is worth only 12 status points to the oldest cohort compared with 25 points for men who started work in the period of postwar economic growth. The differences are only slightly less for the two middle cohorts. A similar increase in the importance of education for job beginnings has been observed in the United States (Blau and Duncan, 1967, p. 180; Lane, 1975; Featherman and Hauser, 1976a). Such trends are consistent both with increased credentialism in job placement (Berg, 1970) and with the fact that the occupational structure has become more differentiated and technically specialized.

Summary

Of the several social processes underlying the basic model of status attainment, how successful or unsuccessful men are in converting their educational attainments into initial occupational status seems the most problematic. Immigrants seem disadvantaged in this respect, whereas upper-middle-class groups are decidedly advantaged. Urban groups are advantaged compared with those from rural origins. Moreover, the nature of the process has changed. Schooling and first job have become more closely linked since the end of World War II. The factors contributing to these differences undoubtedly include job discrimination, lack of language skills and unrecognized qualifications among immigrants, personal networks of influence among higher-status groups, restricted occupational opportunities in rural areas, and an increasingly differentiated and specialized occupational structure. In an era when education and the possession of formal credentials were less important, immigrants from non-English-speaking countries and rural migrants to the cities fared better in the job search, or at least fared no worse than men with different characteristics.

These general findings highlight the importance of education for career beginnings and its responsiveness to social background and wider social and economic conditions. To the extent that groups are especially advantaged or disadvantaged in their occupational careers, whether because of social origins, residence, culture or the impact of major social events, the most vulnerable link is entry into the labour force when educational resources are first traded for occupational status. Thereafter the process of status attainment seems relatively stable and insulated from more remote inequalities associated with social origins, migration, farm background or the general economic climate when a man first started work. Ascribed benefits or handicaps thus established persist, but they do not continually register fresh credits or debits on the attainment balance sheet.

We can now largely settle the question of whether sub-group differences are sufficiently large to throw doubt on the general applicability of the basic model. Do specific groups have such different experiences that they must be analysed separately in order to avoid serious misrepresentation of social processes? Two related considerations need to be balanced. How much does knowledge of group membership *add* to the explanatory power of the basic model? Do group differences in status attainment processes diverge sufficiently from the basic model to invalidate an analysis carried out in terms of a single model for the total sample? On the first point, knowledge of group membership adds between a minimum of 0·8 per cent and a maximum of 4·4 per cent to explained variance, depending on which groups and which dependent variables are involved. These are neither trivial nor substantial improvements in explanation, and where appropriate such differences will be explored in later analysis, especially the schooling/first job link. On the second point, it is clear that elaborations to identify specific groups do not greatly change the overall picture. In view of the small increases in explanatory power and the fact that no large or consistent group differences in social processes were found, the analyses that follow concentrate on status attainment processes in the male Australian workforce as a whole. However, the subsidiary analyses reported here serve to alert reader and researcher alike to variations on the major theme, especially the vulnerability of the link between schooling and career beginnings.

TABLE 2.7   Socioeconomic origins:[a] basic model coefficients and tests for group differences[b]

Dependent variables	DADED	DADJOB	MOMED	WLTH	FAMSZ	BASED	JOB1	ADDED	JOBN	Intercept	R sq.	R sqf	f-t%	N
BASED	0·081	—*	0·277	0·434	−0·278*					4·569*	0·272	0·252		276
	0·137	−0·004	0·195	0·411	−0·284*					9·405	0·256		4·1	196
	0·092	−0·006*	0·169	0·623	−0·130					4·294	0·230	0·293		323
	—	—	0·161	0·414	−0·125					7·202	0·156			657
JOB1	—*		0·159			30·617*				97·644*	0·475	0·331		
	−5·647*		—			17·261				337·057	0·225		2·8	
	−4·440		0·232			17·227				245·919	0·258	0·359		
	3·346		—			20·533				180·196	0·276			
ADDED		—		—	—*	—				1·469	0·028	0·018		
		−0·003		—	—	−0·097*				2·046	0·087		3·3	
		0·002		—	−0·080*	—				1·498	0·034	0·051		
		—		—	—	−0·001				−0·408	0·023			
JOBN				13·598	—	12·947	0·403	31·326		149·475	0·481	0·408		
				—	—	13·080	0·438	23·577		123·359	0·389		0·8	
				11·457	—	6·044	0·598*	24·498		170·902	0·397	0·416		
				—	−3·188	10·725	0·443	29·664		178·018	0·314			
INCOME		—*		—*		—	0·132	—	0·320*	−75·503*	0·419	0·279		
		—	−4·230*	—		—	—	6·455	0·211	−24·286	0·302		3·1	
		—	—	—*		—	—	—	0·274*	−119·069*	0·264	0·310		
		−0·133	3·044	11·259		3·768	0·128	5·714	0·129	−13·413	0·247			
Means	10·881	674·901	9·234	0·730	3·372	11·190	538·108	0·699	603·897	170·015				
	9·039	566·710	8·862	0·334	3·994	10·131	517·537	0·691	563·985	140·209				
	8·596	478·024	8·277	−0·156	4·338	9·808	481·966	0·624	526·975	128·291				
	7·777	420·456	7·947	−0·181	4·644	9·351	466·294	0·559	508·749	123·772				
Standard deviations	4·607	97·851	2·557	1·063	1·586	2·756	131·185	1·093	137·962	85·992				
	2·740	82·431	2·663	1·044	2·235	2·463	101·502	1·026	120·500	72·581				
	2·648	41·654	1·613	0·892	2·457	2·065	80·131	1·087	106·438	63·025				
	1·749	41·958	1·600	0·925	2·580	1·713	73·496	0·914	103·167	59·501				

[a] Socioeconomic groups are defined in terms of DADJOB as follows: professional, managerial (N = 276); clerical (N = 196); skilled manual (N = 323); semiskilled, unskilled and service workers (N = 657).

[b] Tests for group differences are by comparison with semiskilled, unskilled and service workers group. Graziers, farmers and farm workers are omitted.

* An asterisked coefficient differs significantly from that for the semiskilled, unskilled service workers group.

54

TABLE 2.8 *Worker categories:[a] basic model coefficients and tests for group differences[b]*

Dependent variables				Independent variables						Intercept	R sq.	R sqr	R sqf	f-r%	N
	DADED	DADJOB	MOMED	WLTH	FAMSZ	BASED	JOB1	ADDED	JOBN						
BASED	0·154*	—*	0·164	0·498	-0·144					7·506*	0·253	0·266		2·8	699
	0·165*	0·003	0·254	0·455	-0·121					5·405	0·346		0·294		209
	—	0·004	0·285	0·453	-0·152					6·088	0·267				873
JOB1	—	0·207		8·753		17·375				218·466	0·285	0·331		1·9	
	—	—*		—		28·381*				208·341	0·475		0·350		
	—	0·171		—		18·728				242·621	0·304				
ADDED	0·037	—	—	—		—*	—*			0·049	0·040	0·020		2·8	
	0·066	—	-0·126*	0·078		-0·082	—			2·192*	0·113		0·048		
	—	—	—	—		-0·046	0·001			0·384	0·022				
JOBN	—	—	0·127*	12·993*	-3·527	10·874	0·387	22·559		147·537	0·375	0·422		0·8	
	—	—	—	14·466	—	8·510	0·487	23·633		224·121	0·505		0·430		
	—	—	—	—	-3·131	12·587	0·456	31·307		151·864	0·420				
INCOME	—	—	—	—	—	—	—		0·221	-45·089	0·237	0·282		1·0	
	-3·581	—	—	10·255	—	—	0·109		0·353*	-76·549	0·432		0·293		
	—	—	—	6·749	—	3·266	0·092		0·191	-50·046	0·270				
Means	8·268	560·623	8·141	0·416	4·721	9·488	497·380	0·433	543·985	134·283					
	9·828	533·936	9·002	0·225	3·832	10·707	516·783	0·651	562·423	156·146					
	8·198	468·484	8·064	-0·236	4·402	9·622	476·675	0·565	511·119	125·608					
Standard deviations	2·710	99·231	2·012	1·061	2·477	2·221	89·675	0·903	118·333	75·651					
	3·352	122·593	2·323	1·036	2·265	2·579	125·257	0·990	125·757	79·630					
	2·543	93·787	1·709	0·879	2·450	2·092	82·476	0·918	106·168	62·901					

[a] Worker categories are defined as follows: fathers neither self-employed nor supervisors ($N = 873$); fathers not self-employed but supervisors ($N = 209$); fathers self-employed ($N = 699$).

[b] Tests for group differences are by comparison with fathers who were neither self-employed nor supervisors.

* An asterisked coefficient differs significantly from that for the group of fathers who were neither self-employed nor supervisors.

TABLE 2.9 Farm/rural/urban origins:[a] basic model coefficients and tests for group differences[b]

Dependent variables	DADED	DADJOB	MOMED	WLTH	FAMSZ	BASED	JOB1	ADDED	JOBN	Intercept	R sq.	R sqr / R sqf	f-r%	N
BASED	0·215*	—*	0·179	0·403	-0·113					6·930	0·197	0·266		285
	0·163*	—*	0·259	0·283	-0·168					6·281	0·263	0·291	2·5	528
	0·067	0·003	0·199	0·462	-0·133					6·624	0·270			983
JOB1	0·257*		-6·599*	11·476		13·317*				276·675*	0·213	0·331		
	0·166		—	—		14·679*				288·144*	0·238	0·356	2·5	
	0·105		—	—		24·638				173·913	0·413			
ADDED	—			—	—	—*				0·196	0·011	0·020		
	0·051			0·073	-0·034	—*				0·329	0·023	0·048	2·8	
	—			—	—	-0·069				0·927	0·023			
JOBN	-9·364*	0·287*		16·194	—	15·380	0·248*	—*		167·988	0·277	0·422		
	—	—		12·357	-3·546	13·459	0·423	26·908		157·297	0·413	0·438	1·6	
	—	0·064		7·957	—	8·965	0·489	29·253		145·037	0·478			
INCOME	—			10·104		—	—*	0·185	0·250	25·694*	0·145	0·282		
	—*			11·317*		3·854	—	0·230	0·452	-21·538*	0·280	0·298		
	0·044			—		—	0·132	0·219	0·656	-82·693	0·354			
Means	7·619	591·433	7·849	0·328	5·045	9·028	499·831	0·250	540·774	125·665				
	8·034	492·679	7·805	-0·096	4·835	9·293	476·421	0·452	508·436	126·528				
	8·860	498·722	8·523	0·088	4·079	10·129	493·615	0·656	539·369	138·197				
Standard deviations	1·890	71·174	1·590	0·992	2·500	2·030	77·656	0·578	113·115	77·803				
	2·512	106·380	1·769	0·960	2·551	2·108	81·428	0·961	109·941	69·236				
	2·850	109·465	2·035	1·040	2·328	2·265	109·954	1·002	117·150	68·926				

[a] Origin groups are defined as follows: respondents living on a farm at age 14 (N = 285); respondents living in a village or country town at age 14 (N = 528); respondents living in a medium or large size city at age 14 (N = 983).

[b] Tests for group differences are by comparison with the urban group.

* An asterisked coefficient differs significantly from that for the urban group.

TABLE 2.10 First job cohorts:[a] basic model coefficients and tests for group differences[b]

Dependent variables	DADED	DADJOB	MOMED	WLTH	FAMSZ	BASED	JOB1	ADDED	JOBN	Intercept	R sq.	R sqr / R sqf	f-r%	N
BASED	—*	—*	0-309	—	-0-123					6-309	0-241			156
	0-115	—*	0-260	—	-0-080*					6-021	0-192	0-266		471
	0-144	—	0-182	0-247	-0-151					7-190	0-177	0-310	4-4	476
	0-128	-0-003	0-203	0-187	-0-189					6-683	0-235			694
JOB1	—*	0-218	-10-701*	—		12-004*				325-382*	0-232			
	—*	0-177	—	—		13-697*				265-195*	0-215	0-331		
	—*	0-097*	—*	10-429		14-444*				308-583*	0-188	0-361	3-5	
	-3-397	0-198	3-594	—		24-754				149-449	0-431			
ADDED	—*	-0-002	—	—	—	—	—			1-018	0-084			
	—	0-106	—	—	—	—	—			0-764	0-050	0-020		
	—	—	—	—	-0-038	-0-044	0-001			0-310	0-019	0-035	1-5	
	—	—	—	—	—	—	—			0-693	0-020			
JOBN	—	—	6-628*	—	-6-450	—*	0-578	—*		218-573	0-242			
	—	—	—	22-093	—*	6-635*	0-322	24-273		245-105*	0-278	0-422		
	—	0-098	—	14-760	-3-759	12-182	0-459	34-887		112-775	0-398	0-443	2-1	
	—	0-075	—	12-281	-3-251	14-735	0-460	27-332		125-222	0-556			
INCOME				—	—		0-257	0-219	513-106	-93-080	0-241			
				—	—		—	0-246	514-558	-36-462	0-279	0-282		
				7-242	—*		0-099	0-220	524-382	-53-806	0-266	0-296	1-4	
				6-671	—		0-099	0-208	549-586	-65-311	0-290			
Means	7-636	513-416	7-660	-0-589	5-433	8-479	475-639	0-437	513-106	110-592				
	8-111	510-118	7-885	-0-299	4-912	9-026	467-777	0-537	514-558	121-022				
	8-139	505-516	8-067	-0-084	4-514	9-408	482-451	0-493	524-382	135-721				
	8-974	516-676	8-630	0-577	3-891	10-644	513-101	0-579	549-586	144-155				
Standard deviations	1-790	106-145	1-715	0-640	2-616	1-748	67-493	0-783	106-493	72-784				
	2-406	102-799	1-777	0-835	2-578	1-819	71-916	1-047	102-616	61-467				
	2-353	107-133	1-653	0-937	2-438	1-942	82-694	0-833	114-153	69-581				
	3-064	115-018	2-148	4-030	2-219	2-422	109-567	0-981	123-585	75-008				

[a] Cohorts are defined as follows: JOB1 before 1929 (N = 156); JOB1 in period 1929-39 (N = 471); JOB1 in period 1940-8 (N = 476); JOB1 after 1948 (N = 694).

[b] Tests for group differences are by comparison with group entering labour force after 1948.

* An asterisked coefficient differs significantly from that for the group entering labour force after 1948.

3 Education and career beginnings

In status attainment research, as in social research generally, deciding what information to secure and how to ask about it limits the range of issues that can be addressed. The way that variables are constructed from raw data further limits the real-world processes that any theoretical model can represent. Obviously, if information on apprenticeship is not collected, its effect on status attainment cannot be assessed. More subtly, to construct a variable representing education in terms of up to sixteen years of schooling assumes that each year of school has an equal effect on later attainment. That assumption may be false, but alternative conceptions are not always considered. This chapter explores a variety of ways of relating education to status attainment, to see which conceptualization best explains occupational success.

Measuring education

In status attainment research education is usually represented in one of two forms. The first is years of schooling completed. Sewell and his colleagues (Sewell and Hauser, 1975, p. 20), Featherman and Hauser (1976a, p. 465) in their replication of Blau and Duncan, and Alexander *et al.* (1975, pp. 327—8) have all used such a measure in a series of influential studies. Another closely related procedure is to group years of education, and sometimes qualifications, into a series of ordinal categories. Blau and Duncan (1967, pp. 165–6) used an eight category scale which, they say, 'hardly differs from a simple linear transformation, or "coding", of the exact number of years of school completed'. Two of their steps ('high school, four years' and 'college, four years') measure both years completed and signal the formal completion of secondary and tertiary education respectively. Some such categorical measure is employed in all studies that use cross-tabulations to examine relationships among status variables, for example Australia (Broom and Jones, 1976), Finland (Pontinen and Uusitalo, 1975), Germany (Müller, 1973, pp. 245–51), Sweden (Fägerlind, 1975) and the United States (Alexander and Eckland, 1975).

Both years of schooling and educational categories share an assumption that the steps, whether from year to year or category to category, can be regarded as interval scales. In correlation techniques such as path analysis, each step on the scale is treated as if it has the same value as every other step. For example, if the path coefficient for years of schooling on occupational status is 0·3, it means that moving from the first to second grade or from the last year of college to a post-graduate year is worth the same (0·3 status units). The possibility that the effects may be different for different kinds or amounts of education is ruled out in such a simple, linear analytic model. However, there is no reason in principle why a more complicated real-world process can not be incorporated into analysis.

Are educational effects non-linear?

Most contemporary researchers are explicit about the limitations and assumptions of their measures and analytic models. Olneck (1976), for example, refers to 'average' effects of years of education because effects are averaged across a range of years in which each step might have different effects. Sorensen (1976, p. 79) similarly observes that one of his models is probably not appropriate for educational attainment because it 'predicts rapid change at the start of the process and less change later on. If educational attainments are measured in years of schooling, this pattern does not conform to what is observed in bureaucratic school systems.' While he does not elaborate this observation, there are three reasons why the effects of education on status and income may not be linear: different rates of learning, credentialism and alternative forms of education.

Rates of learning

The cognitive learning that takes place in schools varies from year to year because of institutional differences in curricula, variations in teacher quality and school philosophy, as well as because of individual differences in ability, personality, rate of maturation and motivation. The interaction between institutional conditions and personal characteristics may also affect job-relevant skills learnt at school. For example, if an employer wants to hire welders and welding is taught in the fourth year of secondary school, the employer will be interested in hiring school-leavers who have attained at least that level. Furthermore, it is unlikely that all comparable considerations somehow average out across the occupational spectrum.

In the United States it has been claimed that tertiary education carries an unusually high premium for status and income compared with lower levels of education. Arrow (1973) speaks of 'higher education as a filter' and suggests that it affects job placement in a different way from secondary education. Berg (1970, p. 86) also reports from his discussions with employment officers that 'there was, of course, abundant testimony concerning the worth of college graduates, and in this testimony the unifying theme was the diligence and stick-to-it-iveness of a young man who can endure four years of college.'

So far as empirical evidence on this speculation is concerned, Olneck (1976) and Featherman and Hauser (1978) have shown that treating years of tertiary education differently from primary and secondary schooling is an improvement over a simple measure of years of schooling completed. However, within the two categories of primary-secondary schooling and tertiary schooling, they still assume that steps from one year to the next are of equal importance.

Credentialism

Olneck (1976, p. 14) includes a dummy variable to represent 'the additional advantage of completing the fourth year of college over and above the average effect of an extra year of higher education'. He argues that a formal certification of educational achievement is a crucial criterion for status attainment. Although he finds support for an effect of graduation over and above the effects of attendance, he does not directly consider the issue of credentialism. Berg on the other hand observes that 'most of the respondents made it perfectly plain that the content of a college program mattered a good deal less than the fact of successful completion of studies.' 'To a man, the respondents assured us that diplomas and degrees were a good thing' (1970, pp. 86, 88).

It is frequently claimed that in the United States there are three crucial transitions involved in schooling: completing grade school, finishing high school and graduation from college. Almost no one who successfully completes the twelfth year fails to graduate from high school, although in some countries this pattern does not hold. In Australia, throughout the period when respondents in the 1973 survey were at school, public State-wide examinations were conducted which certified both the level of education achieved and whether it qualified a person for entry to higher levels. Such examinations varied historically and between States in their titles and timing, but in general one examination was taken at the end of compulsory education, about ninth or tenth year, and another in the final year of secondary school about two years later. The former is most often called the intermediate certificate and the latter the matriculation certificate, because it was typically required for university entrance. In the last decade or so, however, these State-wide examinations have been de-emphasized in favour of internal assessments. Trends away from end-of-year public examinations and towards continuous assessment and school-based certification in Australia have been too recent to have any effect on the careers of men in our sample.

The importance of public examinations is well documented and obvious even from job advertisements (see the examples in Rooney, 1966). They were required for entrance to higher or alternative types of education such as apprenticeships and are important in other ways. As late as 1975, Nuttall could say of the United Kingdom that, although no large-scale survey of personnel selection policies had been carried out, 'it is quite apparent that employers set considerable store by the results of public examinations' (1975, p. 72). McLaren makes similar observations about Australia: 'public examinations yield tangible rewards in the form of marketable qualifications' (1968, p. 2); 'better wages and security of employment enable parents to keep their children longer at school and give them a better chance than they ever had, by which they mean getting a higher certificate than they ever had' (1968, p. 16); and he refers to 'the annual examinations to which we are as a nation so passionately addicted' (1968, p. 38).

We need to allow for the probability that education affects status attainment through a series of thresholds which must be crossed before additional investment in schooling yields results in later job status. Moreover, in an education system, there are usually several streams, not just one, with each stream designed to have different status and income effects: some produce plumbers and others doctors. These streams can be distinguished in our data only if they involved some post-school or further education, and we address that problem in the next section.

Alternative forms of education

The understanding of how far on-the-job training, apprenticeships and other alternatives to formal educational attainment affect job status is not well advanced. In Switzerland Girod *et al.* (1977) have investigated the consequences of vocational education for occupational aspirations but not for job outcomes. Sewell and Hauser

(1975, p. 20) arbitrarily assume that vocational or technical education can be treated as though it was just one more year of schooling. Müller (1973, p. 226) speaks of 'number of years of formal schooling and formal occupational training' in one study and assigns arbitrary weights in a second (1977, p. 553). In these studies job training is assumed to have the same general effect as formal schooling. Featherman and Hauser (1975, p. 237) recognize the problem but feel it is of peripheral importance: 'While we would have liked to ascertain the effects of nonregular schooling (e.g. business, technical, vocational, on-the-job formal training) on socio-economic achievements, we were unable to justify the inclusion of these items on the basis of the relatively few respondents who had such training (fewer than 25 percent of all men on any single item).'

Since different streams of education produce different types of job skills and different status and income prospects, to group them together and calculate their return to education may be a gross over-simplification of actual social processes. Moreover, other types of training usually ignored in status attainment research may also be important. For instance, Thurow (1975, p. 78) refers to an American study which found that 'only 40 percent of the workforce reported that they were using any skill that they had acquired in formal training programs or in specialized education. Most of this 40 percent reported that some of the skills they were using had been acquired in informal, casual, on-the-job training. The remaining 60 percent acquired *all* of their relevant job skills through informal, casual, on-the-job training.'

Because of such considerations the ANU 1973 survey included a series of questions designed to allow an assessment of the effects of post-school training on initial status, its relationship to later status, the role of credentials in status attainment, and the influence of other forms of training in the job market.

Primary and secondary schooling

In this section we examine the impact of primary and secondary schooling on career beginnings in order to see whether years of schooling have different kinds of effects from the attainment of formal certificates. Is simply being at school for a given number of years as important as also having a piece of paper confirming a specific level of achievement? As we show below, so far as secondary education is concerned certification is of greater importance. How a person performs at secondary school opens or closes doors to other kinds of educational experience. Both social expectations and official requirements control who enters more advanced formal courses, at least during the period covered by our survey.

Years versus certificates

As already mentioned, in the 1973 survey information on years of education comes from a question about age at leaving school, from which six years is subtracted. Information on certificates is obtained from responses to the question: 'Can you tell me the highest level of schooling that you had completed [at age left school]?' The four types of responses presented to the respondent are listed in Table 3.1. For the last two categories several alternate names were presented because of varying nomenclature in different States of Australia. Men who completed their schooling overseas were asked to nominate the nearest Australian equivalent.

TABLE 3.1   *Level of schooling by country (in percentages)*

Level	Australia	Elsewhere	Total
Primary only	25	33	27
Secondary, no cert.	27	21	25
Inter. cert.	32	20	29
Matric. cert.	16	26	19
N (100%)	1,834	713	2,547

As Table 3.1 shows, most men educated in Australia achieved at least some secondary schooling. Men educated overseas are disproportionately represented in the lowest and highest categories, primary education (33 per cent) and matriculation (26 per cent). These differences are plausible, given Australia's policy of recruiting both unskilled and skilled immigrants over the period under consideration (cf. Martin, 1972).

The distribution of certificates corresponds less well to age at leaving school. Table 3.2 cross-classifies age at leaving school by highest certificate obtained. Seven per cent of men educated in Australia and 20 per cent of the others claimed to matriculate at what seems a young age. While it is possible[1] that a small minority of Australian men had matriculated before their sixteenth birthday, the higher proportions of overseas-educated men claiming matriculation at ages fourteen or fifteen suggests that immigrants may have had difficulty in translating their school qualifications into Australian equivalents.

From these data, there is no way of saying whether information on age at leaving school is more accurate than answers on certificates. There is no strong tendency for older respondents to nominate an early matriculation age more often than younger men. Among older respondents (men born 1903 to 1923) 40 per cent of

TABLE 3.2   *Age at leaving school by certificate and country (in percentages)*

| | Certificate obtained | | | |
| | Australia | | Elsewhere | |
Age left school	Inter.	Matric.	Inter.	Matric.
Up to 13	1	0	1	0
14	13	1	29	5
15	46	6	33	15
16	31	27	24	23
17	9	40	8	19
18	1	27	4	38
N (100%)	590	298	141	186

the matriculants left school before age seventeen; among younger respondents the comparable figure is 36 per cent. Foreigners, especially younger ones, tend to claim that they matriculated before they were seventeen. Lapses of memory and difficulties of converting overseas equivalents may account for part of this difference.

We can incorporate these educational data into a status attainment model in different ways. For instance, the categories of Table 3.1 can be used as an ordinal scale or, with fewer statistical assumptions, dummy variables could be used to represent the three higher levels. Table 3.3 presents six alternative models for the effect of schooling on first job. The first model includes both a conventional measure of years of education and three dummy variables representing levels of education. The second model has dummy variables only for level and the third only for the number of years. In each case, the models include the five social background variables, but their coefficients are omitted because they are similar to those reported in earlier analysis and do not bear on the credentialism issue. The dummy variables are constructed so that a respondent who answered 'some secondary' is coded 1, others 0. The second dummy is coded 1 if an intermediate certificate was reported, 0 otherwise, while the third is scored 1 only if matriculation was reported. Because everyone has at least some primary education, everyone starts with a minimum job status represented by the intercept of Table 3.3. Those with more education gain the extra status represented by the coefficient for highest level of education obtained.

These models are discussed rather fully here because they exemplify wider interpretive principles. The simplest model, the third in the table and labelled SED (short for primary-secondary-education), has six variables: the five social background characteristics of father's job, mother's and father's education, family

TABLE 3.3 *Six models of how education affects first job*[a]

Model	Yrs of SED	Variables Binary for Sec.	Inter.	Matric.	Inter-cept	R sq.
Full	2·7	−6·1	8·8	79·3	357	0·269
Binary		−4·1	16·9	74·2	377	0·268
SED	14·3				246	0·200
2 Binary			15·0	89·2	374	0·268
Mixed	4·0			74·8	349	0·265
SED sq.	0·86				307	0·208

[a] All coefficients are net of social background. Underlined coefficients are not significant at the 5 per cent level.

possessions scale and family size, for which no coefficients are shown; as well as years of primary and secondary education, which ranges from a minimum of six years to a maximum of twelve. Its coefficient in the third model indicates that, independent of the effects of home background, a year of education improves a man's first job status by 14·3 points. In other words, someone with ten years of primary and secondary schooling on average had a first job 143 status points, or nearly one and a half standard deviations, higher than a (hypothetical) man from a similar social background with no formal schooling. In this model each year of education is worth the same as any other year. Alternatively, the coefficient of 14·3 can be considered as an 'average' of effects which might or might not be the same for different years of schooling. This issue is examined below, but at this point we need note only the size of the coefficient and the explanatory power of this simple model: combining the six variables in this way accounts for 20 per cent of the variance in the status of first job.

To test whether schooling has linear effects we included the square of SED.[2] If its effect is smoothly curvilinear this squared term should increase the variance explained, but in fact the R sq. for this model is only trivially higher (0·008) than for the simple SED model. This non-difference indicates that the effects of primary and secondary schooling are probably not linear, because the squared term does as well as the linear term. On the other hand they are also more complex than a simple curve because the squared term does not explain more of the individual variation in first job status than the simpler model.

If education affects job status through a set of well-defined thresholds, some kind of step function would be appropriate. In

Australia, the most important steps are entering secondary school, obtaining an intermediate certificate at about the minimum leaving age, or completing secondary school with sufficient marks in the final examination to qualify for university entrance.

These steps can be represented by dummy variables. The first variable (labelled 'Sec'.) has a value of 1 for all those who have some secondary education but did not report a certificate. All others take the value of zero on this dummy, whether they have more or less education. The second dummy ('Inter'.) is scored 1 for those who have an intermediate certificate, zero otherwise. The third ('Matric'.) is constructed in a similar fashion and represents possession of a matriculation certificate. A model using only these variables to represent the effects of education ('Binary' in Table 3.3) explains substantially more of the variance in early job status, almost 7 per cent more than the simpler model, a one-third increase in explanation.

The intercept in this model is about 130 status points higher than in the SED model because the effects of primary schooling are now included in the intercept: everyone starts with at least primary schooling. The insignificant but negative coefficient for some secondary simply means that getting a little secondary schooling without certification confers no advantage by comparison with men who completed primary but did not enter secondary school. The other two significant coefficients indicate that the intermediate certificate is worth 17 status points, and the coefficient for matriculation over four times as much.

The 'full' model includes both SED and dummies for certificates, but there is no increase in the amount of variance explained. But because the model with only years of school explains much less of the variance in career beginnings, it is obvious that some measure of certification is necessary to account for differences in early status attainment. In no model does the dummy variable for 'some secondary' achieve significance. As a comparison with the model labelled '2 Binary' shows, it adds nothing to explaining first job status. This model can also be compared with one containing the years variable and the dummy for matriculation ('mixed' model). Its R sq. is only slightly lower (0·003) than the full or binary models.

Other models using dummy variables for each year of schooling completed, both with and without certificates, were tested. When dummy variables for certificates are introduced, all the year coefficients are reduced to insignificance. The intermediate certificate dummy, although small, is statistically different from zero but most of the status effect is carried by the matriculation certificate. There is also an increase in R sq. of 5 per cent, indicating a significantly better fit.

We therefore conclude that merely staying in school does *not* improve the status attainment of first job unless a certificate is obtained. An additional year spent at school without obtaining a formal qualification adds about 1 point to first job status. Achieving a matriculation certificate adds almost 100 times that amount. Only formal certification seems to have a significant effect on first job status, and the effects of secondary schooling can be represented solely in terms of whether a man obtained an intermediate or matriculation certificate, or their equivalents.

Completing school overseas

About a quarter of the sample (28 per cent) completed their secondary education outside Australia, and in a variety of analyses we have tried to establish whether their lack of Australian schooling put them at a disadvantage. The model which emerged as most effective in the preceding section is presented in Table 3.4, where secondary education is represented by two dummy variables for intermediate certificate and matriculation. As usual, regression coefficients are net of social background.

TABLE 3.4   *Three models for assessing the relative values of Australian certificates[a]*

Model	Inter.	Matric.	Education completed Australia	Inter. Aus.	Matric. Aus.	Intercept	R sq.
Full	18·4	51·1	−6·7	−3·0	61·4	372	0·284
Simple	15·0	89·2				374	0·267
Restricted	15·7	55·9			55·3	367	0·283

[a] All coefficients are net of social background. Underlined coefficients are not significant at 5 per cent level.

In general, migrants have lower status than the native-born, and to establish whether their schooling has different effects on career beginnings we include in the full model a dummy variable for completing school in Australia, another for completing intermediate certificate in Australia and a third for matriculating in Australia. Only the last has any significant additional effect: matriculation in Australia adds 112 status points to first job status (51·1 plus 61·4 in the full model) compared with only 89 points when country is not identified. Again we cannot accept any simplistic discrimination thesis, or even non-recognition of overseas qualifications, because men who matriculated overseas almost always took their first job overseas. Some countries may be less merito-cratic than Australia, or less credentialist. Or it may simply be that men educated overseas misclassified their educational credentials. Whatever the reasons, in the rest of this chapter it is assumed that the effects of primary and secondary education on status and in-come are captured by three characteristics: whether a person obtained an intermediate certificate, whether he gained a matric-ulation certificate and whether he matriculated in Australia or overseas.

Post-school education and training courses

The remainder of this chapter examines the role of post-school education and other types of formal occupational training. The 1973 ANU survey secured a great deal of information about such education and training, because many kinds of post-school courses are relevant to job placement and promotion. To ascertain each respondent's involvement with education and training after starting work, interviewers were instructed to ask about nine specific kinds of post-school training ranging from on-the-job training to university courses. They also listed when and where the course was taken, its content and title, how long it lasted and whether any qualification was obtained. Space was allowed for recording up to six post-school courses. Only 22 members of the entire sample of 4,939 persons reported more than six. We assumed that much of this material would not be incorporated into a status attainment model, because avocational courses and courses of brief duration have little significance for occupational careers.

Number of post-school courses

Table 3.5 presents a distribution of respondents by number of courses begun in the same year as first job, compared with courses begun at any stage of the occupational career. Courses begun before or concurrently with workforce entry were added to basic education (see chapter 2). This chapter focuses on basic education, and the impact of post-school training on careers is considered in chapter 4. A comparison of the two distributions indicates that there are substantial differences in patterns of basic and additional education. Whereas 34 per cent of all men reported no post-school course of any kind, 65 per cent said they had not taken such a course before, or at the same time as, they started work. A high proportion of men with only one course took that course in the same year as their first job (83 per cent), and it is mainly men with multiple

TABLE 3.5 *Post-school education undertaken in the same year as first job*

No. of courses	Percentage of sample with course	
	At workforce entry	At any time during career
0	64·9	34·0
1	31·5	38·2
2	3·1	14·7
3	0·3	7·4
4	0·1	3·6
5	0·0	1·3
6	0·0	0·8
N (100%)	2,560	2,560

courses who are also recorded as having undertaken courses in later years.

Information on early courses not shown here indicates that only 39 people initiated multiple courses immediately after their secondary schooling, mostly in the university sector (22 men). Half of them were involved in programs of study that routinely award two degrees: 11 out of 22 reported arts-law or science-medicine combinations, and for them the professional qualification is the relevant information. The remaining cases show no general pattern. By deleting irrelevant courses, ignoring dual degree courses and higher degrees, and consolidating related courses, each of the 807 men with post-school courses can be treated as if only one kind of post-school education or training were involved.

Correspondence, 'other' courses, professional articles and on-the-job training were combined to form the group of 'informal' courses listed in Table 3.6. Apprenticeships and technical courses are of analysable size as they stand, but teacher-training colleges and CAEs were merged with university to form the 'tertiary' category. This decision may dilute the impact of tertiary education because teacher training is relatively brief and the qualifications are lower, but teacher-training courses are more like university than any other. Arguably, professional articles might be combined with this group, but close inspection revealed no evidence of tertiary-level work, and so they were classified as rather specialized instances of on-the-job training. Courses of less than one year were not retained for further consideration. Only about one in twelve lasted more than six months. Some were as short as two days, others lasted two weeks and many were not vocational. Their exclusion is therefore no real loss.

TABLE 3.6   *Characteristics of post-school courses begun at or before entering workforce*

Type of course	Average duration (years)	Percentage full-time	Percentage overseas	Percentage with qualification	N
Informal	3·1	12	38	58	146
Apprentice	4·2	0	36	86	443
Technical	2·9	40	27	57	100
Tertiary	3·5	86	29	80	166

Four groups of courses are compared in Table 3.6. Apprenticeships last longest because they are done part-time while working, and very few men who undertake such courses fail to gain a trade qualification. The average length of tertiary courses is reduced by teacher-training courses, which are usually two years compared to the university average of about four years; unlike apprenticeships most tertiary courses are taken full-time. Again, a very high percentage gain a qualification, typically a professional one. As Table 3.6 shows, about one-third of men with basic post-school education were enrolled in overseas institutions, somewhat more than for secondary schooling (cf. Table 3.1). The high proportion of overseas-educated men in this 'informal' category undoubtedly includes some whose courses could not be coded accurately into the ABS classification. Migrants are also over-represented in the apprentice category, but this reflects migrant selection policies and the recruitment of skilled workers.

Characteristics of post-school students

Because the status attainment model evaluates the role of education independently of other social characteristics, it is necessary to consider what distinguishes men with different kinds of education and training from those who took no further training at the time they started work. Table 3.7 presents participation rates for the four types of education and training, both for the total sample and for sub-groups defined in terms of six characteristics. The rate of informal training varies little, with the most extreme difference (4 percentage points) between men born in Australia and those born in other English-speaking countries, but this difference probably results in part from the difficulty of coding the level of foreign courses.

As already noted, men born overseas are more likely to have been apprentices. The pattern is different for tertiary education

TABLE 3.7   *Participation rates in post-school courses by various characteristics[a]*

Characteristic	Informal	Apprenticeship	Technical	Tertiary
		Type of course		
Total	6	17	4	6
Community type				
Farm	4	4	3	2
Rural	5	15	2	4
Urban	7	22	5	9
Birthplace				
Australia	5	15	4	6
Other English-				
language country	9	26	4	6
Non-English	7	19	4	9
Secondary certificate				
Inter.	6	30	6	1
Matric.	9	10	7	31
Australian certificate				
Inter.	6	29	6	1
Matric.	7	3	8	36
Father's SES quartile				
Lowest	4	23	2	3
Second	6	22	4	5
Third	5	16	5	5
Highest	7	10	5	13
Age cohort				
60–9	7	11	3	6
40–59	5	16	4	5
30–9	6	23	4	9

[a] Percentage of respondents with various characteristics involved in each type of course.

where men born in non-English-speaking countries report the highest rate of involvement. Not surprisingly, an intermediate certificate is generally all that is required to enter an apprenticeship, whereas matriculation is almost universally required for tertiary study. Few men who undertook apprenticeships have the matriculation certificate, especially if their education was completed in Australia.

Social background also influences the kinds of courses undertaken. The lower the status of father's job at age fourteen, the greater the likelihood of becoming an apprentice. The two lowest-origin quartiles have similar participation rates, the third is about average, while the top group is less than half the rate of the lowest status group. The rates for tertiary education show the reverse pattern. The last three rows of Table 3.7 indicate how participation rates in post-school training have changed. Apprenticeships show a steady increase, with twice as many younger men involved than is the case for older men. The increase in tertiary courses is confined to the youngest, postwar cohort. There is no apparent trend in the other two types of training.

Table 3.8 presents means for six background and four achieved characteristics for six groups: men with no post-school basic education, men with one of four different kinds of post-school education, and the total sample. As a guide for evaluating differences, the sample standard deviations are also presented. These data allow an initial examination of the relationship of social background to post-school training, and of training to careers and earnings.

Respondents with no further education are in general somewhat below average in terms of social background. They are the only group in which the number of children in the family of origin exceeds the sample average. The chance of undertaking further education immediately after leaving school is clearly related to family size, and it is instructive that family size decreases as the academic level of the course increases. It is also interesting that men with 'informal' (largely avocational) courses generally come from somewhat advantaged family backgrounds. For instance, their fathers had, on average, about half a year more schooling, slightly higher status jobs, more material possessions and slightly fewer children. Respondents undertaking 'informal' courses are also advantaged compared with the overall sample in terms of their own schooling, jobs and earnings, but the differences are not as marked as they are among some other groups.

Men with technical education have backgrounds and attainments similar to those with only 'informal' courses to their credit. They are a little more advantaged both when they start and when they finish. They come from rather better-off backgrounds, their first job is about 30 status points higher than average, and their current status is 51 points higher. Apprentices are much like the general average. They come from slightly smaller families and are more urban (see also Table 3.7), but their fathers' average status is the lowest of any group. Their career paths are somewhat below average as well, starting 9 status points and ending 25 points lower. Men who began as apprentices earned about the average income for men in 1973 ($130 per week). Men with apprenticeships, some informal training or technical education have almost identical socioeconomic profiles.

71

Men with tertiary education are generally about one standard deviation above the average on background characteristics except, of course, for family size, which is negatively related to attainment. These men start work in jobs with very high status and increase that high initial status by around 40 points over their careers, just above the increase of 36 points in the sample as a whole. Their average earnings are close to double those of men who gained no post-school training before starting work.

These patterns suggest that not every kind of post-school education serves as an important independent channel for mobility. Men with no immediate post-school training do not fare appreciably worse than men who enter long apprenticeships, whereas men who undertake more formal training such as university courses come from more advantaged backgrounds in the first place. How far does further education affect careers independently of social origins?

Post-school education and its effects on status

Post-school education might influence status and income in two major ways. Merely being involved in further education could improve the chances of getting a better first job and entering a different sort of career; in that case every year of further education would matter. Or, as is the case with secondary education, completing courses and gaining formal certificates might affect later status. This question is explored mainly in relation to career beginnings when education exerts its strongest effect. First job in turn is the most important cause of later status and income. In any event, analyses of other status outcomes give equivalent results.

Table 3.9 presents data on four ways of examining the effect of post-school education on first job status. Each model includes the five social background and three secondary education variables discussed above, and the coefficients shown are again net of social background. The first model, 'Duration', is constructed from four variables indicating the number of years the respondent had spent in an informal, apprenticeship, technical or tertiary course, regardless of whether it was finished. The R sq. for this model (0·44) can be compared with 0·30 for the basic model in chapter 2, and it is clear that by including post-school training, half as much again of the variation in career beginnings is explained. From this model one would conclude that apprenticeship has a slight effect on initial status (10 status points), informal and technical training raise the status of first job by about twice as much, while tertiary education adds a very large increment, almost half a standard deviation (47 points) to first job status. In interpreting these differences it is important to bear in mind that each type of course differs in its

TABLE 3.8 *Mean values for ten status characteristics by post-school education*

Post-school education	DADED	DADJOB	MOMED	WLTH	FAMSZ	SED	JOB1	JOB10	JOBN	INCOME
None	8·0	510	7·9	−0·10	5·0	8·6	468	486	503	118
Informal	9·1	530	8·8	0·16	4·4	9·4	502	529	554	142
Apprentice	8·4	482	8·1	−0·07	4·0	9·0	477	492	507	127
Technical	9·1	547	9·0	0·33	3·9	9·6	516	541	573	150
Tertiary	11·2	597	10·0	0·81	3·4	11·0	664	684	704	212
Total sample	8·4	513	8·2	−0·00	4·7	8·9	486	503	522	129
Standard deviation	2·7	109	1·9	1·0	2·6	1·5	90	100	114	70

TABLE 3.9 *The effects of post-school education on first job status[a]*

Model	Intercept	Years				Qualification obtained				R sq.
		Informal	Apprenticeship	Technical	Tertiary	Informal	Apprenticeship	Technical	Tertiary	
Duration	396	18·8	9·9	16·3	46·7					0·437
Qualified	384					22·0	10·9	35·9	173·8	0·426
Duration-qualified	392	18·5	14·8	11·8	28·7	2·3	−6·5	19·4	83·1	0·447
Duration-tertiary	392	19·3	10·3	16·8	28·6				82·9	0·447

[a] All coefficients are net of social background. Underlined coefficients are not significant at the 5 per cent level.

average duration. The gap between apprentices and men who took technical courses is much reduced when the coefficients in the 'Duration' model are multiplied by the average durations of Table 3.6.

The second model, 'Qualified', includes dummy variables indicating whether a respondent obtained any qualification from the course. The R sq. for this model is only slightly lower than for 'Duration', but technical, and especially tertiary, education have relatively larger effects. When both duration and qualifications are included, as in the third model, the duration variables reduce all the qualification variables to insignificance, except for tertiary. The coefficient for technical education is reasonably large, but not significant. Because duration and completion of apprenticeships are so highly correlated, their coefficients cannot be interpreted in this model.

A final model includes duration measures for each type of education and the completion measure only for tertiary education. The R sq. for this model is the same as the preceding model and is significantly higher than for any other model. Each year of informal training adds about 20 status points to first job, apprenticeships are worth half as much again, while technical education has slightly less impact than informal education. Each year of tertiary education is worth almost 29 status points, but obtaining a tertiary qualification adds 83 points. Thus, a person who attended university for four years and obtained a degree would expect to have a first job status nearly 2 standard deviations (200 points) higher than someone who had only matriculated.

Elaboration of the role of education in status attainment

Table 3.10 brings together in comprehensive fashion the results of the preceding analysis. As in previous tables the five coefficients for family background are not reported, although they have been included in the calculations. For this reason the first line for each dependent model has no coefficients, but the R sq. and the intercept are shown to represent the direct effects of background. To allow the reader to assess total, direct and indirect effects (see Alwin and Hauser, 1975), each successive step in the causal model is represented by a new line for each dependent variable.

So far as the status of first job is concerned, more than half the effect of matriculation is indirect and mediated by post-school education, primarily tertiary. Very little (8 per cent, the proportional reduction from 15·7 to 14·4) of the effect of intermediate certificate is indirect through other training. The final R sq. for this equation is 0·45, which can be compared to 0·30 in the basic model.

TABLE 3.10 A summary model of the effects of secondary and post-school education on status attainment[a]

Dependent variables	Inter-cept	Inter.	Matric.	Matric. in Aus.	Years of informal	Years of apprent.	Years of technical tertiary	Years of tertiary	Qual. from tertiary	JOB1	ADDED	JOBN	R sq.
JOB1	350	15·7	55·9	55·3									0·16
	366	14·4	26·9	34·5									0·28
	392				19·3	10·3	16·8	28·6	82·9				0·45
ADDED	0·57												0·02
	0·49	3·2	2·3	2·7									0·06
	0·49	3·7	3·5	2·9	−1·6	−2·1	−2·1	−1·2	−0·5				0·08
	0·32	3·6	3·3	2·7	−1·6	−2·2	−2·2	−1·4	−0·8	0·00			0·08
JOB10	400	33·0	54·3	89·5									0·18
	407	32·4	35·8	75·5									0·34
	425	27·0	25·9	62·8	14·7	5·0	13·5	16·6	59·3				0·39
	280	22·6	21·9	59·5	7·6	1·2	7·3	6·0	28·7	0·37			0·45
	276				9·6	3·8	9·9	7·6	29·7	0·36	12·1		0·46
JOBN	407	43·2	60·4	90·2									0·19
	409	44·2	41·2	75·2									0·32
	433	39·8	33·0	64·8	16·7	−1·1	12·6	22·3	44·3				0·37
	315	31·1	25·0	58·3	10·9	4·2	7·5	13·6	19·2	0·30			0·40
	307				14·8	0·9	12·7	16·8	21·2	0·29	23·9		0·45
INCOME	95	19·9	25·5	39·3									0·12
	95	19·5	15·6	32·5									0·18
	62	17·9	12·5	28·6	8·2	3·1	7·3	10·9	22·3				0·21
	60	14·7	9·6	26·2	6·0	2·0	5·4	7·6	12·8	0·12			0·23
	57	7·5	3·7	12·6	7·4	3·8	7·3	8·7	13·5	0·11	8·6		0·24
	−14				3·9	3·6	4·3	4·8	8·5	0·04	3·0	0·23	0·32

[a] Underlined regression coefficients are not significant at the 5 per cent level. Coefficients for ADDED have been multiplied by 10.

The gain of 50 per cent in explanatory power indicates that career beginnings are much more closely related to formal credentials than to years spent at school or post-school institutions.

The R sq. for additional education increases four-fold, from a very small to a moderately small figure, and a comparison of the secondary and post-school effects shows why. All the post-school education variables have negative signs whereas the secondary variables have positive effects. In the basic model these effects largely cancel out, leaving a very small negative effect. In general, those who gain post-school education before starting work do not (or do not need to) obtain it later.

The respondent's occupation ten years after entry into the workforce is included as a dependent variable (JOB10) because it gives an estimate of the residual effects of education after the respondent is firmly established in his career. However, we exclude JOB10 as an intervening variable for JOBN or INCOME to maintain comparability with the basic model. The models for JOB10 and JOBN are very similar, and it is instructive to see how quickly the effects of education stabilize. For both JOB10 and JOBN, secondary education becomes increasingly important relative to tertiary, doubtless because a tertiary qualification places a man in a professional job at the beginning of his career, whereas other kinds of education (except apprenticeships) involve career mobility and exercise a more gradual influence during careers rather than being concentrated at career beginnings. The next chapter shows that professionals and skilled tradesmen have relatively low rates of career mobility.

In the basic model the total effect of BASED on JOB1 is 0·454, whereas the total effect of BASED on JOBN is 0·371. Table 3.10 demonstrates that this decrease results from the combination of two opposing tendencies: the growing impact of secondary education, especially if undertaken in Australia, and the declining impact of post-school education. Less than one-third (28 per cent, the proportional decrease in effect from 43·2 to 31·1 points in the fourth equation in Table 3.10) of the effect of intermediate certificate is indirect, through additional education (20 per cent) and first job (10 per cent). For the most part, matriculation works indirectly (59 per cent), with 32 per cent of its effect transmitted by post-school education and the rest almost equally by JOB1 and additional education. Much the same is true for matriculation in Australia. To calculate the indirect effects for Australian matriculants, the effect of matriculation is added to the effect of the location variable to obtain the total effect of matriculating in Australia. Forty-five per cent of this total effect of 150·6 status points is indirect through post-school education (23 per cent) or first job and additional education (12 and 10 per cent respectively). Men with a reasonably solid secondary education who undertake additional training in early career improve their later statuses.

On the other hand, men who obtain some post-school education before or at the same time as they start work are less likely to undertake additional education. For this reason additional education suppresses the effect of post-school education on later variables, because its negative relationship with post-school education cancels out its positive relationship with current job and income. This result can be seen in the last three lines of the JOBN equation of Table 3.10 and in the middle three lines of the equations for INCOME, where the coefficients for post-school education *increase* when ADDED is included. The indirect effect of post-school education is best assessed by comparing the total effect with the last line for JOBN and the penultimate line for INCOME.

Summary

Matriculation and tertiary qualifications contribute substantially to the status of first job, while other kinds of education have relatively small effects. An Australian matriculation certificate is more important than an overseas equivalent. Tertiary qualifications serve mainly to secure higher initial status, although they exert a continuing effect over the career. Other sorts of post-school education have moderate effects throughout the career, except for apprentices whose statuses are fixed at a relatively early stage.

Representing education in terms of credential thresholds improves the explanation of an individual differences in first job status by half as much again as in the basic model, although for later occupational status the increase is only 15 per cent. This difference highlights the fact that education has its greatest impact on job entry. Thereafter career beginnings rather than education *per se* chiefly affect later status attainments. This finding applies to income as well as to current job. Of the education variables, only the intermediate certificate has a significant direct effect on income but in absolute terms it is not large. In brief, the analysis presented above indicates that the duration of secondary education is unimportant compared to the influence of certification. The effects of further education are best understood in terms of length of study in four different kinds of further education and whether a tertiary degree or diploma was obtained.

Obviously eight variables representing processes of educational certification are too many to retain in detailed analyses of later status attainment. Because we have demonstrated that education has its main effect on JOB1 status, little will be lost by adopting a simplified measure of education in considering the relationship of education to later statuses in the occupational career. In the remainder of this book we can revert to the basic model BASED measure. As these analyses have shown, early job status mediates most of the later effects of education. In general, earlier ascribed and achieved statuses continue to exert small direct effects over the life-cycle and across generations, but with each successive link in the chain of social inequality more distant influences become weaker and weaker.

4 Careers and career contingencies

This chapter examines the socioeconomic life-cycle of Australian men at ten year intervals from the year of their first job to the year of interview, 1973. Because the men in the sample had been at work in some cases for over forty years, changes in status attainment processes can be assessed by carrying out parallel analyses for different career cohorts. Only 41 men had been working for less than a decade when they were interviewed and they are excluded from all but the first analysis reported here.[1] This small group consists of men who continued their full-time education much longer than most of their peers. If they had been retained in the analysis the meritocratic character of the post-war labour market which emerges from our data would be even more marked.

Defining career cohorts and career contingencies

Throughout this chapter the status attainment profiles of four career cohorts are compared in terms of several career contingencies: further education and training, international migration, internal migration, and war service. The smallest cohort, called the 'pre-depression' cohort, is the oldest: 468 men with forty or more years of work experience, 90 per cent of whom were born between 1903 and 1917. Their average age when interviewed was 60, and 72 per cent took their first job between 1920 and 1930. An additional 25 per cent of this cohort took their first job in 1931 or 1932. Their average age at leaving school was 14·6 years, and about one in six subsequently had some form of further education. This cohort has the longest work experience and it appears in all comparisons.

The next oldest cohort, the 'depression cohort', is composed of 725 men with thirty but less than forty years in the workforce. Their average age is 51 years, and 90 per cent were born between 1916 and

1927. About one in four had some further education after leaving school, on average at age 15. Over 80 per cent entered the workforce between 1935 and 1942 and the remainder started work in 1933 or 1934, the depth of the depression. There is no overlap in year of first job between these two oldest cohorts. If the years 1929 to 1939 are taken to span the depression (double-digit male unemployment peaking in 1932 at 31 per cent of the workforce), 68 per cent of this cohort started work during the depression, compared with 43 per cent of the oldest cohort.

The third cohort, called 'early postwar', consists of men with at least twenty but less than thirty years of work experience. When interviewed they averaged 41 years of age. In 1973 90 per cent of them were aged between 36 and 48 years, and 91 per cent entered the workforce in times of high labour demand between 1944 and 1952, when they were aged between 15 and 16, on average.

Finally, there are 668 men, identified as the 'postwar growth cohort', who had been at work for ten but less than twenty years. At the time of interview 90 per cent were aged between 30 and 38. On the average they left school between 16 and 17 years of age and 92 per cent started work in the years 1953 to 1960. These men entered the workforce during a period of rapid economic growth and, as we shall see below, at a time when educational credentials were at a premium.

To those familiar with status attainment research it will be apparent that these career cohorts have not been defined according to the conventions of birth cohort analysis. Obviously, birth cohorts are homogeneous in terms of current age, at least within the constraints of age grouping, usually a span of five or ten years. But because men born about same time leave school at different ages, birth cohorts are heterogeneous with respect to work experience. For the analysis of social change, for example the shifting relationship between education and career advancement, birth cohorts have the disadvantage that the length of the career varies depending on when persons in the same age group left school and started work. Consequently, period and life-cycle effects are confounded. This study defined specific career stages in order to avoid this problem.

When cohorts are defined directly by work experience, it is possible to compare members of different cohorts in terms of the same career period, in the case of this study, ten-year intervals. Given enough resources on the part of the researcher and enough patience on the part of the respondent, this interval could be made as narrow as desired. However, standardizing the stage of a man's career in this way necessarily introduces overlap in the age composition of cohorts: the cohorts are separated in terms of work experience but not by age. Thus, while 90 per cent of the two older cohorts were born in years that do not overlap (1903 to 1917, and 1918 to 1928 respectively), the degree of overlap is somewhat greater for the two younger cohorts: 90 per cent of the 'early postwar cohort' were born between 1926 and 1937, and 90 per cent of the 'postwar growth cohort' were born between 1936 and 1943. They therefore overlap by a year or two, even when the 10 per cent at the extreme of the age range in each cohort are excluded.

The following analysis assumes that the social and economic circumstances of the period when a man left school and started work are more important for understanding the careers of Australian men over the last half-century than the circumstances surrounding their birth, or their experience relative to age peers who left school earlier or later. In other words we assume that period effects on careers are more important than age cohort effects. Of course the two largely coincide because most members of the same birth cohort leave school in their middle teenage years. A definitive test of the relative importance of these two kinds of effects would require a comprehensive life-history approach in which age and work experience could be simultaneously controlled.

The data on occupational careers presented here are in some respects unique in the published literature (see the theoretical studies of Sorensen, 1974, 1975; and the empirical work of Featherman, 1971; Featherman and Hauser, 1973; and Kelley, 1973a, b). Our measures of changes in the level of a man's human capital over his working life extends Sorensen's model, although we cannot consider one variable he considers important, namely, whether a job shift was voluntary or involuntary (Sorensen, 1974, p. 55). On the empirical side, Kelley and Featherman have disagreed about whether early career history directly affects later career or whether only the more immediate past has an impact on current job status and income. Since their debate hinges in part on assumptions about measurement error in proxy and retrospective reports, we cannot contribute to the resolution of this issue. However, in certain historical circumstances such as depressions and wars, job mobility is sufficiently erratic to make a simple causal chain implausible. Earlier statuses of parents and the respondent himself continue to exert small but significant effects well into middle and even late career. These points are documented below.

Post-school training and occupational careers

As explained in chapter 3, the usual definition of schooling was extended in this survey to include post-school training of various kinds. Forty-four per cent of respondents reported that after completing their full-time education they had undertaken some further training. Table 4.1 gives unweighted figures about the kinds of course involved, the number of courses taken, whether the course was full-time or part-time, how long it lasted, and whether a formal qualification was obtained. Note that these courses were undertaken after starting work. Courses taken in the same year as first job are included in BASED (see chapter 2). Thus, whereas four out of five courses involving 'on-the-job' training go into ADDED rather than BASED, only about one-third of apprenticeships go into ADDED because apprenticeships are typically begun immediately upon leaving school. University courses split about evenly between basic and further education, and most of the remainder are counted predominantly as post-school education, as a comparison of Table 3.7 above with Table 4.1 shows.

TABLE 4.1   *Type and number of post-school courses*

Type of course	1	2	3	4	5	6	Total courses
On-the-job training	332	47	14	5	0	0	398
Apprenticeship	194	31	2	2	0	0	229
Professional articles	14	7	1	0	0	0	22
Nursing	7	0	1	0	0	0	8
Technical coll.	269	134	55	16	6	0	480
Teacher-training coll.	23	8	3	0	0	0	34
Coll. of Advanced Ed.	42	23	14	5	0	0	84
University	78	40	19	5	0	0	142
Correspondence course	109	92	55	15	6	1	278
Other courses	125	88	53	34	14	6	320
Total	1,193	470	217	82	26	7	1,995
Percentage part-time	95	94	99	90	96	100	94
Percentage obtained qualification	58	54	46	55	73	43	56
Percentage of courses less than one year	24	23	30	34	31	43	25

The 'total' column of Table 4.1 indicates that 94 per cent of post-school courses were taken part-time, since most men enter full-time work immediately on leaving school. One-quarter of the courses lasted less than one year, and data not reported in Table 4.1 show that about one-third lasted for three years or longer. By far the most common courses were on-the-job and technical training, with lesser numbers taking apprenticeships or tertiary level courses. Correspondence and 'other' courses are also numerous, although many are not vocationally oriented. Only about half the courses led to a qualification, and not every qualification was relevant to current or future job prospects.

In chapter 3 we showed that training certified by a credential contributes most to occupational status, and that tertiary qualifications are more valuable than trade or technical ones. These findings guide our interpretation of further education as well. Whereas ADDED in the basic model included only courses lasting one year or longer, courses lasting less than one year have been retained in this analysis, with a weight of half a year. Courses lasting a year or longer (75 per cent of all post-school courses) were assigned weights of one to five depending on their duration in years. Part-time courses were given one-third the weight of full-time courses (0·33 versus 1·0). The 44 per cent of the sample with further education had full-time equivalent years of ADDED ranging from one-sixth of a year to ten years. For purposes of the present analysis, this variable was truncated to an upper limit of five or more years. Only a dozen men reported more than five years of further education and only one in thirteen had more than two years full-time equivalent of further education.

Because each respondent was asked when he began each course, how long it lasted, and whether or not he gained a qualification from it, ADDED can be placed in the appropriate career stage, and trade and technical qualifications can be distinguished from tertiary qualifications. Courses of doubtful vocational value, that is, ones that cannot be coded into trade, technical or tertiary qualifications, have also been separately identified. As might be expected, most men undertook further education early rather than late in their careers; 52 per cent of all the further education reported by this sample was begun within ten years of starting work and 32 per cent more in the next ten years. Eleven per cent reported taking courses twenty but less than thirty years after first job, and the remaining 4 per cent after thirty years of work experience. If the educational behaviour of these men is a realistic response to the job market, further education and training gained early in a career should have a greater impact on job status than training undertaken in middle or late career.

As already mentioned, 56 of every 100 men who undertook further education obtained a qualification. Qualifications were coded according to the index prepared by the Australian Bureau of Statistics for the 1971 Census, and in this analysis we have distinguished trade or technical qualifications (QUAL1) from tertiary non-degree qualifications, bachelors, or higher degree (QUAL2). Ten per cent of this sample obtained a trade or technical qualification in the first decade of working life and 6 per cent obtained a tertiary qualification. For the second decade of the career, the corresponding figures are 5 and 3 per cent, and for the third, 2 and 1 per cent. Only nineteen men obtained any kind of qualification after thirty years of work experience.

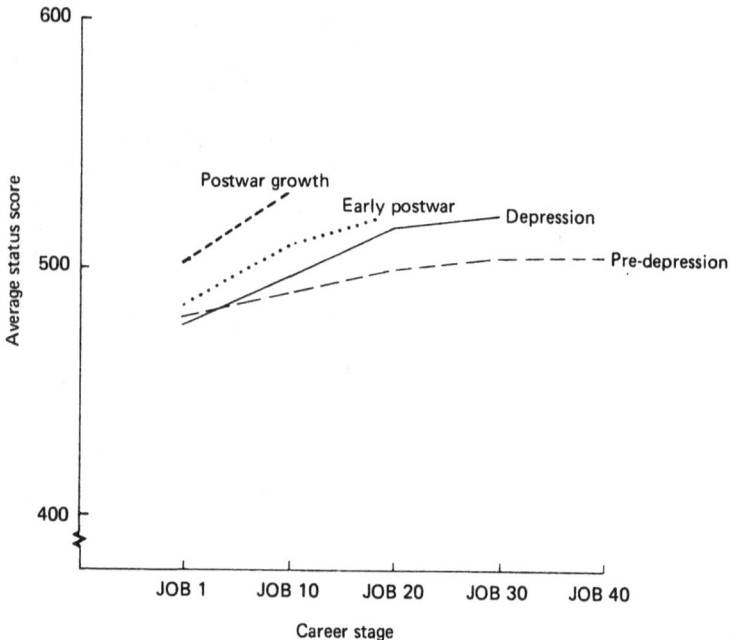

Figure 4.1 Average status of jobs during career for four cohorts.

Before examining how further education affects status, we should note that each cohort, in aggregate, experiences a steady rise in occupational status over the career. More recently held jobs are on average higher in status than earlier jobs. Younger cohorts started work in higher status jobs than older men, and at each stage in their careers they maintained that initial advantage. Figure 4.1 displays data on average status at different stages of the career for the four cohorts. Except for the depression cohort first job status is progressively higher, and at every career stage younger men attained higher average status than older men. The rise in status is most rapid in early career, and flattens out after about twenty years of work experience. As we shall see, the rate of mobility also declines after middle career.

Table 4.2 examines the impact of further education on job status at three stages of the occupational career for different cohorts. All the background variables are measured in the same way as in the basic model, except that the job status scores in this chapter utilize the extended status scale, which differentiates a number of jobs on the basis of self-employment or employer status versus employee status (Broom *et al.*, 1977a, b).

The bottom line of Table 4.2 shows that we can explain more of the differences in early career status among younger than older men, at least for the first decade of the occupational career (we discuss each decade of the career in turn). The early careers of men who started work in the depression are rather unpredictable because they were more mobile. The oldest cohort was almost as mobile. For example, calculating the proportion in each cohort who had a job with the same status score at first job and job ten years later, we find that it follows the same pattern as the coefficient of determination (R sq.): during the first decade of their career 32 per cent of the youngest cohort had the same status score at both the end and the beginning, compared with 27 per cent of the second cohort, 20 per cent of the third and 23 per cent of the oldest.

Generally speaking, workers with the lowest rates of career mobility are professionals, craftsmen and farmers. Thus, the declining rate of career mobility across cohorts partly reflects the increasing importance of the professional category, which accounts for only 3 per cent of first jobs among the oldest group but 15 per cent among the youngest. However, even if the initial job distribution is standardized by cohort, the proportion immobile rises by only two percentage points for the oldest cohort, to 25 per cent. Irrespective of the changing occupational structure, there has been a decline in mobility during early career.[2]

Further inspection of Table 4.2 shows the main reasons why this model better explains the early career experience of younger than older men. Family background variables do not play an important direct role by this stage of the career, and only WLTH continues to exert a significant effect on early job status, an effect roughly equal to the delayed effects of one year of BASED among the older cohorts. So far as the persistent effects of WLTH involve an ascriptive element in the process of stratification, there is evidence of a small shift from ascription to meritocracy over the last fifty years, especially in the postwar period. For example, the relative weights of WLTH and BASED on JOB10 are in the ratio of about two to one for the two oldest cohorts but are about equal for the youngest. On the other hand, in every cohort JOB1 is by far the most important influence on JOB10. Just as the main effects of social background are transmitted via the educational system, so the effects of education are largely mediated by first job.

Further evidence of meritocratic processes in the labour force is provided by the coefficients for further education. Analyses not

TABLE 4.2 Effects of further education on career achievement for four cohorts[a]

Independent variables	Early career: JOB10 Cohort				Mid-career: JOB20 Cohort			Later career: JOB30 Cohort	
	Pre-de-pression	Depres-sion	Early postwar	Postwar growth	Pre-de-pression	Depres-sion	Early postwar	Pre-de-pression	Depres-sion
DADED	2·40	−0·23	1·65	−0·59	−0·52	−0·62	−0·42	0·05	−0·49
DADJOB	0·06	0·08	−0·01	0·10	0·07	0·04	0·02	0·06	0·02
MOMED	−2·70	2·01	−0·10	−1·27	2·66	0·76	2·22	1·91	3·12
WLTH	16·27	13·01	14·13	11·58	6·33	12·52	7·88	1·43	8·35
FAMSZ	−1·23	−1·55	−4·38	−0·67	0·50	−0·88	−2·76	0·27	−0·25
BASED	8·05	6·20	10·62	13·15	2·40	6·11	6·43	4·19	5·51
JOB1	0·47	0·28	0·53	0·52	0·22	0·22	0·07	−0·05	0·07
ADDED	3·86	3·22	−7·13	12·57	−4·12	9·32	3·27	−17·28	1·82
QUAL1	−2·11	15·61	10·12	−5·62	18·70	−5·87	−4·28	−14·84	7·23
QUAL2	43·66	57·35	47·58	68·76	79·98	46·61	14·25	18·19	9·68

TABLE 4.2 *continued*

Independent variables	Early career: JOB10 Cohort				Mid-career: JOB20 Cohort			Later career: JOB30 Cohort	
	Pre-de-pression	Depres-sion	Early postwar	Postwar growth	Pre-de-pression	Depres-sion	Early postwar	Pre-de-pression	Depres-sion
JOB10					0·54	0·52	0·58	0·18	0·07
ADDED					16·45	22·11	18·05	31·15	6·18
QUAL1					26·36	13·91	−13·90	5·48	5·00
QUAL2					59·66	77·20	59·83	−49·75	19·92
JOB20								0·56	0·64
ADDED								0·13	4·25
QUAL1								−3·53	3·51
QUAL2								114·56	47·33
Intercept	180·73	252·64	153·63	81·57	55·72	74·83	112·09	74·50	45·86
R sq.	0·31	0·26	0·44	0·59	0·51	0·52	0·57	0·49	0·66

[a] Underlined regression coefficients are not significant at 5 per cent level.

reported here show that ADDED independently affects job status to a significant degree ten years after workforce entry. But of those men who gained a trade or technical qualification (QUAL1) or a tertiary qualification (QUAL2), only the last has an independent, significant effect on later job status. This finding further confirms the importance of educational credentials in the job market and supports the argument that further education gained early in a career has greater effects on subsequent status than courses taken later.

There are several possible reasons for the tightening bond between education and job status in the early careers of men who started work before or after World War II. It is scarcely surprising that a society which devoted increasing amounts of public and private resources to education and training should utilize those investments in the labour market. Educational credentials are a convenient screening device for potential employers, and credentials serve to certify technical or social skills related to productivity. On the other hand, while education was less important in the period before 1945, the careers of the oldest cohorts were affected by a world depression and a world war, and some of the jobs recorded in their careers are military rather than civilian. Forty-three per cent of the depression cohort and 36 per cent of the pre-depression cohort reported full-time service in the Australian Armed Forces some time between 1939 and 1945. Because questioning about careers is tied to ten-year intervals and the war lasted about half that long, only about half of the respondents with military service report a military job at one of their career points, mostly at JOB10. Very few men from the two younger cohorts reported jobs later coded to 'defence', but about one-fifth of the two older cohorts reported a military job ten years after they started work. It is possible that the movement from civilian jobs to wartime service and back to civilian life again accounts for a large part of the mobility of the two oldest cohorts.

However, war service and the interruption to civilian careers do not materially affect the interpretation of Table 4.2. When men reporting defence jobs are excluded from analysis, the results are little changed. For the oldest cohort, the amount of variance explained rises from 31 to 33 per cent, the coefficient for WLTH falls slightly, and the coefficients for BASED and JOB1 rise trivially. For the depression cohort, the changes are slightly greater, but only in the direction of making the results closer to the oldest cohort. The amount of variance explained rises to 31 per cent, as a result of an increase in the coefficient for JOB10. In other words, most of the observed differences are not due to the impact of World War II on civilian careers. Rather, they can be ascribed to broader trends such as increased reliance on educational credentials in the job market, the growth of the tertiary sector (especially professional and technical jobs) and possibly also the increasing scale of production and bureaucratization of employment, leading to lower rates of mobility between jobs and across employers.

Analyses were also carried out defining career cohorts according to the historical periods discussed at the beginning of this chapter rather than by length of work experience. These analyses were restricted to determinants of status at JOB10, since after that point the relevant career data are sometimes missing because of difference in age and workforce experience. The youngest cohort is obviously a combination of the two youngest cohorts shown on Table 4.2, and the coefficients are close to their average, but more like the younger. Similarly the 1940–9 cohort is like the early postwar cohort, with some leavening from the depression cohort. There is such a high degree of overlap in the other two cohorts, defined either by the number of their career stages or in terms of economic conditions when they started work, that the substantive interpretation of trends is unaffected.

In the following discussion we therefore retain the career cohorts as earlier defined. The coefficients for the family background variables change little regardless of which stage of the career is involved: apart from WLTH they are mainly insignificant, and their effects are largely mediated by BASED and JOB1. For reasons of space coefficients for background variables are not shown in later tables but the reader is reminded that they are included in the analysis and have very similar values to those reported in Table 4.2.

The second panel of Table 4.2 is restricted to three cohorts with twenty or more years of work experience. Again there is evidence of reduced career mobility among younger men, although in all three cohorts more than half the variance in job status twenty years after workforce entry is explained by the variables in the model. As expected, JOB20 status depends heavily on JOB10 status. Whereas an extra 10 status points at JOB1 added between 3 to 5 status points at JOB10, 10 JOB10 points convert to between 5 and 6 points by JOB20. Note that for the two older cohorts whose careers were interrupted by the depression and World War II, there are also significant direct effects of JOB1.

A higher proportion of men held jobs with the same status scores at both JOB10 and JOB20 than during the first decade of the career: for the three cohorts shown the figures are 41 versus 27 per cent, 35 versus 20 per cent and 36 versus 23 per cent. The increase in regression coefficients reflects this lower mobility in the second decade of work experience. JOB1 status and BASED, together with the further education variables, exert small direct influences on

JOB20 status. However, most of the variation in status twenty years after starting work can be explained by JOB10 status, which accounts for 51, 38 and 43 per cent of the variance in JOB20 status for each cohort respectively. Again, the depression cohort experienced most discontinuity in their careers. But by the time they had been at work for twenty years, more men had experienced no shift from the occupational status attained ten years earlier. About one-fifth of the men in all three cohorts were immobile throughout the first twenty years in the workforce, at least in terms of the three time-points for which we have information.

There are several delayed direct effects worth mentioning. WLTH seems to influence careers even after twenty years in the workforce, and basic education and first job status also continue to exert perceptible effects. Tertiary qualifications gained in the first decade of working life also have an impact on mid-career status. In general, these delayed effects are most noticeable for the two older cohorts, who encountered the most difficult economic circumstances. In more orderly times a simple causal chain model may describe the process of career development fairly well because once he is launched into the workforce a man's most recent job is the best predictor of the status of his next job, much as today's weather is the best predictor of tomorrow's weather. At the conclusion of this chapter this generalization is further illustrated with career paths for different occupational groups.

A comparison of the relative effects of job status in different decades of work experience illustrates the hardening of mobility arteries. For the pre-depression cohort, 100 status points at JOB1 convert to 47 points at JOB10, 100 points at JOB10 convert to 54 points at JOB20, and 100 points at JOB20 convert to 56 points at JOB30. For the depression cohort the increase is even steeper: 28 to 52 to 64. JOB20 alone accounts for 61 per cent of the variance in JOB30, by which time the only other significant effect for this cohort is the continuing impact of BASED. About 56 per cent of men in the depression cohort had jobs with the same status at both JOB20 and JOB30, compared with 48 per cent of men in the pre-depression cohort. Part of this difference lies in the fact that about 7 per cent of the pre-depression cohort reported a military job for JOB30 compared with only 2 per cent of the depression cohort.

In sum, the best way to predict the status of a man's later job is to know the status of his earlier job. As a career progresses, the effects of earlier statuses – whether family background, schooling or earlier occupations – are absorbed into and mediated by more recent statuses. Once the status of first and later jobs have been taken into account, other characteristics, whether ascribed at birth or achieved in adolescence, are relatively unimportant for predicting later status. However, this finding does not imply that the other variables have no effect on job status, merely that they have little *direct* importance once a career is reasonably well developed.

Careers and ethnic origin

At various points we have compared the occupational experiences of native-born and foreign-born men. This section compares men from four nativity categories: English-speaking countries (ETH1, New Zealand, the United Kingdom, Ireland, Canada and the United States), north-western Europe (ETH2, Germany and the Netherlands), southern Europe (ETH3, Greece, Italy and Yugoslavia) and a residual category (ETH4, other overseas countries). The experience of each ethnic grouping is compared to that of Australian-born men. The coefficients in Table 4.3 can be interpreted as indicating how much better or worse members of these ethnic groups fared at early career, mid-career and late career. Dummy variables (AUS10, AUS20, AUS30) have been included to indicate whether the man concerned had already emigrated to Australia by the time of the job concerned (coded 1), or was still overseas (coded 0).

Since the coefficients for BASED and JOB1 differ only slightly from the values in the tables already discussed, no further comment is necessary. The striking feature of Table 4.3 is that all but one of the ethnic group coefficients have a negative sign. That is, after controlling for family background, schooling and career beginnings the foreign-born still tend to have lower-status jobs at each stage of their careers than native-born Australians. However, in only eight cases are the negative coefficients statistically significant.

Restricting attention to the coefficients that exceed or approach statistical significance we see that the foreign-born, particularly those from southern Europe (ETH3) and the rest of the world (ETH4), tend to be disadvantaged compared with the native-born. Men in the second category (about 8 per cent of the depression cohort) were especially disadvantaged during the 1930s. Note also that being foreign-born *and* in Australia during the depression compounded that disadvantage ($-48 \cdot 46$ status points for ETH4 and $-32 \cdot 98$ status points for Australian residence, a total negative score of $81 \cdot 44$ points on an occupational scale whose standard deviation is 100). It appears that migrants from countries where English was not the native tongue suffered more than their share of penalties in this period of massive economic dislocation. In the postwar period, however, there is no such double disadvantage. Migration to Australia at an opportune time about cancelled out the

TABLE 4.3 *Cohort and ethnic differences in achievement at three career stages*[a]

Independent variables	Early career: JOB10 Cohort				Mid-career: JOB20 Cohort			Later career: JOB30 Cohort	
	Pre-depression	Depression	Early postwar	Postwar growth	Pre-depression	Depression	Early postwar	Pre-depression	Depression
BASED	8·74	7·74	11·25	13·96	4·23	5·33	6·72	2·34	5·83
JOB1	0·47	0·30	0·54	0·55	0·20	0·24	0·09	−0·02	0·07
JOB10					0·56	0·56	0·58	0·16	0·06
JOB20								0·62	0·67
ETH1[b]	−3·80	−12·33	−18·40	−9·17	−27·42	−30·81	−2·61	−7·46	−16·30
ETH2	2·74	−60·90	−19·71	−7·79	−28·19	−23·04	−1·85	−40·73	−33·91
ETH3	−3·02	−32·33	−30·25	−28·45	7·28	−57·50	−38·68	−78·13	−10·21
ETH4	−23·31	−48·46	−26·08	−29·61	28·00	−33·72	−14·61	−16·01	−31·64
AUS10[c]	4·68	−32·98	−21·72	24·93					
AUS20					−8·54	−38·09	−2·59		
AUS30								−13·58	−16·02
Intercept	175·68	248·10	161·86	55·05	61·66	84·58	105·02	105·15	42·02
R sq.	0·31	0·25	0·44	0·55	0·48	0·47	0·56	0·49	0·65

[a] Underlined regression coefficients are not significant at 5 per cent level. All coefficients are net of social background (see text).
[b] The ethnic variables are: ETH1, men born in English-speaking countries; ETH2, men born in Germany or the Netherlands; ETH3, men born in Greece, Italy or Yugoslavia; and ETH4, men born in other countries.
[c] AUS10, AUS20 and AUS30 are dummy variables which have the value 1 if the man lived in Australia 10, 20 and 30 years respectively after his first job. Otherwise the variable has the value zero.

disadvantage of foreign birth and, in the case of English-speaking migrants and north-western Europeans, turned into a modest advantage.

It should be kept in mind that most of the foreign-born men in the sample have been employed in more than one country. For example, 27 per cent of the depression cohort were born overseas, and two-thirds of these men were still overseas ten years after starting work. Thus, the coefficients in Table 4.3 imply some discrimination in Australia but also indicate that migrants fared relatively less well in their countries of origin than they would have if they had been born, educated and started work in Australia. In other words, the negative effects of foreign birth reflect more than discrimination by Australian employers, because many foreign-born workers had already started work before emigration to Australia.

Most of the ethnic origin coefficients relating to mid-career status are not large, but with one exception they are negative in sign. Again it can be seen that the depression cohort suffered most in the job market. For example, in the 1950s a southern European who had a similar socioeconomic background, about the same amount of education and comparable early career status to a native-born Australian had a JOB20 status about 58 points lower. If he was living in Australia at that time this disadvantage was further compounded. The last panel of Table 4.3 reveals a similar pattern in late career. Clearly, foreign birth is a handicap in the status attainment process. Of course, by JOB30 most of the foreign-born were long settled in Australia. Only 8 per cent of the foreign-born from the depression cohort were still resident overseas by this stage of their career.

Careers and rural–urban migration

There is evidence both that men migrate to improve their job opportunities and that migrants are more successful than men who remain in the region of their birth (Blau and Duncan, 1967, p. 250). However, people move for other than occupational reasons, for example to gain political and religious refuge. So far as rural–urban migration in mid-twentieth-century Australia is concerned, however, we assume that push factors predominated and expect that migration to cities will be associated with status loss because many rural skills do not transfer easily to urban settings. On the other hand, movement from larger to smaller communities is more likely to be in response to pull factors. On this reasoning, rural–urban migrants should suffer status loss whereas urban–rural migrants should experience status gains, compared with city-stayers. Rural stayers probably occupy an intermediate position.

Table 4.4 presents analyses in which geographically mobile men are compared with those who remained in middle-sized or large cities. Three patterns of geographical mobility are distinguished. In the first panel of Table 4.4 RR10 stands for men who at time of JOB1 were living on a farm, in a village or in a country town and were living in a similar setting at JOB10. RU10 stands for men who at JOB1 were also in that kind of community but who by JOB10 had moved to a middle-sized or large city; UR10 represents the reverse movement, from larger to smaller communities. The base for comparison are men who remained in middle-sized or large cities. RR20, RR30 and so on are defined in a similar way except that they refer to mobility in the next two decades of the career.

Obviously there are few significant differences between movers and stayers. Most coefficients are small and their direction is mixed. Only three coefficients exceed twice their standard error, and 17 of the 27 mobility coefficients are negative in sign, the rest positive. The only pattern worth interpreting is for rural–urban migration which is associated with status loss in all cohorts at all stages of the career. Men who moved to cities in the third decade of their working lives, usually in their mid-forties, suffered significant status loss. According to the last panel of Table 4.4, such a migrant experienced a drop in job status of between 35 and 55 points, net of social background, schooling and previous job status. Undoubtedly this effect represents the cost of being forced off farms into urban jobs late in life. There is no significant status gain for urban–rural migrants, and of the 9 relevant coefficients none is statistically significant, 5 are positive in sign and 4 negative.

The only other significant effect found in Table 4.4 is that rural stayers in the pre-depression cohort were advantaged compared with movers or city-stayers. For them JOB10 relates to the depths of the depression when job opportunities were especially scarce in towns and cities. During the 1930s the movement of workers out of farming was temporarily arrested. In 1911 30·2 per cent of the workforce was in primary industry, by 1921 the figure had declined to 25·8 per cent, by 1933 to 24·3 per cent and by 1947 to 17·6 per cent (Ford, 1970, p. 91). Clearly, the intercensal period 1921–33 witnessed a much slower rate of decline in the rural population than the period before or after.

To determine whether these patterns are affected by including the foreign-born, the experience of Australian-born men was analysed separately. The overall results are not altered: the same coefficients are significant and only two non-significant coefficients change sign. We conclude that men who move from cities to smaller

TABLE 4.4 Geographic mobility and career achievement for four cohorts[a]

Independent variables	Early career: JOB10 Cohort				Mid-career: JOB20 Cohort			Later career: JOB30 Cohort	
	Pre-depression	Depression	Early postwar	Postwar growth	Pre-depression	Depression	Early postwar	Pre-depression	Depression
BASED	8·90	7·50	11·33	12·99	2·75	5·24	6·92	2·53	4·77
JOB1	0·47	0·30	0·54	0·56	0·21	0·22	0·09	−0·05	0·06
JOB10					0·58	0·57	0·59	0·17	0·06
JOB20								0·62	0·69
RR10[b]	30·95	11·80	5·89	−5·00					
RU10	−12·05	−22·60	−14·15	−9·88					
UR10	15·35	10·69	−14·99	−3·57					
RR20[b]					−1·06	3·44	2·56		
RU20					−23·69	−14·83	−14·30		
UR20					17·34	−0·12	8·26		
RR30[b]								−1·52	−7·80
RU30								−54·92	−35·07
UR30								−5·76	2·96
Intercept	182·94	236·75	143·39	86·73	52·86	54·04	100·03	84·12	47·01
R sq.	0·34	0·25	0·44	0·54	0·48	0·45	0·55	0·48	0·65

[a] Underlined regression coefficient are not significant at 5 per cent level. All coefficients are net of social background.
[b] RR, RU and UR are dummy variables. They represent rural stayers, movers from rural to urban areas and movers from urban to rural areas respectively. The numerals 10, 20 and 30 refer to early career (first job to ten years later), mid-career (between 10 and 20 years after first job) and later career (between 20 and 30 years after first job). For example RR10 is scored 1 if the respondent lived in a rural area when he started work and was in a similar locality ten years later; if not it is scored zero. RU10 indicates mobility from a rural to an urban location in the first decade of the career. UR10 indicates reverse mobility in the same decade.

communities did not as a group experience any net advantage or disadvantage in their occupational careers compared with men who began and continued their careers in cities. On the other hand men who moved from farms, villages and country towns to middle-sized or large cities suffered relative disadvantage, especially if they moved in late career. No consistent pattern emerges for men who remained in smaller communities, except that during the depression of the 1930s they enjoyed some status advantage over city dwellers.

Careers and war service

As already mentioned, about two-fifths of the men in the two oldest cohorts served full-time in the Australian Armed Forces, mostly during World War II. With few exceptions, this period of war service came between their jobs ten and twenty years after starting work. Two countervailing effects of war service on later occupational careers seem plausible. On the one hand, the interruption of civilian careers might have hindered occupational advancement. On the other hand special privileges in the form of postwar reconstruction schemes and informal or formal preferences to ex-servicemen in civilian employment may have helped their later careers (see Smith *et al.*, n.d., for an account of repatriation and rehabilitation proposals under discussion in 1945).

An American study of early career achievement found that veteran status had very small effects on job status or wages eight years after workforce entry, except among blacks, whose earnings were higher than otherwise expected (Ornstein, 1976, p. 169). However, this finding pertains to men aged between 30 and 39 in 1968, and veteran status refers not to service in World War II but to compulsory military service during the 1950s and 1960s. None the less, it shows that some groups may gain skills in military service that are beneficial later in civilian life.

Table 4.5 presents the results of a multiple regression analysis which shows that war service had a significant positive effect on the status of JOB20 among members of the depression cohort, whereas for men in the older pre-depression cohort the effect was statistically insignificant but negative. This difference between the cohorts may have come about because men in the younger cohort were able to take better advantage of educational assistance programs offered to ex-servicemen. But the evidence does not bear out that surmise. The difference between the cohorts persists even when ADDED and qualifications are taken into account. That is, war service improved the later job status of men in the depression cohort independently of both other background characteristics and any further education they may have gained after demobilization. It therefore seems that this difference relates to a more general effect: war service that occurs relatively early in a man's career is apparently less disruptive of his subsequent civilian career, and because younger men are less established in their careers and had fewer family responsibilities when they entered the services they may have been able to take greater advantage of later occupational and educational opportunities.

TABLE 4.5   *Effects of war service on mid-career achievement[a]*

Independent variables	JOB20	
	Pre-depression cohort	Depression cohort
BASED	2·61	5·61
JOB1	0·19	0·22
JOB10	0·59	0·58
WAR[b]	−6·98	22·45
Intercept	59·99	46·81
R sq.	0·49	0·46

[a] Underlined regression coefficients are not significant at 5 per cent level. All coefficients are net of social background.

[b] WAR is a dummy variable which takes the value of 1 if the respondent served in the Australian Armed Services between 1939 and 1945, zero otherwise.

If this interpretation is correct, more men in the depression cohort should report that war service helped rather than hindered their civilian careers. Seven questions in our survey were concerned with the qualifications and occupational benefits respondents derived from war service, and whether war service had helped or hindered them in their subsequent civilian careers. The responses show that men in the depression cohort believe war service was beneficial to them. Excluding the one in five in both cohorts (18 and 21 per cent respectively) who answered that war service neither helped nor hindered their civilian career, twice as many men in the depression cohort reported that their time in the Australian Armed Services helped rather than hindered their civilian career (55 versus 26 per cent). For the pre-depression cohort the split was 39 per cent in each category. Thus, respondents' recollections support the statistical analysis. This finding gives added credence to our analytic procedures and further confirms the validity of the occupational status scale as a measure of the general desirability of jobs and the subjective experience of workers.

Patterns of career mobility

Career contingencies such as decisions to undertake further education and training, to migrate to another country or region, or to volunteer for military service all influence later status attainment to varying degrees. But as already demonstrated, the overwhelming determinant of later occupational status is earlier occupational status. Career beginnings and early career mobility largely determine later occupational status.

This final section uses a graphic form of data presentation to delineate the main paths that men with the same first jobs follow over their careers, and the main routes followed by men who in 1973, the year of the survey, had the same kinds of job. To maintain sufficient numbers of cases to reveal meaningful patterns the whole sample is used. First job, job ten years later and job at time of interview are examined. Eight broad occupational categories are defined: professional, managerial, clerical, skilled manual, semi-skilled, unskilled, farmers and farm workers. These categories are taken from the ANU 1 status scale and form a status hierarchy in terms of the ANU 2 scale within the nonfarm and farm sectors. For simplicity only civilian careers are examined and periods of full-time war service are ignored. That is to say, men whose JOB1, JOB10 or JOBN were in defence are excluded.

Figures 4.2a–4.9 outline the main career mobility patterns both in terms of the different destinations reached by men who started out in the same general kind of work and in terms of the diverse origins of men whose 1973 occupations were much the same. For most occupational groups outflow and inflow data are presented, but so few men started out as managers or farmers that only inflow data are presented for these two groups. Similarly, for farm workers only outflow patterns are shown because very few men in the sample were still farm workers in 1973. Figure 4.2a traces any career path which involved five men or more. For larger origin or destination groups a number larger than five is used. In general, only paths involving at least 3 per cent of a group are shown.

A comparison of Figures 4.2a and 4.2b shows that while a considerable proportion of the sample began work as professionals (a broadly defined category including technical workers), their number was augmented by men who gained additional qualifications during their careers. The number of professionals at time of interview is about half as large again as the number who were professionals at the outset of their careers.

Men who begin as professionals are very likely to continue as professionals: about two out of three who start in this category remained in it during the first decade of their working life and were

Occupational category	JOB 1	JOB 10	JOB 73
Professional		102	
Managerial			7
Clerical			
Skilled manual		6	
Semiskilled manual			
Unskilled manual			
Farmers			
Farm workers			

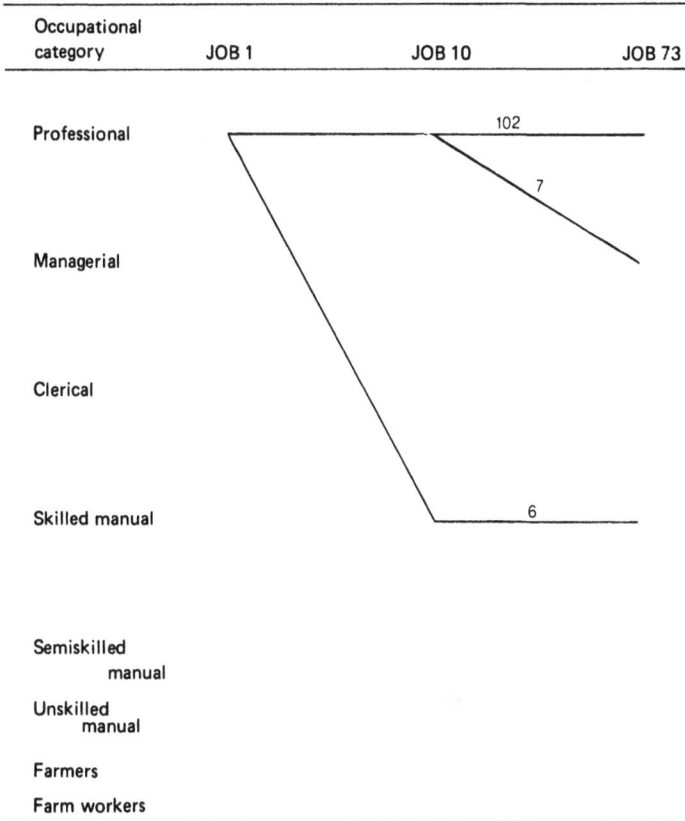

Figure 4.2a Major career paths of 160 men whose first job was professional. This figure excludes minor career paths involving 45 men.

still so occupied when interviewed. The only other discernible patterns involved movement into managerial jobs and skilled work. The latter are downwardly mobile men who began their careers as technical workers. The remaining twenty-two patterns account, on average, for two cases each. Only twelve men who started out in the professional category experienced downward mobility into semi-skilled or unskilled manual work.

Figure 4.2b shows that recruits into professional and technical ranks come mainly from skilled manual and white collar beginnings, in early and mid-career. Five major paths account for three out of four men in the professional-technical group in 1973; the remaining 26 paths, which are not shown, accounted for only 57 men. Only 8 men from unskilled beginnings entered a professional-technical

Occupational category	JOB 1	JOB 10	JOB 73
Professional		102	
Managerial	28		
Clerical		15	
	14		
Skilled manual		19	
Semiskilled manual			
Unskilled manual			
Farmers			
Farm workers			

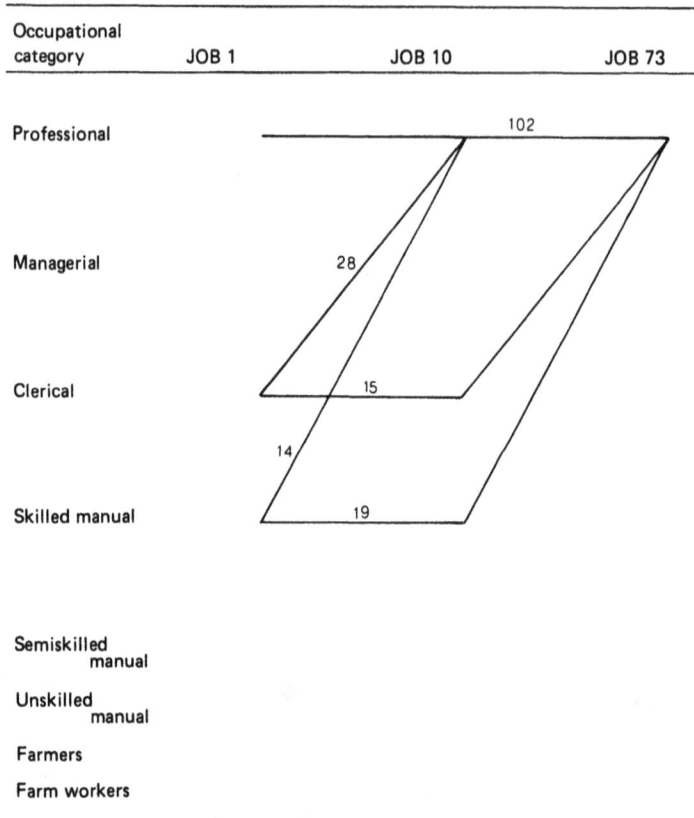

Figure 4.2b Major career paths of 234 men whose 1973 job was professional. This figure excludes minor career paths involving 56 men.

occupation. The professional category is more closed than any other: 64 per cent of the 102 men who began as professionals remained in the category at all three career stages, the highest percentage in any group. Of 234 men who were in the professional group in 1973, 44 per cent started out in that category, a proportion exceeded only in the recruitment of skilled manual workers (see Figure 4.6b).

As already mentioned, so few men start work as managers (only thirteen in this sample) that no generalizations about outflow mobility can be sustained. However, by time of interview fully 12 per cent of the total sample had followed a wide variety of routes into managerial positions. Figure 4.3 presents five career paths involving more than seven men, accounting for half the managerial group. Most men achieved managerial status after at least a decade of work experience; only about 20 per cent reached that level in the first ten years of their career. The white-collar workers and the few semiskilled workers who were already managers by the end of the first decade of their career constitute a minority of their peers with the same career beginnings. Promotion to a position of authority over other workers depends in part on skills learned on the job. It is hardly surprising that managerial status is largely reserved for mature workers, especially in the bureaucratic setting that characterizes most white-collar work. By contrast, the paths to managerial status for manual workers are more often through self-

Occupational category	JOB 1	JOB 10	JOB 73
Professional			
Managerial			
Clerical			
Skilled manual			
Semiskilled manual			
Unskilled manual			
Farmers			
Farm workers			

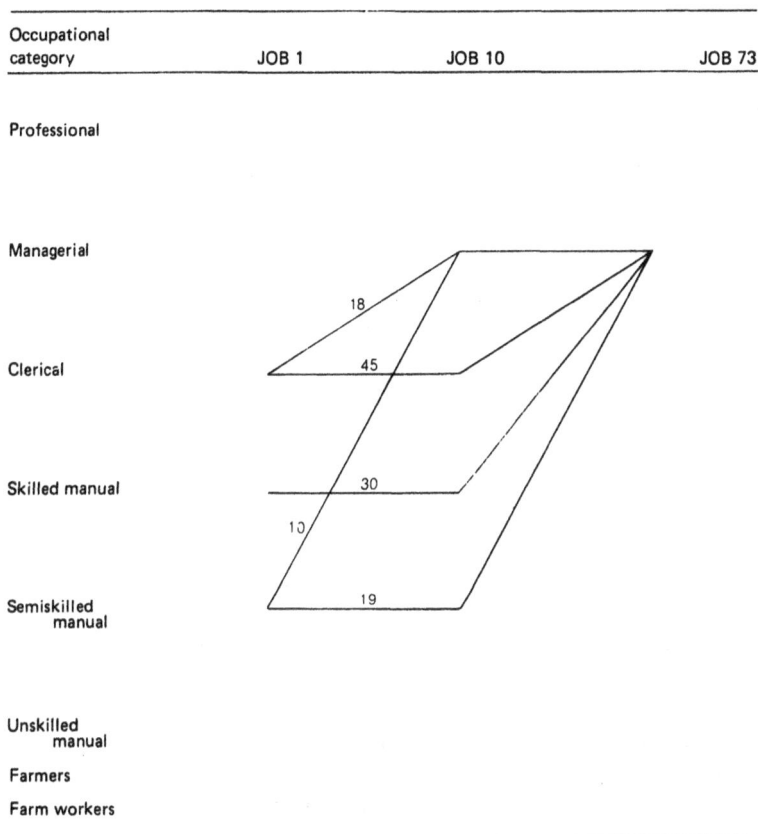

Figure 4.3   Major career paths of 248 men whose 1973 job was managerial. This figure excludes minor career paths involving 126 men. No figure showing managerial origins is presented because few men begin work as managers.

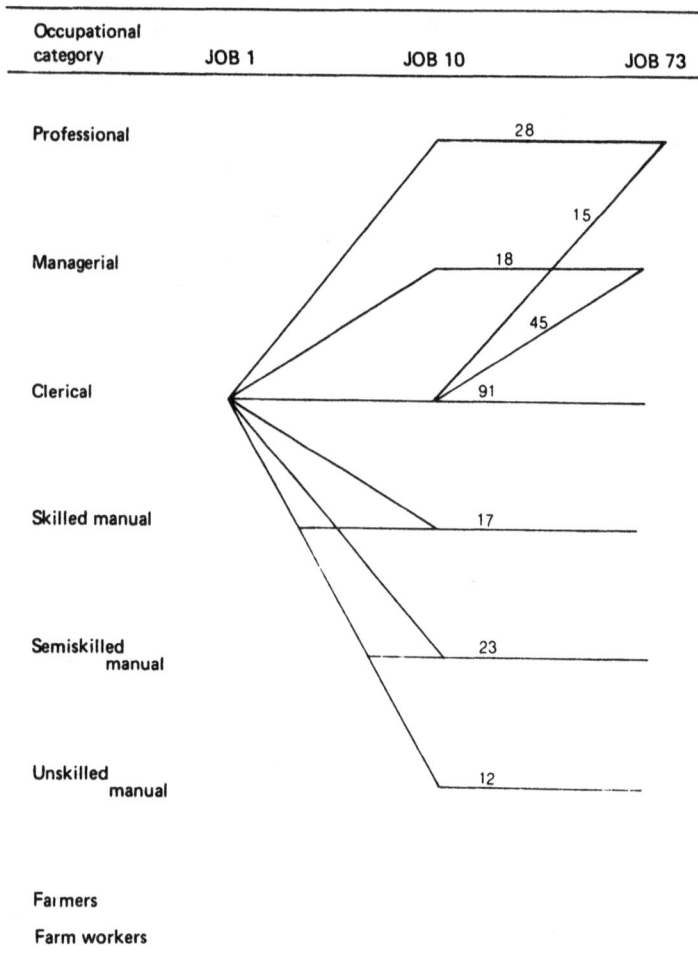

Occupational category	JOB 1	JOB 10	JOB 73
Professional		28	
			15
Managerial		18	
			45
Clerical		91	
Skilled manual		17	
Semiskilled manual		23	
Unskilled manual		12	
Farmers			
Farm workers			

Figure 4.4a Major career paths of 343 men whose first job was clerical.
This figure excludes minor career paths involving 94 men.

employment in building and construction or in commerce, although with the increasing scale of commercial enterprises many managers are salaried. In fact two-thirds of all managers in our sample were salaried, and of the remainder a large proportion were owner-managers of small enterprises (fewer than twenty-five workers).

Clerical work is characteristically an entry job and Figure 4.4a traces paths involving ten or more men. As can be seen they lead both upwards and downwards to every other nonfarm occupational group. Most of these moves begin early and the careers of about half

Occupational category	JOB 1	JOB 10	JOB 73
Professional			
Managerial			
Clerical			
Skilled manual			
Semiskilled manual			
Unskilled manual			
Farmers			
Farm workers			

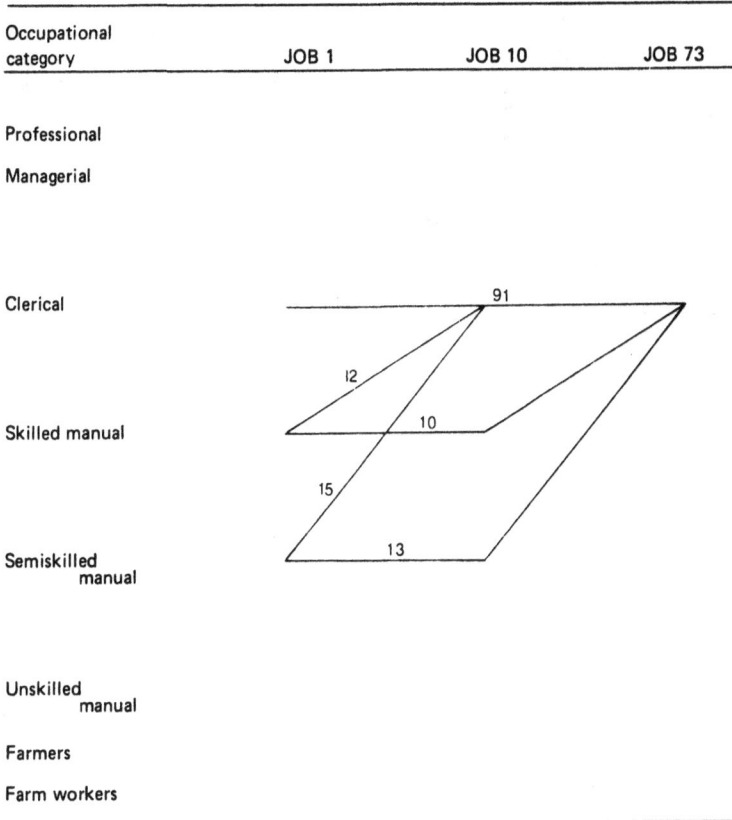

Figure 4.4b   Major career paths of 231 men whose 1973 job was clerical.
This figure excludes minor career paths involving 90 men.

this initial group are represented by the eight main paths shown. The largest path, those who remained in the clerical group at all three points, accounts for 27 per cent of the total, a rather low proportion by comparison with professionals. The next largest paths, already discussed in relation to Figures 4.2b and 4.3, are inflows into managerial positions and into professional and technical jobs. In addition there are smaller downward flows from clerical into manual work. In terms of inflow, there is no appreciable recruitment from higher white-collar beginnings into clerical work. The five main patterns shown in Figure 4.4b account for 61 per cent of men with clerical jobs in 1973, and are fairly evenly distributed between movement out of the skilled and semiskilled strata in both early and mid-career. Some of these shifts involve moves from the shop floor into the office.

Apprentices by definition start work in skilled trades, which is the single largest category of first jobs: one-quarter of all men in the sample began as skilled manual workers. There was a net movement out of this group, but relatively little movement into it. Just over half the men who were skilled workers in 1973 began work as skilled workers and were still so employed ten years later (Figures 4.5a, 4.5b). Outflow mobility was mostly downward: three of the four mobility paths shown are to lower skill levels. Some of

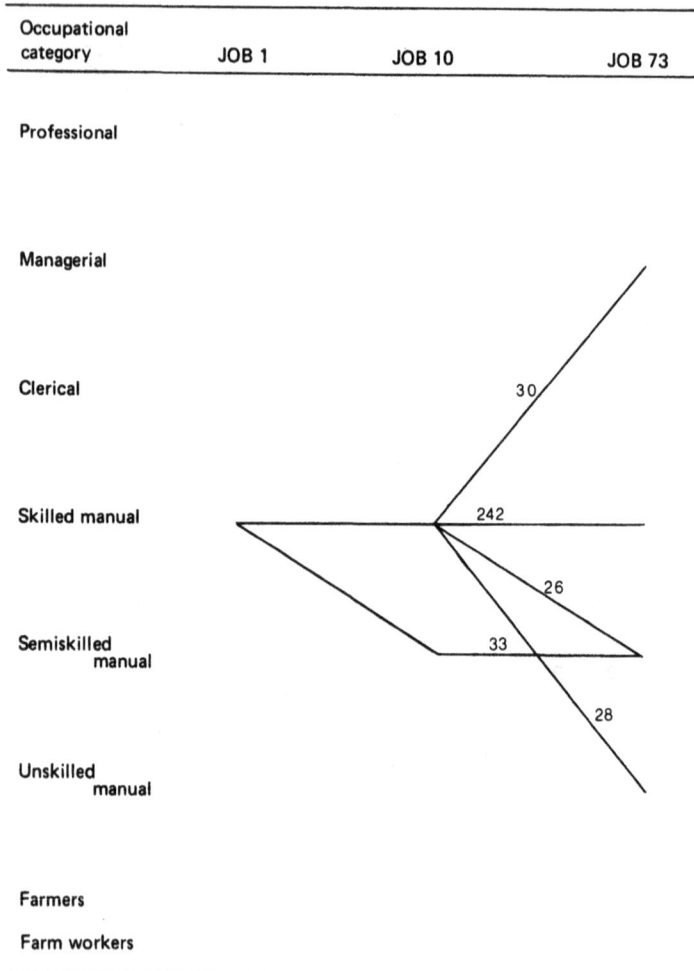

Occupational category	JOB 1	JOB 10	JOB 73

Professional

Managerial

Clerical   30

Skilled manual   242

                                                                 26

Semiskilled
      manual   33

                                                                 28

Unskilled
      manual

Farmers

Farm workers

Figure 4.5a   Major career paths of 552 men whose first job was skilled manual. This figure excludes minor career paths involving 193 men.

Occupational category	JOB 1	JOB 10	JOB 73
Professional			
Managerial			
Clerical			
Skilled manual			
Semiskilled manual			
Unskilled manual			
Farmers			
Farm workers			

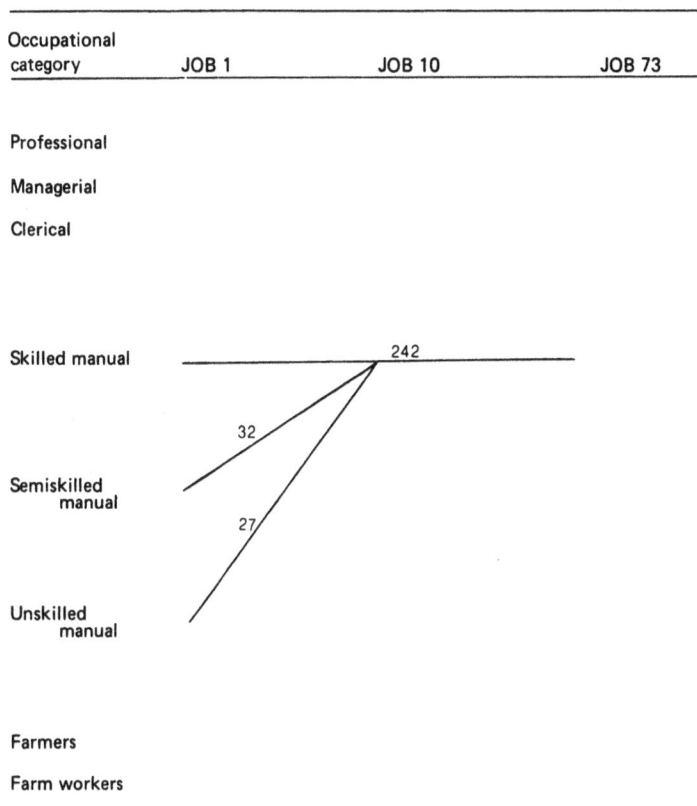

Figure 4.5b   Major career paths of 468 men whose 1973 job was skilled manual. This figure excludes minor career paths involving 167 men.

the downwardly mobile were apprentices who failed to get their papers and went into semiskilled work. Thus, only four of these downwardly mobile men gained a trade or technical qualification in the first decade of their working lives. About one-quarter of them were born in a non-English-speaking country and held qualifications that may not have been recognized in Australia.

The main route of upward mobility is into small businesses. Of the 30 men shown as moving into managerial positions in mid-career. 12 were owner-managers, mostly in firms with few employees. From an inflow perspective, only two career mobility paths account for more than 20 men in this group: men who started off in jobs with few skills and by dint of on-the-job training and further education upgraded themselves into skilled work. Of the 59

105

upwardly mobile workers shown in Figure 4.5b, over one-third undertook further education and, by the time they had been at work for a decade, 20 had earned a trade, technical or tertiary qualification.

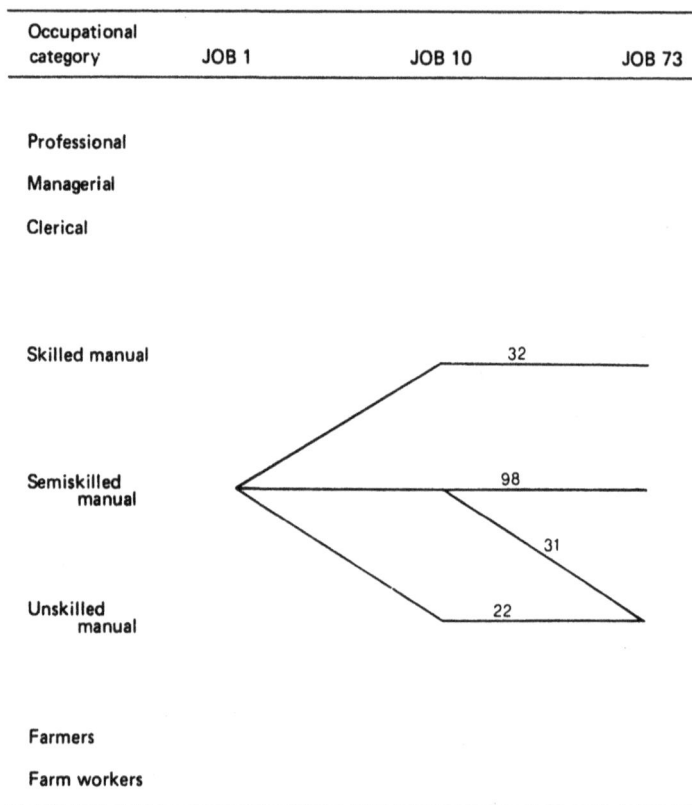

Occupational category	JOB 1	JOB 10	JOB 73
Professional			
Managerial			
Clerical			
Skilled manual		32	
Semiskilled manual		98 / 31	
Unskilled manual		22	
Farmers			
Farm workers			

Figure 4.6a Major career paths of 385 men whose first job was semiskilled manual. This figure excludes minor career paths involving 202 men.

The semiskilled category has fairly heterogeneous origins. It includes some white-collar workers such as shop-assistants, but also other kinds of service workers. It has a high rate of outflow, with only about one in four of the initial group remaining in the same stratum over their careers (cf. Broom and Jones, 1976, p. 93 for figures from the 1965 survey).

Although this category is about the same size at both first job and current job, it is composed of a cluster of jobs which attract new

Occupational category	JOB 1	JOB 10	JOB 73

Professional

Managerial

Clerical

Skilled manual

Semiskilled manual

Unskilled manual

Farmers

Farm workers

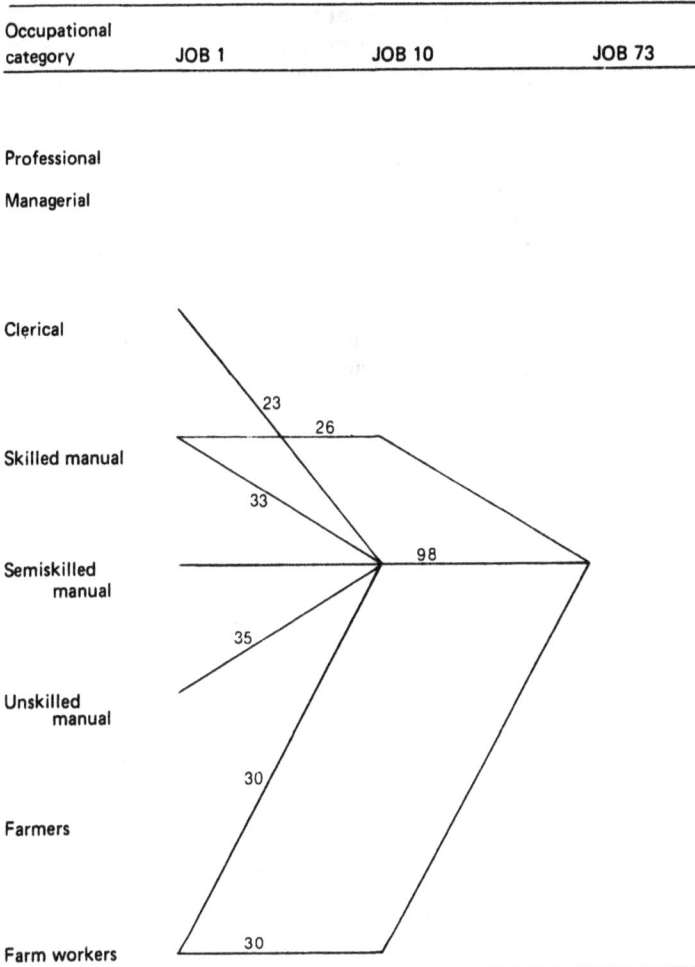

Figure 4.6b Major career paths of 421 men whose 1973 job was semiskilled manual. This figure excludes minor career paths involving 146 men.

entrants and lose existing workers over time. Some semiskilled workers enter higher and lower skill occupations within the manual stratum, but there is also an inflow of older men who leave skilled manual work as their physical capacities decline, and an inflow of white-collar workers moving into the service sector.

With rare exceptions workers who enter the workforce with few skills are locked into low-status manual work for the rest of their working lives. The three immobile or downwardly mobile career paths shown in Figure 4.6a represent two out of every five men who started work in this stratum. There are few paths of upward mobility into the top two groups, apart from self-employment. Of 60 such upwardly mobile men, 47 arrived by various routes at managerial and entrepreneurial statuses. The 'openness' of this stratum is further evidenced in Figure 4.6b, where for the first time paths from farm work appear. Because factory operatives are in this stratum, the proportion of men from southern Europe following such career paths are twice as numerous as expected: 15 per cent compared with only 7 per cent in the sample as a whole.

Unskilled workers have neither the human nor the material capital to go on the land except as farm workers, and their main prospects are a rise to higher manual levels. To make such a move

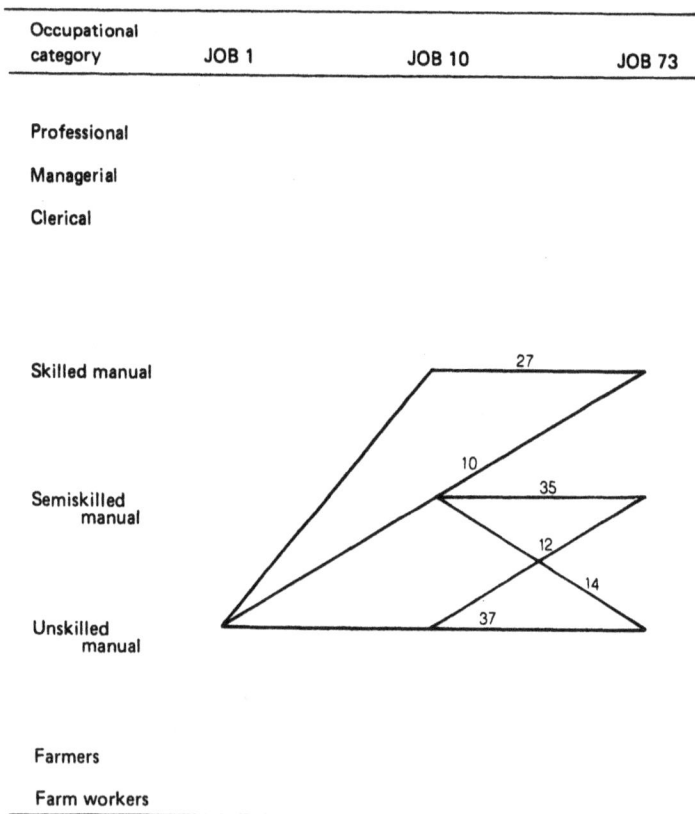

Occupational category	JOB 1	JOB 10	JOB 73

Professional

Managerial

Clerical

Skilled manual   27

Semiskilled manual   10   35   12

Unskilled manual   37   14

Farmers

Farm workers

Figure 4.7a   Major career paths of 218 men whose first job was unskilled manual. This figure excludes minor career paths involving 83 men.

requires early investment in human capital. Of the five paths showing upward mobility, four begin before the end of the first decade of working life, with one path representing counter-mobility back to unskilled work in 1973 (see Figure 4.7a). About one-quarter of those men who achieved semiskilled status at JOB10 were again unskilled by 1973. Their downward mobility is almost exactly matched by men who after a decade or more of unskilled work entered the semiskilled stratum.

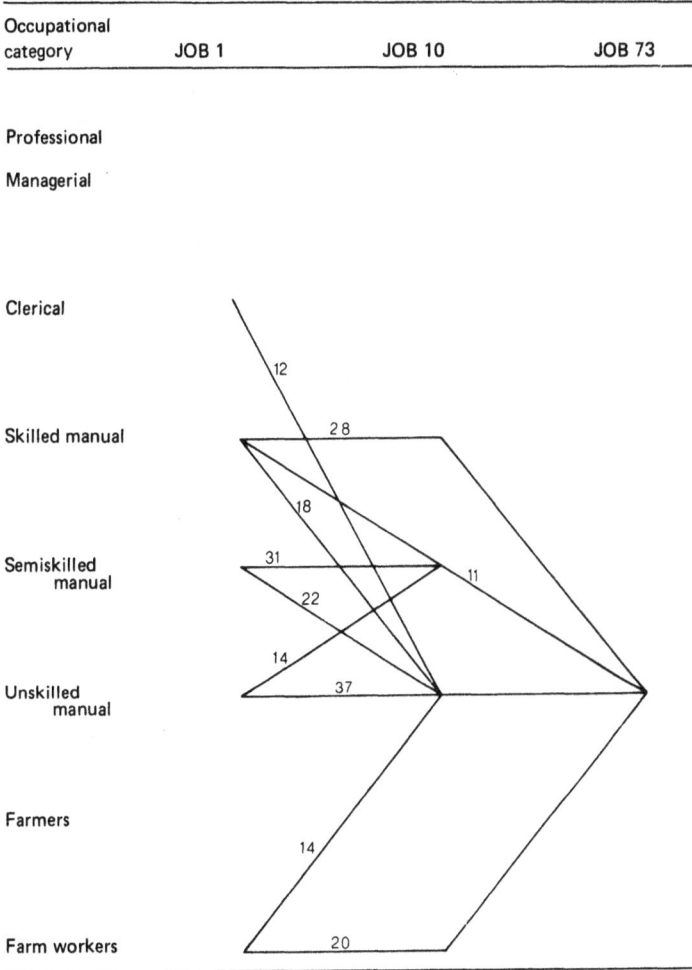

Occupational category	JOB 1	JOB 10	JOB 73

Figure 4.7b Major career paths of 295 men whose 1973 job was unskilled manual. This figure excludes minor career paths involving 88 men.

Of the 218 men who started work in unskilled jobs, only one-fifth had crossed the manual/nonmanual divide by 1973. Not surprisingly, fewer men choose to start their working lives in unskilled work than the number who eventually find themselves occupying such jobs. About one in ten of this sample started out in an unskilled job, but by 1973 the proportion was one in seven. To some extent this shift is a response to industrialization and the declining importance of employment in the farm sector, but it also reflects downward mobility as manual skills deteriorate. Note also that rural–urban migrants also enter unskilled work (Figure 4.7b). However, according to Figure 4.9, semiskilled work is a more important destination for men who start out as farm workers.

Figures 4.8 and 4.9 present inflow figures for farmers (including farm managers) and outflow figures for farm workers. As already

Occupational category	JOB 1	JOB 10	JOB 73

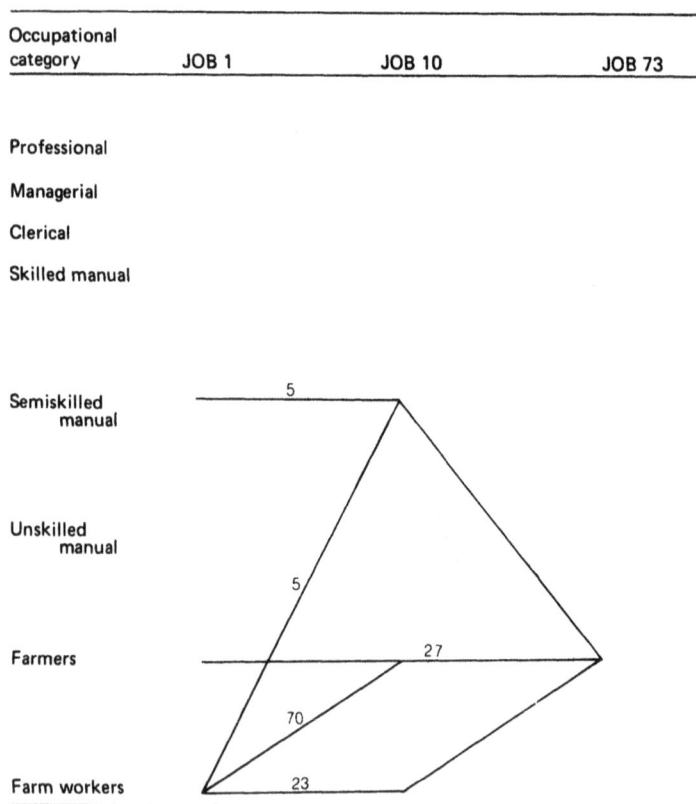

Professional

Managerial

Clerical

Skilled manual

Figure 4.8 Major career paths of 166 men who were farmers in 1973. This figure excludes minor career paths involving 36 men. Few men begin work as farmers and no such figure is presented.

110

Occupational category	JOB 1	JOB 10	JOB 73
Professional			
Managerial			
Clerical			
Skilled manual			
Semiskilled manual			
Unskilled manual			
Farmers			
Farm workers			

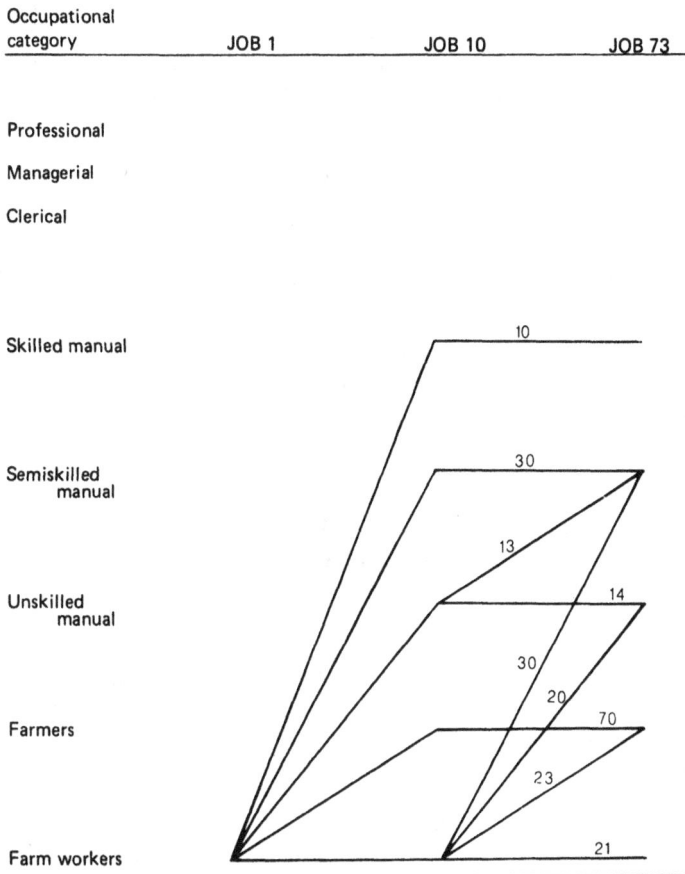

Figure 4.9 Major career paths of 378 men whose first job was farm work.
This figure excludes minor career paths involving 147 men.
Relatively few men enter farm work in the course of their
careers. Thus no separate figure for farm work as a destination
is presented.

mentioned, relatively few men start out as farmers or farm
managers, because most men in farming begin as farm workers on a
family farm (Broom *et al.*, 1977a, p. 128). The 65 men who started
as farmers are too few to justify outflow analysis. Since only 51 men
were still farm workers in 1973, no inflow data are presented for this
group. Note the familiar decline in the number of farm jobs. If the
farm stratum is taken as a whole, 20 per cent of the sample started
out in farming, but by 1973 farmers and farm workers amounted to
only about 11 per cent.

As Figure 4.8 shows, there is only a small cluster of immobile farmers, one in six of this group in 1973. For the most part they began as farm workers and became farmers on their own in early or mid-career. However, four of the five career paths shown are within the farm stratum, and in total account for 75 per cent of men employed as farmers in 1973. The only other path involving five or more men was a trickle in mid-career from the semiskilled category. Most of the men in this cluster worked in jobs linked with primary industry. Two were butchers in provincial towns who later went into beef-raising and dairying; two others were shop assistants in country towns who made the same move; and the last was an English migrant who, in his fifties, left his job in an electronics firm to own a poultry farm jointly with his son.[3] Otherwise, the farm stratum was insulated from inflow from the nonfarm sector. Only 48 men, or 22 per cent of the total in farming, had begun work in another stratum. Of those, 23 had fathers in farming and returned to take over a family farm.

Although farming recruits few men from nonfarm pursuits, it provides a steady flow of workers to the cities. We have already seen that they compete at a disadvantage with urban workers. Even when other background factors are taken into account rural–urban migration entails a loss of occupational status. Figure 4.9 makes this explicit: no major career path out of farming leads to white-collar jobs, and the flow into skilled jobs is the smallest of those shown. The mobility flows depicted split evenly between mobility within the farm stratum (114 men, or 30 per cent of all farm workers) and mobility into the manual stratum, mostly semiskilled or unskilled work (117 men). The remaining two-fifths of this group follow diverse patterns of mobility. Indeed, farm workers show the highest rate and most varied pattern of career mobility. In addition to the nine patterns depicted, forty-six other patterns occurred, accounting for an average of three men. In other words, fifty-five of the sixty-four logically possible mobility patterns were actually followed by at least one man in this sample. No other entry stratum of comparable size manifests such a variety of occupational experience or such a high degree of out-mobility.

These analyses demonstrate that many Australian men become locked into more or less stable career paths, and in some cases highly segmented labour markets, early in their occupational careers. Professional, skilled and farming jobs are most fully insulated from other occupational groups, in the first two cases because of the qualifications barrier to entry and in the third because of the inheritance of family farms. The extent to which men with similar career beginnings follow similar paths can be seen from the graphs, which reveal that 9 per cent of a possible 384 paths shown on the outflow graphs account for 1,272 men, or 62 per cent of the sample. Similarly 9 per cent of a possible 448 paths shown on the inflow paths account for 66 per cent of the sample. Both these graphs and the regression analyses demonstrate how strongly occupational paths are influenced by where men start out. This segmentation of the labour market is examined further in relation to earnings in the next chapter, but before proceeding to that more technical analysis the present findings are summarized in the form of a standard career mobility table. The farm sector is omitted because of its insulation from nonfarm jobs, at least in terms of inflow.

Tables 4.6 and 4.7 present analyses of early mobility from first job to JOB10 and later mobility from JOB10 to 1973 respectively. The strata are constructed from the ANU 2 status distributions with the objective of delineating the top and bottom segments of the status hierarchy (roughly the 12·5 per cent at either extreme) and three middle groups (the remaining three quartiles). Because the status distributions at JOB1, JOB10, and JOBN differ (entry jobs have lower average status than current jobs), the categories are not exactly defined by these splits, as the marginals of each table show. However, the actual dividing points are the same at each career point to avoid counting a person with the same job status at JOB1 and JOBN as 'mobile'. The dividing points used were status scores below 410, scores from 411 to 460, 461 to 550, 551 to 651, and scores of 652 or higher. Because of the low rates of mobility between manual and nonmanual jobs, the third and fourth groups were further subdivided. The extreme categories are exclusively manual and nonmanual respectively, and the 'semiskilled manual' group is almost entirely manual (84 per cent at JOB1, 93 per cent at JOB10 and 95 per cent at JOBN). The other two groups are, as the tables show, somewhat mixed in terms of the nonmanual/manual split, especially for first job.

The first decade of work is characterized by substantial status immobility. In the sample as a whole, there was an almost even split between mobility and immobility, with 51 per cent remaining in the same group at both points and 49 per cent shifting positions. If careers were random and followed no set pattern, that is, if the kind of job a man had after ten years bore no systematic relationship to his first job, four out of five men would have changed groups instead of one in two. If each broad stratum is examined in turn, and allowances are made for the differences in stratum size at JOB1 and JOB10 (for example, there are about twice as many men in the top two strata by JOB10 as there are at JOB1), the overall symmetry of exchanges between strata is impressive. Thus, mobility into and out of the lowest status group is largely confined to the two next higher

TABLE 4.6 *Patterns of early career mobility*[a]

Occupational status at JOB1		Occupational status at JOB10							N (100%)
		1	2	3a	3b	4a	4b	5	
1	Lower skilled, manual	*38·4*	31·2	15·8	3·7	4·3	5·1	1·6	244
2	Semiskilled, manual	16·2	*46·6*	15·0	8·0	3·8	8·4	2·0	454
3a	Middle manual	5·7	16·9	*59·8*	1·9	6·3	6·9	2·5	387
3b	Middle nonmanual	4·5	9·8	5·3	*48·4*	0·8	19·3	11·8	242
4a	Independent trades	4·3	13·4	8·4	2·5	*55·3*	8·3	7·8	68
4b	Lower professions, administrative	7·9	8·3	8·6	8·4	3·5	*41·1*	22·3	85
5	Higher professions, administrative	2·6	3·3	5·0	3·5	1·2	5·2	*79·2*	91
	Total	13·5	25·2	23·5	11·6	6·1	10·8	9·4	1,571
	N	212	396	368	182	95	169	147	

[a] For detailed description of occupational categories, see text. Underlined figures (the diagonal) indicate the percentage immobile.

TABLE 4.7 *Patterns of later career mobility[a]*

| Occupational status at JOB10 | Occupational status at JOBN | | | | | | | N (100%) |
	1	2	3a	3b	4a	4b	5	
1 Lower skilled, manual	<u>43·4</u>	29·7	13·1	2·8	1·1	6·1	3·9	212
2 Semiskilled, manual	13·7	<u>46·7</u>	13·5	7·1	5·1	9·3	4·7	396
3a Middle manual	5·8	12·3	<u>55·7</u>	2·6	10·4	7·2	6·1	368
3b Middle nonmanual	3·2	7·2	3·4	<u>48·1</u>	0·0	11·9	26·1	182
4a Independent trades	4·4	5·6	13·6	2·3	<u>57·1</u>	6·0	11·0	95
4b Lower professions, administrative	3·7	8·2	2·5	9·3	1·7	<u>53·8</u>	20·7	169
5 Higher professions, administrative	0·7	2·6	1·8	1·9	1·6	10·5	<u>80·9</u>	147
Total	11·8	21·0	19·9	9·7	7·7	13·4	16·6	1,571
N	185	330	312	152	121	210	261	

[a] For detailed description of occupational categories, see text as for preceding table. Underlined figures (the diagonal) indicate the percentage immobile.

manual strata: 85 per cent of men who began work in low skill, manual jobs remain in the three bottom strata ten years later, while 90 per cent of men in this lowest level at JOB10 began work in one of the same three strata. The chances of rising far from a low-status job are slight indeed. Similarly, for the next stratum, very high proportions of both outflow and inflow mobility are confined to the same three strata: 78 and 89 per cent respectively. However, the chances of moving upwards into middle nonmanual and lower professional or administrative jobs are about twice as favourable for men who started work in the second lowest stratum.

The middle manual level, by contrast, shows more immobility, and slightly higher than expected mobility into the independent trades. In addition there is some exchange with all other strata, but downward mobility into the lowest skill group is unlikely, less likely in fact than for men who started out in lower professional or administrative positions. However, there are few men in this last category and the difference is not statistically significant.

Men beginning in white-collar jobs with similar social status (Group 3b, Table 4.6) show a quite different mobility pattern. Slightly more are mobile, not so much into blue-collar jobs (only about one in five) as into administrative and professional jobs (see Figure 4.4a). Few men start out as independent tradesmen (a generic label for manual workers with relatively high status), but those who do are relatively immobile. Over half remained in jobs with the same or similar status ten years later, and the main paths of mobility are into managerial positions. Men in the next highest stratum export a very high proportion of their number into the highest status bracket during the first decade of the career. In terms of mobility ratios,[4] this represents the highest flow of upward mobility in the table, partly because there is substantial recruitment into high status administrative jobs over time. As one might expect, starting out in a high-status first job provides insurance against downward mobility. This last group shows the lowest rate of out-mobility, although, as already noted, it recruits new members to its expanding ranks, mainly from white-collar origins.

It is useful to summarize the patterns of Table 4.6 by calculating conventional mobility ratios (Jones, 1975), and relating observed mobility to what might be expected on the basis of chance. Such a procedure starts from the concept of statistical independence of origins and destinations and the assumption that jobs ten years after workforce entry are distributed randomly in respect of career beginnings. These are not empirical assertions but hypothetical assumptions which provide a baseline from which real world processes can be measured.

Mobility ratios as such are not presented since they can be easily inferred from the percentages in Table 4.6. If the status of a job ten years after starting work was independent of career beginnings, 13·5 per cent of men in all origin groups would be found in the 'low skill, manual' group, 25·2 per cent in the second group, 23·5 per cent in the third, and so on across the last line of percentages in Table 4.6. Of course, such expectations are not realized in practice because later jobs do depend on earlier jobs, as we have already shown. Thus, ten years later, 38·4 and not the 'expected' 13·5 per cent of men who started work in the bottom group were still at the bottom. This figure is almost three times the 'expected' figure and yields a mobility ratio of 2·84 (38·4 divided by 13·5). All the diagonal figures, which identify immobility, exceed expectation on this criterion.

In similar fashion, ratios of observed to expected career mobility can be calculated for the off-diagonal cells, and the degree of openness of any particular stratum can be assessed. On this criterion, the least open groups are 'higher professions, adminis-trative' and 'independent trades', followed by 'middle, nonmanual' and 'lower professions, administrative'. The most 'open' strata are the second and third lowest groups on the table, since they export and recruit across a wide status range. After allowance is made for the expansion and contraction of specific status groups over the first ten years of the career, there remains a remarkably consistent pattern of exchange between categories. Outflow and inflow are very nearly balanced, and discrepancies between adjusted flows from one cell to another in the table average only two or three cases. In other words only two to three cases would need to be added to or subtracted from any off-diagonal cell in order to have a perfectly symmetrical pattern of interchange. Patterns of early career mobility display a high degree of structure, and the probability of movement is approximately inverse to the social distance involved: the greater the difference in the relative status of each occupational level, the smaller is the number of men who move between them.

Later career patterns show an even higher degree of structure. Although the general outlines in Table 4.6 and 4.7 are remarkably similar, it should be remembered that the average interval between JOB10 and JOBN in Table 4.7 is about nineteen years instead of the ten years covered by Table 4.6. For the youngest cohort, the period between JOB10 and JOBN is on average about five years, but for the oldest it is more than thirty years. Yet with few exceptions the patterns of exchange mobility are so similar that it is not necessary to rehearse the earlier discussion. There is slightly greater overall *immobility* in later career despite the longer average duration of the career span. The link between earlier and later jobs remains strong. More importantly, although no stratum is entirely closed the chances of mobility are very strongly influenced by the position in the status hierarchy from which a man starts the next stage of his career.

To take an extreme example, the chances that a man whose JOB10 was in the highest status group would still be in this highest group in 1973 (JOBN) are more than forty times greater than the chances that a man whose JOB10 was in the bottom group would be upwardly mobile into the highest stratum. This segmentation of the labour market by career beginnings and levels of skill and status is further examined in the next chapter, which documents how far current status and earnings are determined by social background, schooling, career beginnings and other factors.

5 Status and income

Chapter 2 presented an account of how inequalities in social background and early achievement affect later job status and earnings. This chapter elaborates and extends that analysis in relation to different conceptions of the labour market and different groups of workers.

Theories of the labour market

Human capital theory

Status attainment research shares a common theoretical perspective with neoclassical labour economics: 'the marginal productivity theory of demand based on profit-maximizing behavior of employers and a supply theory based on utility maximization of workers' (Cain, 1976, p. 1216). Status attainment research focuses primarily on the second problem and on how human capital is converted into earnings (Schultz, 1961; Becker, 1964; Mincer, 1974). The basic point of view is straightforward (Sorensen, 1975, p. 339):

> the resources of an individual can be regarded as a stock of capital that determines the individual's productivity and hence his earnings. This stock can be augmented by investments in training and education. These investments in human capital increase productivity and hence earnings, and the earnings increase constitutes a return on the investments.

Such a generalization involves a departure from a strict human capital model in that it is necessary to consider a wider range of factors, for example, social background as well as personal resources (cf. Sahota, 1978, pp. 3–7).

Three main forms of human capital can be distinguished: investment in formal education before the individual enters the labour force; education undertaken to upgrade qualifications or skills after beginning work; and productivity-enhancing skills gained on the job. The first two components have already been examined within the basic status attainment model.

In chapter 2 the determinants of status and income were assumed to be additive in their influence: one year of BASED increased JOBN by 12 status points, independently of the influences of JOB1 status, years of additional education and social origins. To treat education and experience in the same way here would similarly imply that a specific level of education combined with any amount of work experience had the same overall effect on status and income. In other words, extensive work experience with little education would produce as much prestige and income as the same work experience with more education. Both evidence and commonsense argue otherwise (Becker, 1964; Thurow, 1975; Stolzenberg, 1975a, b): 'education with a little experience is not worth as much as education with a lot of experience, and the more education one has, the more valuable, in terms of impact on earnings, is the experience to which one is exposed' (Stolzenberg, 1975a, p. 304). Such a statement implies that education and experience interact in their effects on later statuses, and the basic model presented in chapter 2 is elaborated to take such a possibility into account.

This chapter also departs from a strict construction of human capital by relaxing the assumption that income (and status) are determined by productivity, or potential productivity, in a perfectly competitive labour market. The existence of separate job markets for specific clusters of skills modifies such relationships.

Segmented labour market theories

Some theorists of the labour market have postulated multiple labour markets. The number of such markets ranges from two (e.g., Doeringer and Piore, 1971) to an indefinitely large number, as in Stolzenberg's (1975a, b) 'occupations-as-markets' formulation. Doeringer and Piore distinguish primary and secondary markets. In the primary market, workers enter occupations that are protected from market-wide competition, either by employers who invest in training their employees, or by professional or union organizations that control entry requirements and bargain with employers about wages and conditions. Such markets may be specific to industries, occupations or even firms. In contrast, the secondary labour market consists of low-skill, low-paying jobs for which employers offer little or no training, job competition is relatively open, there is little job security and labour turnover is high. In this market, unskilled workers are essentially 'industrial fodder'. The cycle of poverty among such groups as blacks in the United States and Aborigines in Australia is sometimes seen as an outcome of such secondary labour markets.

At the other extreme, Stolzenberg asserts that there are several basic sources of segmentation and that there are as many labour markets as there are occupations. First, workers acquire occupation-specific and non-transferable skills which are an investment in human capital but also induce the worker to remain in that occupation. Second, jobs are organized in different ways, and vary in such matters as, say, the degree of union influence on wages, promotion, hours of work and conditions of employment. Third, some industries, for example extractive industries in remote locations, experience idiosyncratic supplies and demands for labour. For these and other reasons the processes generating the income distribution in segmented 'occupations-as-markets' may vary widely between occupations. For example, the second set of factors mentioned above might affect income by age among manual compared with nonmanual workers. As has already been observed, in blue-collar occupations productivity depends more on physical labour, peak earnings are achieved relatively early, and income declines as physical capacities wane.

Economists working from a Marxist perspective (Bowles, 1972; Bowles and Gintis, 1976) are also skeptical about the single labour market thesis, but for quite different reasons. As one might expect, they emphasize differences arising from relations to the means of production and assume that processes governing the distribution of income will differ for wage labour compared with managers, entrepreneurs, and salaried staff. Wright and Perrone (1977) and Robinson and Kelley (1979) offer empirical support for such a view. However, status attainment models are not designed to address the central problems of class theories such as the existence and nature of a ruling class. A ruling class is by definition too small to affect the overall results of a status attainment model or even to be identified in a mass survey (Broom and Jones, 1976, pp. 60–1, 70–1; Heyns, 1978, p. 1004).

Labour markets and human capital

Cain's (1976) recent detailed review concludes that any adequate theory of labour markets and income determination needs to draw upon both neoclassical and segmented labour market conceptions. We take a similar view. Although we emphasize the importance of human capital, we allow for the existence of multiple, occupationally-defined labour markets with differing processes of status attainment. In this way the influence of structural characteristics of the labour market on income and industrial and regional differences in the supply of and demand for labour are taken into account.

The 'occupations-as-markets' perspective is adopted here in principle, but limitations of sample size do not permit detailed occupation-by-occupation analysis. Instead the influences of education and experience on status attainment are examined separately for six broad groups: professional, managerial, clerical, skilled, semiskilled and unskilled workers. If marked inter-occupational differences exist in the supply, demand and social organization of labour, they should be reflected in differences across such groupings. There are of course other aspects of the social organization of labour markets that may affect status attainment, among which three stand out as being of special potential importance: job discrimination on the basis of ethnic background (cf. Australian Government Commission of Inquiry into Poverty, 1975, p. 20), the influence of organized labour and the power of ownership.

Data sources and variable construction

Some analyses in this chapter are limited to the weighted 1,739 economically active men for whom there is complete information on all relevant variables. Fortunately this selected group has similar social characteristics to the wider sample, as a comparison of means and standard deviations in Tables 2.1 and 5.1 shows. The restricted sample is characterized by slightly more prosperous social origins and marginally higher attainments than the remainder of the sample, but these slight differences do not impair the generality of the findings. Because we are primarily interested in how individuals convert earlier resources into later attainments, we start with a simple model with additive effects only. The ten basic model variables used are those defined in chapter 2. Seven additional variables are defined below.

Labour force experience (LFX)

This variable is the number of years between the year of first entry into the labour force and 1973, the year of the survey, less the number of years spent in further education.

Occupational group

Nine occupational groups are defined according to the ANU 1 scale

122

(see Broom and Jones, 1969b): professional, managerial, clerical, skilled, semiskilled, unskilled, graziers, farmers and farm workers. The three rural groups are represented only in Table 5.1 because of their small numbers: 53, 87 and 36 respectively.

Industry

The ABS Industry Classification (ABS, 1971b) was used to distinguish twelve industry categories: agriculture, forestry, fishing and hunting; mining; manufacturing; electricity, gas and water; construction; wholesale and retail trade; transport and storage; communication; finance, insurance, real estate and business services; public administration and defence; community services; entertainment, recreation, restaurants, hotels and personal services.

Mother-tongue

For present purposes it was considered sufficient simply to separate respondents born in an English-speaking country from all others.

Rural/urban residence

Respondents living in a farm, village or country town were classified as rural. Those living in a medium-sized city or large city were classified as urban.

Union

Respondents who said they were members of professional associations, trade unions and the like were distinguished from non-members.

Owners, managers and workers

Respondents were categorized as owners, managers or workers according to criteria described in chapter 2. Those who employed others or were self-employed were defined as owners; those not self-employed but in supervisory positions were labelled managers; others were designated workers.

Group differences in status and income

Before we proceed with analysis, some basic descriptive data on status and income are presented. Table 5.1 gives means and standard deviations for the ten basic model variables plus labour force experience both for the total 1,739 respondents appearing in later analyses and for nine occupational groups.

Ignoring the three farming groups for the time being, we find as expected that the means of all ascribed and achieved characteristics, except family size, decrease systematically from the highest to the lowest status group. Professional workers come from families with the highest educational, occupational and economic achievements, and have the fewest siblings competing for family resources. On average they have the highest levels of education, begin work in higher-status jobs, get more additional education and occupy the most highly paid and prestigious occupations – more prestigious, in fact, than those of their fathers. At lower occupational levels, semiskilled and unskilled workers gain fewer benefits from their family of origin, they do not match their father's occupational attainments, and their incomes are roughly half those received by professionals. Moreover, the standard deviations tend to be smaller for groups with lower social status, indicating the greater relative homogeneity of these job categories (see Broom and Jones, 1969b, p. 657).

Age, status and income

Table 5.2 presents data on the distribution of status and income by age for total sample and for the six nonfarm sub-groups.[1] By definition occupational prestige decreases from left to right across Table 5.2 for each of the five-year age cohorts. Age differences can be assessed by looking down the columns of the table. Apart from a slight decrease in occupational status among older men in the total sample, differences within occupational groups are irregular and unremarkable, indicating that the status mix within each group is fairly constant by age but that older men in general have lower-status jobs than younger men.

In contrast to status, income is systematically related to age. The incomes of white-collar workers increase up to their mid-forties and then begin to decline. This familiar age-income profile (Mincer, 1974) is especially noticeable among the three manual groups, although the increase among younger men is not as evident. Of course, these are cross-sectional data, and younger men may have started on higher income streams. But we would expect income to increase with age for white-collar workers because of promotion and structured career paths within bureaucracies, whereas blue-collar workers, whose income is more affected by shift-work, overtime and physical effort, experience a decline in income with age.

TABLE 5.1 Occupational differences for variables in the basic model

	MOMED	DADED	DADJOB	FAMSZ	WLTH	BASED	JOB1	ADDED	LFX	JOBN	INC	N
					Means							
Professional	9·16	9·78	558·01	3·35	0·59	12·38	611·65	1·22	21·44	723·36	187·73	216
Managerial	8·55	9·22	534·61	3·97	0·32	10·10	496·20	0·72	28·41	25·18	173·02	208
Clerical	8·50	8·83	503·28	4·08	0·17	9·76	479·72	0·65	27·26	527·16	136·46	229
Skilled	7·94	8·23	481·33	4·36	−0·16	9·60	471·17	0·49	28·22	492·74	115·58	382
Semiskilled	7·77	7·72	490·15	5·04	−0·18	8·79	453·82	0·28	29·71	425·79	111·37	328
Unskilled	7·82	7·87	481·51	5·24	−0·25	8·88	455·14	0·27	31·74	428·77	97·98	200
Graziers	8·26	7·97	618·24	4·72	0·72	8·84	504·74	0·10	33·34	659·20	143·41	53
Farmers	8·23	7·73	580·71	4·62	0·43	8·94	500·06	0·08	32·78	599·47	144·35	87
Farm workers	7·79	7·41	515·88	5·84	−0·19	8·41	467·20	0·51	30·33	443·13	96·28	36
Total	8·21	8·43	511·67	4·43	0·08	9·71	489·98	0·53	28·40	531·11	132·22	1,739
					Standard deviations							
Professional	2·41	3·50	132·59	1·86	1·05	2·86	145·16	1·53	10·71	90·48	80·45	216
Managerial	2·21	3·45	118·42	2·26	1·12	2·19	80·28	1·04	9·47	66·06	86·36	208
Clerical	1·78	2·78	100·76	2·16	1·05	1·69	60·71	0·89	10·61	56·23	59·09	229
Skilled	1·74	2·33	96·93	2·44	0·89	1·69	62·08	0·78	10·01	46·18	48·32	382
Semiskilled	1·60	1·90	92·52	2·54	0·91	1·71	57·34	0·56	10·21	33·15	54·20	328
Unskilled	1·63	2·11	96·02	2·79	0·85	1·64	57·88	0·53	10·42	49·83	37·11	200
Graziers	1·78	2·18	75·87	1·98	0·95	1·61	64·90	0·34	10·53	9·54	93·66	53
Farmers	2·03	2·09	83·25	2·39	1·03	1·75	67·80	0·33	10·79	37·78	97·39	87
Farm workers	1·44	1·56	90·50	3·00	0·95	1·19	58·50	1·53	9·49	22·85	47·76	36
Total	1·93	2·69	109·12	2·45	1·02	2·22	92·02	0·95	10·68	114·71	71·03	1,739

TABLE 5.2 Mean occupational status and income by age and occupational group

| | Occupational status at JOBN | | | | | | | Income at JOBN | | | | | | | |
Age	Prof.	Manag.	Cler.	Skilled	Semi-skilled	Un-skilled	Total	Prof.	Manag.	Cler.	Skilled	Semi-skilled	Un-skilled	Total	N
30–4	723	616	518	494	427	425	533	170	166	129	115	113	104	132	448
35–9	722	636	530	483	421	427	520	190	167	142	120	110	102	133	407
40–4	726	633	541	488	423	429	522	213	173	159	116	115	102	136	410
45–9	691	628	520	488	426	431	525	194	179	125	112	109	107	134	401
50–4	744	630	544	488	428	417	519	200	171	139	105	106	88	128	351
55–9	707	609	530	490	423	428	518	185	162	125	104	92	82	115	271
60+	740	627	515	489	432	424	513	198	167	132	97	83	84	111	272

TABLE 5.3 Mean occupational status and income by basic education and occupational group[a]

| | Occupational status at JOBN | | | | | | | Income at JOBN | | | | | | | |
Years of basic education	Prof.	Manag.	Cler.	Skilled	Semi-skilled	Un-skilled	Total	Prof.	Manag.	Cler.	Skilled	Semi-skilled	Un-skilled	Total	N
–7	616	679	513	455	431	397	439	85	180	95	85	87	78	88	103
7	676	576	525	473	416	412	476	170	169	124	98	89	90	105	174
8	644	608	507	482	424	425	483	122	132	123	104	102	90	111	704
9	672	631	521	487	425	433	508	157	169	126	112	110	103	125	574
10	700	623	539	498	434	435	539	170	167	142	123	126	105	136	410
11	697	633	539	499	420	441	545	184	178	149	113	110	108	141	257
12	707	649	538	498	435	443	578	166	201	146	124	129	101	149	138
13+	764	651	554	514	432	441	683	226	215	166	134	126	91	200	200

a Underlined values based on fewer than ten cases.

Education, status and income

Table 5.3 presents data on status and income differences by levels of education. As expected, the 200 individuals educated beyond high school (the last row of the table) are in occupations characterized by the highest status and income. At the other extreme, respondents with fewer than seven years of basic education occupy the lowest-status jobs and earn the least income. Two other observations are of interest. First, in the professional group, where job skills are acquired mostly through formal education, the relationship between education and status attainment is strongest: the differences between those with little education (eight to nine years) and those with the highest (thirteen or more years) are 120 status points and $104 in weekly income. By comparison, within-group differences in the other five groupings do not exceed 75 status points or $46 in income. Second, within education levels, status and income differences between occupational groups are progressively larger from the lowest to the highest levels.

Experience, status and income

Table 5.4 presents comparable data broken down by years of labour force experience. Of most interest is the apparent decline in status and income with experience, which occurs relatively early among manual workers. Because age and experience are highly correlated it is impossible to disentangle their relative influence in simple analyses of this kind, and that problem is taken up in more complex analyses below (see Table 5.10).

Mother-tongue, status and income

Table 5.5 presents a breakdown of the same data according to respondent's mother-tongue: men born in English-speaking countries versus others. Within occupational groups, status differences are not remarkable although they favour native English-speakers. The fact that the overall difference (40 status points) is greater than the unweighted average for the six occupational groups (12 status points) simply indicates that men from non-English-speaking backgrounds work in lower-status jobs. Income differences range from $10 a week for skilled workers to $20 a week for managerial workers, all favouring the English-speaking group. In short, ethnic differences, crudely defined, make some impact on status and income even within the same kinds of occupations.

TABLE 5.4 Mean occupational status and income by labour force experience and occupational group[a]

Years of labour force experience	Occupational status at JOBN							Income at JOBN							N
	Prof.	Manag.	Cler.	Skilled	Semi-skilled	Un-skilled	Total	Prof.	Manag.	Cler.	Skilled	Semi-skilled	Un-skilled	Total	
–11	747	*645*	*510*	*503*	*451*	*480*	698	179	*236*	*197*	*105*	*111*	*180*	178	52
11–15	727	641	540	505	431	437	574	186	180	136	115	122	113	145	226
16–20	711	622	519	488	424	430	519	199	167	137	116	113	101	134	401
21–5	729	634	536	484	420	426	518	204	170	146	124	111	101	135	406
26–30	700	650	521	487	421	427	510	197	201	133	114	111	108	131	362
31–5	721	621	531	491	431	426	526	213	156	132	105	113	93	130	366
36–40	704	615	526	490	424	417	512	162	174	142	110	98	90	124	324
41–50	*664*	597	524	479	424	428	498	*140*	142	112	100	87	79	101	212
46+	*686*	628	514	486	434	422	495	*165*	153	130	85	85	83	111	209

[a] Underlined values based on fewer than ten cases.

TABLE 5.5   *Mean occupational status and income by mother-tongue and occupational group*

Occupational group	Occupational status at JOBN		Income at JOBN	
	English mother-tongue	Non-English mother-tongue	English mother-tongue	Non-English mother-tongue
Professional	720	721	192	176
Managerial	630	604	173	153
Clerical	526	536	136	125
Skilled	492	478	114	104
Semiskilled	426	420	108	196
Unskilled	430	415	99	86
Total	530	490	133	110
N	2,093	467	2,093	467

Industry, status and income

Table 5.6 presents data on differences for twelve industry divisions in status and income. For the total sample, the range of inter-industry differences is 170 status points and $78 in weekly income. However, because these industries differ in occupational mix, the gross differences are not easy to interpret. Comparisons within occupational groups are more meaningful. Within occupational groups, between-industry differences in status range from 26 points for semiskilled workers to 152 points for managerial occupations, and income differences from $31 to $71 per week. The prestige and income accorded to similar occupations depend in part on the industries in which they are located. In view of differences in the relative size and profitability of different firms and industries, it is not surprising that the managerial category shows the widest industry differences for income. These variations suggest that labour market segmentation is important in Australia, and that issue is examined below.

Unions, status and income

Organized workers might be expected to win higher incomes and status through collective bargaining, but union membership seems to offer little status advantage in the sample as a whole or within specific occupational groups. Table 5.7 presents relevant data on 1,346 employees. Only in managerial occupations does union or association membership appear to contribute significantly to status and income. However, this difference may be attributable to the

129

TABLE 5.6 *Mean occupational status and income by industry and occupational group*

Industry[a]	Occupational status at JOBN							Income at JOBN							
	Prof.	Manag.	Cler.	Skilled	Semi-skilled	Un-skilled	Total	Prof.	Manag.	Cler.	Skilled	Semi-skilled	Un-skilled	Total	N
Agriculture	724	643	527	483	414	432	575	157	128	95	97	114	96	132	254
Mining	746	677		488	418	405	535	230	226		170	115	118	168	44
Manufacturing	686	670	519	483	414	406	490	162	192	113	109	100	88	117	691
Electrical	772	640	525	527	431	396	499	202	203	126	132	112	79	124	85
Construction	756	638	542	477	417	441	485	204	184	114	108	114	118	119	294
Trade	737	575	566	501	435	420	516	164	135	120	106	116	86	120	331
Transportation	686	602	510	503	440	414	469	174	177	113	119	109	89	113	207
Communication	665		459	546	433	363	481	155		109	130	98	65	112	60
Business	763	694	559	522		455	639	223	206	166	121		107	185	151
Administration	679	682	516	492	429	416	530	177	198	160	101	104	78	145	153
Services	716	654	510	533	463	447	633	186	185	128	157	94	97	161	196
Entertainment	615	542	511	521	469	439	483	225	156	89	100	96	79	107	82

[a] Agriculture also includes forestry, fishing and hunting; electricity also includes gas and water; trade includes both wholesale and retail trade; transportation includes storage; business includes finance, insurance, real estate and business services; administration includes public administration and defence; services includes community services; entertainment also includes recreation, restaurants, hotels and personal services. Underlined values based on fewer than ten cases; blank cells contain no cases.

higher average status and earnings of managers in bureaucratic settings compared with managers in small enterprises.

TABLE 5.7   *Mean occupational status and income by union membership and occupational group[a]*

Occupational group	Occupational status at JOBN		Income at JOBN		Number	
	Members	Non-members	Members	Non-members	Members	Non-members
Professional	718	723	191	186	229	67
Managerial	649	610	184	160	122	166
Clerical	522	533	135	135	162	141
Skilled	489	489	112	111	370	186
Semiskilled	423	430	102	115	340	174
Unskilled	418	439	97	93	222	136
Total	520	526	128	129	1,537	1,014

[a] Excludes self-employed respondents.

Owners, managers and workers

Status differences across the three categories in Table 5.8 are not marked, with the exception of professional occupations which show almost a 100-point difference between the average status of owners (most of whom are independent professional employers), and the

TABLE 5.8   *Mean occupational status and income by worker category and occupational group*

	Occupational status at JOBN			Income at JOBN		
	Owners	Managers	Workers	Owners	Managers	Workers
Professional	796	724	697	262	208	159
Managerial	597	646	606	163	176	159[a]
Clerical	593	522	523	187	149	126
Skilled	482	502	486	126	129	101
Semiskilled	437	422	424	157	124	94
Unskilled	459	426	419	116	105	86
Total	567	550	492	155	150	108
N	587	557	1,337	587	557	1,337

[a] Includes 30 respondents, mainly purchasing officers and inspectors, in managerial occupations without supervisory responsibilities.

average status of workers (most of whom are salaried professionals). So far as income differences are concerned, apart from managers and skilled workers, owners of enterprises earn the most, and workers earn the least. Managers occupy an intermediate position. Managers enjoy somewhat higher average salaries than owner-managers ($176 versus $163) because many owner-managers operate small businesses as shopkeepers, contractors, and self-employed tradesmen. Differences in the skilled worker group are even smaller ($129 versus $126), for much the same reasons.

The basic model with labour force experience

We now estimate how far achieved human capital in the form of education, additional education and labour force experience influences status and income attainment. To begin with, the model is treated as if labour force experience had only an additive linear effect on status and income. Table 5.9 provides estimates for equations to JOBN and log-INCOME extended in this way. Separate estimates are provided for the group as a whole and for each of the six occupational groups discussed earlier.

Log transformation of income (LINC)

In these and subsequent analyses, we use the natural logarithm of income rather than income as such, a practice in research of this kind justifiable on both statistical and substantive grounds (see Heckman and Polachek, 1974; Hill, 1959). Through the log transformation the partial regression coefficients can be interpreted as proportional differences in income instead of simple dollar increments. Welch (1973, p. 183) points out, however, that the regression coefficients in equations predicting log-income can be interpreted approximately as the percentage *increment* in earnings associated with a one-unit difference in the independent variable under examination.

Additive effects of labour force experience

For the total group, labour force experience (LFX) hardly improves the performance of the basic model. A year of labour force experience is worth a little more than 1 status point after other factors have been taken into account, but it has an unexpected negative effect (-0.003) on LINC. Other things equal, there is a 0.3 per cent decline in income with each year of workforce experience. Within each of the six occupational groups the effects of labour force experience on status are insignificant or substantively trivial

TABLE 5.9 Effects of social background, early attainment and labour force experience on occupational status and income by occupational group[a]

	MOMED	DADED	DADJOB	FAMSZ	WLTH	BASED	JOB1	ADDED	LFX	JOBN	R sq.
Occupational status at JOBN											
Professional				12·814		6·553	0·295	10·944			0·399
Managerial			−4·944					15·861			0·127
Clerical						8·053					0·086
Skilled						5·873	0·214	13·302			0·195
Semiskilled					5·344			7·789	0·472		0·052
Unskilled						4·558		16·989			0·117
Total	0·076			−3·702	14·970	11·532	0·445	27·732	1·066		0·426
Log-income at JOBN											
Professional		0·001					0·001			0·002	0·427
Managerial							0·001			0·003	0·272
Clerical					0·033			0·068		0·001	0·209
Skilled									−0·006	0·003	0·154
Semiskilled					0·045					0·001	0·124
Unskilled										0·001	0·161
Total					0·030	0·017	0·001	0·025	−0·003	0·002	0·251

[a] Non-significant regression coefficients are not shown.

(e.g. each year of LFX adds half a status point for semiskilled workers). Even allowing for reduced sample size in each group, LFX is clearly not a major additional determinant of current job status.

In the six comparable equations for LINC the unexpected negative effect of LFX in the total group appears only in the skilled worker group. However, LFX effects are also negative (but insignificant) for the other two blue-collar occupational groups. These results suggest that income is tied more closely to productivity than is status. Increasing age is accompanied by a decline in productivity and also a decline in income. That there is no comparable decline for status is possibly artefactual: for a particular job designation status is by definition fixed, whereas income can, and does, vary within a specific job title.

The basic model in context

We now estimate an extended model in which the effects of industry, region, union, ethnicity and worker categories are constrained to be additive. To test whether status attainment processes vary for different occupational groups, separate analyses are presented for each. Table 5.10 presents additive equations for JOBN and LINC in an extended model for the total group and for each of six occupational sub-groups.

The coefficients relating to industry are not shown because, being dummy variables, they have no easily interpreted meaning. However, the coefficients for workers and managers are included as they can be interpreted by reference to the omitted category of owners. We show also the proportion of variance explained by three models: the basic model with LFX estimated in Table 5.9 (model 1); this model together with ethnicity, rural/urban residence, worker category and union membership (model 2); and model 2 differentiated by industry (model 3). Because the regression coefficients for industry are not directly interpretable, we adopt the added-variance approach to make limited inferences about inter-industry differences.

Occupational status

The coefficients for JOBN in the total group can be interpreted as follows: each sibling in the respondent's family of origin reduces current occupational status by just over 3 points. One standard deviation difference in 'wealth' between families confers an advantage of about 7 status points. A year of basic education is worth a little more, about 10 points; a year of additional education

TABLE 5.10 *An extended model of status attainment processes incorporating sub-group differences*

	Occupational status at JOBN							Log-income at JOBN						
	Prof.	Manag.	Cler.	Skilled	Semi-skilled	Un-skilled	Total	Prof.	Manag.	Cler.	Skilled	Semi-skilled	Un-skilled	Total
MOMED		4·256												
DADED														
DADJOB									0·001					
FAMSZ							-3·442							
WLTH							6·684							0·027
BASED	7·999		7·721	4·439			10·455	0·001						
JOB1	0·228			0·189			0·361			0·001				
ADDED	14·553			10·846		15·918	23·758							
LFX							0·531				-0·006			-0·004
JOBN								0·002	0·002	0·002	0·002		0·001	0·001
ETHNIC							21·049							
URBAN					16·769		14·288							-0·066
UNION									-0·094					
WORKER	-56·632	-57·240		14·690		-26·209	-45·907	-0·255		-0·194	-0·444	-0·163		-0·219
MANAGER	-48·491	21·356				-29·444	-14·246							
R sq. model														
1	0·399	0·127	0·086	0·195	0·052	0·117	0·426	0·427	0·272	0·209	0·154	0·124	0·161	0·251
2	0·458	0·269	0·141	0·219	0·112	0·178	0·472	0·496	0·288	0·248	0·202	0·299	0·224	0·286
3[a]	0·523	0·675	0·336	0·292	0·197	0·262	0·531	0·547	0·307	0·400	0·243	0·319	0·335	0·315

[a] Coefficients for industry variables are included in the model but are not shown. Workers in farm occupations are shown in the *Total* columns but not separately because of small sample size.

more yet (24 points); but a year of labour force experience contributes a mere half point once these other factors have been taken into account. Individuals differing by 100 status points on entry into the labour force (JOB1) will still differ by 36 points at JOBN. Being born in Australia or another English-speaking nation confers about the same advantage as a year of ADDED. Residing in an urban area adds 14 points to current status. Compared with owners, managers lose 14 points and workers 46 points, other things being equal.

Beyond the effects of the main variables in the basic model, which are fairly consistent throughout these analyses, four stand out: the disadvantaged status of migrants from non-English-speaking backgrounds and from rural areas, the apparent ineffectiveness of union membership and the disadvantages of managers and workers compared with owners.

Ethnicity, rural/urban residence, union membership and worker categories increase explanation by 4·6 per cent for the total group, and from 2 to 14 per cent across the six occupational groups. Dummy variables representing industry add further to the explanation of current occupational status: 6 per cent for the total group, and up to 40 per cent for managerial occupations, a job grouping within which status scores are explicitly differentiated by broad industry category (Broom et al., 1977a, pp. 95–6). It is hardly surprising that 'industry effects' are most noticeable because they are built into the status scale.

Income

The pattern of effects on log-income (LINC) is simpler than for current job. In general, direct effects of social background variables are negligible, since income variation is explained mainly by attainments gained after labour force entry. As we saw earlier, the most consistent influence on income is current occupational status: 10 status points increase income by 1 per cent. Among the basic model variables the negative effect of labour force experience noted in Table 5.9 persists, at about the same level in both cases: −0·004 for the total group and −0·006 for skilled workers.

LINC differences by ethnicity, rural/urban residence and union membership are small. An ethnicity effect appears only for the total group, where men from English-speaking countries experience a 7 per cent advantage. Rural/urban effects are statistically insignificant in all cases. Union membership appears to make a difference only among clerical workers: unionized clerical workers earn less than non-union members with similar characteristics. Managers differ little from owners, but workers are much worse off: in the total group by 22 per cent, among professionals by 26 per cent, for skilled workers by 19 per cent and among unskilled workers by 44 per cent. Clearly, the economic returns to ownership and self-employment are much higher than to wage and salary workers.

In terms of adding to an understanding of status attainment processes, ethnicity, rural/urban residence, union membership and the worker classification add between 1 and 7 per cent to the explanation of LINC for all groups, except semiskilled workers where the increase is much higher, 17 per cent. The semiskilled group contains many self-employed service workers as well as factory operatives.

Taking account of industry adds between 2 and 15 per cent to the explanation of variations in LINC, especially among clerical workers (15 per cent) and unskilled workers (11 per cent). In short, individuals in occupations with similar characteristics are paid according to the industry in which they work: the highest paid clerical workers are in communication, finance, insurance, real estate, business services; public administration and defence; and community service industries. For unskilled workers the best paying industry is mining.

The relationship between education and experience

The additive models estimated in Tables 5.9 and 5.10 extend the basic model by considering additional influences on status and income and focus on variables that might reflect labour market differences in the supply and demand of labour and its social organization. We turn now to an analysis of how the achieved resources of formal education and workforce experience influence status and income attainment. Earlier it was suggested that returns to investment in either are interdependent: 'education with a little experience is not worth as much as education with a lot of experience, and the more education one has, the more valuable . . . is the experience to which one is exposed' (Stolzenberg, 1975a, p. 304). If we take this argument seriously we cannot assume that the relationships among education, experience, status and income are simply linear and additive.

Establishing nonadditive and nonlinear effects

If BASED, ADDED and LFX have nonadditive and nonlinear effects on status and income, the presence (but not the nature) of these effects can be established with the conventional added-variance approach incorporating both product and higher order terms. Such a formulation is represented by the following equation (cf. Stolzenberg, 1975a, p. 305):

$$Y = \sum_i b_i X_i + (U_0 + U_1\text{BASED} + U_2\text{BASED}^2)^*$$
$$(V_0 + V_1\text{LFX} + V_2\text{LFX}^2)^*$$
$$(W_0 + W_1\text{ADDED} + W_2\text{ADDED}^2) + e \quad \ldots \ldots 5.1$$

Y is either JOBN or LINC, and the Xs are variables listed in Table 5.10 constrained to have additive effects on Y (excluding BASED, ADDED and LFX). The nonadditive nature of the education/ experience effect is represented by multiplicative relationships between BASED, ADDED and LFX, and the possibility of nonlinear effects is allowed for by quadratic terms (e.g., LFX^2). By expanding the multiplicative terms, the equation reduces to an additive form in which the equations of Table 5.10 are extended to include 23 additional product or quadratic terms of the form (BASED*LFX*ADDED), (BASED*LFX^2*ADDED^2), (BASED^2*LFX*ADDED), (BASED^2), and so on. If a complex extension of this kind explains more of the variation in status and income than the simpler additive model, the existence of interdependent effects of education and experience is supported. For reasons of space only general findings for the sample as a whole and for the six occupational sub-groups are reported.

The additional variance explained by the nonadditive, nonlinear terms in the JOBN equation amounts to a statistically significant increase for the total group, from 42·6 to 44·1 per cent. Across six occupational groups the variance added ranges from 5·6 per cent (professionals) to 11)1 per cent (clerical workers), with an average of 8·5 per cent. Although these increases seem substantial, they are not statistically significant because of small sample size. While the 1·5 per cent additional variance contributed by nonadditive, nonlinear terms is significant for the total group ($N = 1,739$), and the 10·7 per cent is significant for semiskilled workers ($N = 328$), for clerical workers ($N = 229$) the 11·1 per cent fails to reach statistical significance.

Similarly, for the LINC equation there is a significant increase in the amount of variation explained for the total group (from 25·1 to 28·7 per cent). Across the six sub-groups increases range from 7·9 per cent among professionals to 16·4 per cent among unskilled workers, averaging 10·2 per cent across all sub-groups. However, these increases are statistically significant only for skilled and unskilled workers.

In sum, the substantive advantage of assuming complex interactions between education and experience is equivocal. On the one hand, nonadditive, nonlinear effects add significantly but not dramatically to understanding status attainment in the sample as a whole. On the other hand, these increases for occupational subgroups are statistically reliable only for semiskilled workers (JOBN) and skilled and unskilled workers (LINC). On balance, we are inclined to accept these results as general support for nonlinear, nonadditive education and experience effects on JOBN and LINC, for two reasons. Their inclusion adds significantly to explaining variation in statuses in the sample as a whole; and the statistical insignificance of the larger effects probably results from small sample sizes rather than substantive unimportance.

A human capital model of status and income attainments

We now develop a statistical model in which the effects of education and experience on status and income are consistent with human capital theory; that is, the effect of any one of the three components of human capital is contingent on the other two. For example, the monetary returns to a year of basic education depend on how long a man has worked and on how much further education he has completed. This more complex relationship between human capital and status attainment is examined in the context of the extended model estimated in Table 5.10.

The following discussion departs from a conventional status attainment analysis by omitting initial occupational status from both the JOBN and LINC equations because we want to estimate the *total* influence of education and experience on current status and income rather than their direct effect net of career beginnings. In other words, the total effect of education and experience will not be partitioned into direct effects and indirect effects. Moreover, because JOB1 intervenes causally between education, experience and further education, controls on JOB1 would introduce ambiguity into the structure of the estimated model. For similar reasons, JOBN is excluded from the income equations to permit an estimate of the total effect of education and experience on income. In short, BASED, LFX and ADDED are considered as forms of human capital with nonadditive effects. However, social origin variables from the basic model are retained as ascribed resources. The social organization of labour is represented in part by union membership, ethnicity and the worker classification, and potential variations in the supply and demand for labour by the rural/urban dichotomy. We estimate this model for the total of 1,739 respondents, and for each of six occupational sub-groups to establish the extent of labour market segmentation.

Education, experience, and human capital

Because we postulate nonadditive education/experience effects it is appropriate to think of a single *joint* effect of all three education/experience variables. In other words 'human capital', represented as accumulated experience and investment in education, is converted into status and income, or 'returns' on capital. It is obvious, however, that the components of human capital may not be of equal importance. In addition to knowing the total effect of the human capital term, it would also be useful to know the relative contributions of BASED, LFX and ADDED to human capital. Thus we estimate equations for JOBN and LINC following Stolzenberg (1974):

$$Y = b_0[\text{BASED}^{b1}*\text{LFX}^{b2}*\text{ADDED}^{b3}]\,e_1 +$$

$$\sum_i b_i X_i + e_2 \qquad \ldots \ldots 5.2$$

Y is either JOBN or LINC; the Xs comprise the five social origins variables plus ethnicity, dummy variables for worker categories, union membership, rural/urban residence and industry, and are constrained to have additive effects on Y; b_0 is the coefficient representing the overall effect on Y of the human capital term, which is a multiplicative function of BASED, LFX and ADDED (shown in brackets) in keeping with the nonadditive formulation proposed; and the exponents b_1, b_2 and b_3 represent the relative importance in the human capital term of each of its three components.

To compare the experience of men in different kinds of occupations the three components of human capital, ADDED, BASED and LFX, were dichotomized around the median (for details of the calculations see Appendix to this chapter). Comparisons are therefore made in terms of an eight-cell classification of men with less rather than more basic education, men with some rather than no further education, and men with more rather than less labour force experience. The results of estimating equations of this kind for both JOBN and LINC in the total group and for each of the six sub-groups are shown in Table 5.11. The first R sq. is the square of the multiple correlation coefficient for equation 5.3 and indicates the proportion of variance in JOBN or LINC explained overall. The second R sq. is derived from equation 5.5 and shows the proportion of variance in the adjusted means for JOBN or LINC explained by the human capital term.

Since the metric of the coefficient representing the joint effect of education and experience is unknown, concrete interpretations of the coefficient for H are not possible. While we could say, for instance, that for the total sample one unit of human capital is worth

254 status points, we do not know the literal meaning of one unit of human capital. Even so, we can make comparisons among the six different occupational groups. The three partial regression coefficients estimated from equation 5.5 (b_1, b_2, b_3) are exponents of BASED, LFX and ADDED respectively, and because they are in the same metric (years) they can be interpreted as the *relative* contribution of each to the overall human capital term.

TABLE 5.11   *The contribution of human capital to status and income*

| | | Current occupational status (JOBN) | | | | | |
	Total	Prof.	Manag.	Cler.	Skilled	Semi-skilled	Unskilled
H^a	254·0167	327·0784	553·9088	422·8003	441·9956	387·5326	448·3167
BASED[b]	0·2272	0·2359	*	0·1264	0·0950	0·0330	0·0392
LFX[b]	0·0186	*	−0·0154	0·0332	0·0113	0·0197	−0·0112
ADDED[b]	0·0069	0·0052	0·0015	0·0009	0·0022	0·0012	0·0048
R_1^2	0·4287	0·4524	0·6941	0·3484	0·2429	0·2143	0·2878
R_2^2	0·8472	0·7357	0·3637	0·8166	0·6118	0·3111	0·8258

| | | Log-income (LINC) | | | | | |
	Total	Prof.	Manag.	Cler.	Skilled	Semi-skilled	Unskilled
H^a	4·9382	4·2182	4·3180	4·2346	5·5428	4·4562	5·1717
BASED[b]	0·0215	0·0873	0·0401	0·0555	0·0347	0·0683	0·0468
LFX[b]	−0·0195	0·0083	−0·0133	*	−0·0132	−0·0152	−0·0367
ADDED[b]	0·0008	*	0·0019	0·0018	0·0002	0·0007	0·0025
R_1^2	0·2503	0·4387	0·3039	0·3553	0·1839	0·3428	0·3674
R_2^2	0·8089	0·7709	0·4671	0·6121	0·6619	0·7812	0·8324

* not significantly different from zero.
[a] the coefficients for H (human capital term) represent the joint effect of education and experience.
[b] the coefficients for BASED, LFX and ADDED represent their relative contributions to H.
R_1^2 represents the proportion of variance explained by equation 5.3.
R_2^2 represents the proportion of variance (in adjusted means) explained by equation 5.5.

So far as current occupational status is concerned, human capital pays off most for those in managerial occupations (554 points), and least for those engaged in professional occupations (327 points). In the case of log-income there is a similar range of variation but the pattern is different: skilled workers benefit the most and professional workers the least. While these results provide further support for the existence of multiple labour markets each characterized by somewhat different processes of status attainment, our data do not allow us to identify the specific causes of these differences.

Education and experience contribute to human capital much as expected: years of basic education is the most valuable form of human capital; labour force experience has an effect ranging from zero for those in professional jobs up to 60 per cent of BASED for semiskilled workers; and the effects of additional education are minor, averaging 3 per cent of BASED in the sample as a whole up to a maximum of 12 per cent among unskilled manual.

The substantial variation in the relative contributions of ADDED across the six groups indicates that the skills, or potential productivity, that accrue from formal schooling are differently valued in different occupational settings as are skills learned by on-the-job experience. For example, the skills required of individuals in professional occupations are acquired for the most part in formal education, and so formal education is a highly valued form of human capital in these occupations, at least for the allocation of prestige. Entry to professional work guarantees a high minimum level of status. By contrast, the skills required by workers in lower status jobs are acquired through apprenticeships and on-the-job training, so that formal education, although still the most valuable form of human capital, returns less occupational status. However, as noted in chapter 4, education that falls short of completed secondary has no appreciable occupational returns: men who get a few years of secondary schooling enter much the same kind of jobs as those with less schooling.

The coefficients for education, whether obtained before or after starting work, are all in the expected direction, and even the zero coefficient for managers is not surprising since they are a very mixed group, including self-made men as well as managers in hierarchical, bureaucratic settings. However, two coefficients for labour force experience, those for managers and unskilled workers, are negative. The latter indicates that older unskilled workers enter jobs with progressively lower status, whereas the former indicates that across a wide range of industries the growth of large bureaucracies has created managerial jobs with higher average statuses than before, and that younger men are disproportionately represented in such positions by virtue of this recent expansion. In Table 5.10, no such negative coefficients emerged for JOBN, although they did for LINC.

In interpreting the coefficients for LINC, we need to bear in mind that the log transformation of income means that coefficients represent *proportional* changes in income, or percentage increments in actual income. Thus, what appear to be small differences in the coefficients between groups represent substantial differences in effects on *actual* income. In fact, for the total group, one unit of human capital produces a five-fold increase in income. Similarly, over the six groups one unit of human capital increases income four- to five-fold. This finding is consistent with our previous observations on the apparently segmented nature of the labour market and with differences in the social processes relating to status attainment in different occupational groups.

Two general observations about the relative contributions of BASED, LFX and ADDED to human capital are pertinent. First, in contrast to the equation for JOBN, the ratio of the relative effects of BASED and LFX is much smaller in the LINC equation, indicating that education and experience are more equally valued forms of human capital where income is concerned. Second, five of the six significant coefficients for LFX are negative: all three coefficients for the blue-collar occupational groups are negative and are largest for lower blue-collar work. These negative effects of labour force experience have appeared consistently in the various analyses of LINC but not for JOBN. The probable explanation of this difference is that variation in income does exist within a specific occupation such as a carpenter, whereas all carpenters by definition receive the same status score. Another contributing factor to this difference is that because age and experience are so highly correlated ($r = 0.96$), negative LFX coefficients express the effects of declining productivity on income in blue-collar jobs brought about by declining physical capacities associated with ageing. Only professionals seem able to augment their incomes throughout their careers.

The facts that BASED is a more important component of human capital for occupational status than it is for LINC and that LFX generally has negative effects in the LINC equation suggest two conclusions. Years of basic education completed provide a guide to employers about an individual's *potential* to learn job-specific skills that enhance productivity. Basic education thus serves as a cheap screening device for allocating individuals to positions with varying prestige. This generalization supports the judgment of Thurow and Lucas (1972, p. 68) that 'the function of education is not to confer skill and therefore increased productivity and higher wages on the worker; it is rather to certify his "trainability" and to confer upon him a certain status.'

On the other hand, when it comes to getting paid for services rendered, *actual* productivity looms larger and work experience becomes a more important form of human capital. Job-specific skills increase rapidly in early career but the rate of learning tapers off with age and experience, skills become obsolescent, and productivity may suffer. Our sample consists primarily of individuals in their mid and late careers. Their average age is forty-four years and they have been at work for twenty-eight years on average. For the total group the decline in physical capabilities with age and experience and the obsolescence of job-specific skills have presumably overtaken the possible benefits of earlier labour-force experience, with the result that LFX has on balance negative effects on income. This interpretation is consistent with the typical age-income profile: productivity, like income, increases during the early career, reaches a peak in mid-career and declines in late career (Stolzenberg, 1975b, p. 659).

Further considerations: age, unions, and worker categories

The way BASED, LFX and ADDED are defined throughout these analyses means that age can be defined very nearly as the simple sum of BASED, LFX and ADDED, plus six pre-school years. Although individuals of the same age started school at about the same time, they became differentiated in terms of BASED and LFX (and possibly ADDED) because they attended school for different lengths of time. Some left at the minimum legal age, others at younger or older ages. Consequently, they entered the labour force at different times, converted their achieved personal resources into status and income during different periods, and were at different stages of their careers when interviewed. Therefore, current age may be a confounding influence in these analyses.

To test for this possibility all basic model variables except LFX were adjusted for the effects of age by using residuals from their regression on age; the age-adjusted analogues of tables 5.10 and 5.11 were then estimated. The changes to the LFX coefficients due to age-adjustment proved to be minor in the equation explaining variation in occupational status. If anything, adjustment decreases the size of coefficients and more of them are negative. In the case of income, the coefficients for labour-force experience similarly are smaller, and all except that for professionals are negative. In other words, age-adjustment shows that the contribution of labour force experience to human capital is consistently negative for the total group and for five of the six sub-groups. Thus, far from being a confounding influence, a consideration of age effects strengthens the observation that ageing depletes the store of human capital.

The negligible effects of union membership on status and income run counter to the idea that trade unions are able to achieve special benefits for their members. However, it is possible that union influence appears negligible because it affects status and income in a more complex way than was assumed. Therefore an analysis was performed in which union membership was allowed to interact statistically with other variables in the model. This analysis indicated with a single exception that processes governing status and income attainment are the same whether or not one belongs to a trade union.

The one difference, for which we can offer no convincing

explanation, is that among union members each year of basic education adds 18 points to the status of JOBN compared with only 9 for non-union members. A hypothesis that migrants and rural workers might be over-represented in the nonmember group is not supported by the data. Migrants from non-English backgrounds make up about 15 per cent of both groups, and rural workers about 20 per cent. Apart from this one difference, we are left with findings contrary to expectations and labour lore: belonging to a labour union adds little in the way of status and income advantages. It seems that in Australia union-influenced wage determinations flow on to workers irrespective of union affiliation, at least at times of almost full employment, as in 1973, the year of the survey.

In contrast to union membership, the worker categories (owners, managers and workers) show fairly consistent effects on status and income. For the most part, the findings are expected. Compared with owners, managers and workers are disadvantaged. Because these effects emerge so consistently, we also allowed for *differences* in processes of status and income attainment among the three groups.

For JOBN the coefficients for three variables show significant differences among these three groups. DADJOB has a significantly greater effect for owners than for managers or workers, whereas the two educational attainment variables, BASED and ADDED, are most important for managers and workers. Each year of BASED or ADDED contributed about three times as much JOBN status for these two categories than for owners (for example, 15 to 16 status points for each year of BASED, compared to 5 for owners). These findings are clear evidence of stronger ascriptive influences in the status attainments of the self-employed and employing group. Other things equal, the status origins of owners translate into greater advantages in current status: 100 points of father's status add 22 points to current status compared with negligible effects for the other two groups. The same difference can also be observed in the correlations between the status attainments of fathers and sons (0·46 for owners, but 0·22 for managers and 0·18 for workers). The greater similarity in jobs among owners and their fathers provides futher evidence of ascriptive forces in part of the labour market, whereas the stronger influences of BASED and ADDED among managers and workers are evidence of achievement and meritocracy among salaried and wage employees.

These interpretations receive further support in the analysis for LINC. Worker category directly affects earnings in favour of entrepreneurs, whereas among workers and managers current occupational status has somewhat more influence on LINC. As in the JOBN equation, individual career achievements are more important influences on economic attainments for men who sell their labour. The 'meritocratic' status attainment model, based as it is on human capital theory, explains more of the variance in income among managers and workers than among those who employ themselves or others. Status and income attainment among owners is not a wholly meritocratic process but contains a substantial ascriptive component: the social inheritance of status and income. On the other hand, for those who sell their labour the meritocratic status attainment model seems more appropriate: lower father-son correlations reflect higher intergenerational mobility; achieved 'human capital' resources exert a greater influence on current statuses; and, at least for income, the model explains two to three times more of individual variation in earnings.

These findings, together with those reported earlier, support the conception of multiple labour markets. Social and economic statuses are attained somewhat differently depending on industry and region of residence, differences that are related to the functioning of specific labour markets. Status attainment processes are also influenced by wider aspects of social organization such as ethnic origin and the private ownership of firms and businesses. None of these differences, however, is so striking or systematic as to challenge the broad validity of the human capital model, particularly for workers who sell their skills for wages and salaries. Of the three forms of human capital examined, formal education is the single most valuable component, but the way it relates to labour force experience varies according to the status outcome under consideration. Education, or potential productivity, has a stronger influence on the allocation of individuals within job status hierarchies, whereas actual productivity is more important for the distribution of income. These results emerge both in our more complex analysis of the three components of human capital and in a more conventional analysis in terms of an extended status attainment model. The last chapter returns to the status attainment perspective, extended to three generations. An attempt is made to answer the question of how far status attainment in Australia is governed by ascription or achievement, and what changes can be observed in those processes over the last sixty years.

Appendix: Estimating the Effects of Education and Experience

Estimating the coefficients in equation 5.2 above proceeds in three steps. First, to allow for the nonadditive effects of BASED, LFX and ADDED, we set up a multiple cross-classification of these three variables. Since the objective is to compare different occupational groups, we are restricted by sample size to simple dichotomies made at the median for each distribution. Thus, the cross-classification of BASED by LFX by ADDED creates eight cells, each of which can be represented by a dummy variable. Individuals below the median on all three variables would be scored '1' on the dummy variable representing this cell, with everyone else scored zero. Similarly, men below average on both education variables but above average on labour force experience would be scored so as to distinguish them from respondents with other profiles. This procedure is consistent with the assumption that the variables act jointly since each dummy variable provides an estimate of the separate effect of a particular combination of BASED, LFX and ADDED.

This set of dummy variables can be used in the next step to estimate the following equation:

$$Y = b_0 + b_i D_i + b_i X_i + e_1 \qquad \ldots \ldots 5.3$$

Again, Y is either JOBN or LINC; the Ds are dummy variables representing the cross-classification of BASED by LFX by ADDED with one cell omitted to avoid linear dependency in the equation; and the Xs are assumed to have only additive effects. This equation provides estimates of the mean of Y in each of the eight cells, *net of the influence of the Xs*. These adjusted means are derived directly from the constant term (the omitted cell), or by the sum of the constant and a coefficient for one of the remaining seven cells, since those coefficients represent a deviation from the omitted cell.

The final step focuses on the human capital term itself, net of all extraneous factors controlled for in the second step. The adjusted means for the eight cells defined above are used to estimate the final equation:

$$Y^* = b_0 [\text{BASED}^{b1} * \text{LFX}^{b2} * \text{ADDED}^{b3}] e_1 \qquad \ldots \ldots 5.4$$

Y^* is the adjusted mean of JOBN or LINC in each of eight cells, and BASED, LFX, and ADDED are the means of these variables in each of the eight cells. The original equation (5.2) is now in a form that can be estimated by taking the logarithm of both sides to transform it to an additive equation whose parameters can be estimated with weighted ordinary least squares in which the eight cell ns are the weights. Equation 5.5 shows the form of this equation:

$$Ln\, Y^* = Ln\, b_0 + b_1\, Ln\, \text{BASED} + b_2\, Ln\, \text{LFX} +$$
$$b_3\, Ln\, \text{ADDED} + Ln\, e_1 \qquad \ldots \ldots 5.5$$

The three partial regression coefficients from this equation (b_1, b_2

147

and b_3) are the exponents of BASED, LFX and ADDED in the previous equation. Since all three variables are in the same metric (years) they may be directly compared and interpreted as the relative contribution each has to the overall human capital term.

6 Status attainment over three generations

Earlier chapters have been chiefly concerned with influences affecting the education, occupational careers and earnings of Australian men. Analysis is now broadened from a two-generational span embracing a respondent and his parents to the three generations of a respondent, his parents, and his children.

The three-generation model serves several purposes. First, it permits comparison of the status attainment patterns of respondents with those of their children, thus throwing light on changing social processes. Second, historical depth makes it possible to assess whether grandparental characteristics, independently of parental influences, affect the careers of grandchildren. Finally, the longer time-span may permit assessment of the relative merits of stratification and class theories of inequality.

Since respondents were asked about all their children, it is also possible to compare the occupational experience of sons and daughters. This extension, which does not require a three-generational span, should disclose whether social background and education exert similar effects on the careers of sons and daughters. A full exploration of status attainment processes among Australian women is reserved for a later publication.

No three-generation analyses of the kind presented here have been published, although a few studies have approached a three-generation treatment. For example Mukherjee (1954), examined grandfather to father to son occupational mobility in England. As in the present study, the respondent was in the middle generation but a limited amount of information was secured and only on the eldest and youngest sons. Svalastoga (1959) in Denmark and Lopreato and Hazelrigg (1972) in Italy based similar analyses on respondents' reports about fathers and grandfathers, not about fathers and sons. The latter strategy is inevitably plagued by unreliability because

149

grandsons may not accurately recall or know about essential information from a distant family past. Svalastoga's documentary records in many cases lacked grandparental job information. Furthermore, grandfather's job can not be specified to a definite stage of the life-cycle and is therefore difficult to interpret. Because of these problems and differences in method, comparisons with the findings of such three-generation studies are not attempted. In the absence of genuinely comparable evidence, interpretations of social mobility over a long span and specifically in the context of social change must be confined to our own analysis.

The inheritance of inequality

It is argued that in capitalist countries social inequalities are essentially reproduced from generation to generation. For example, Bottomore holds that the social class system 'operates, largely through the inheritance of property, to ensure that each individual maintains a certain social position, determined by his birth and irrespective of his particular abilities' (1965, p. 16). As stated, this proposition is falsifiable, but Bottomore enters the following qualification: 'This state of affairs is only mitigated, not abolished, by various social influences' (1965, p. 16). Thus it is unclear what would count as sufficient mitigation to warrant abandonment of the original proposition. If Bottomore means simply that families influence the social position of their offspring, there is little to quarrel with, but the strength of the association between the social characteristics of parents and their children is the hub of the matter.

In similar vein Connell (1977, p. 183) distinguishes two kinds of social reproduction, first

> processes which distribute people among positions in the class structure and second (and more fundamentally) processes by which a structure of positions and relations among them is maintained in its everyday working. 'Occupational inheritance' and 'social mobility' are concepts that refer to the first of these forms of reproduction, presupposing the second. The concept of the 'reproduction of the relations of production' in Marxist theory refers to the second, and is independent of the first. There can be stability or change in one without the other.

Much of this statement is unexceptionable. Process versus structure, dynamics versus statics, are standard distinctions. Clearly it makes no sense to talk about movement within a structure of occupational positions in the absence of a structure. It also makes little theoretical sense to talk about a structure of positions apart from the social mechanisms by which they are filled. The concepts of process and structure are obviously complementary, but many commentators who emphasize structure tend to give little attention to social mobility. This is a curious omission since mobility flows reveal the rigidity or fluidity of the social order. We incline to the view that the structure of social inequality in industrial societies is largely reproduced *as a structure* from one generation to the next (Broom and Jones, 1976, p. 6). To put it more simply, in the absence of major social upheavals or revolutions, societies have historical continuity. But even if a particular society changes only slowly in its general structure there may be considerable changes in the positions occupied by individual families and family members from one generation to the next.

The inter-relatedness of structure and process can be illustrated in a simple diagram, which serves to emphasize that both concepts are necessary to understand the dynamics of social reproduction and social change.

Position of kin group over time	Structure of positions	
	Same	Different
Same	1	2
Different	3	4

A fully developed class society in the Bottomore or Connell sense would be found in cell 1 of this simple classification. The structure of positions and relations among them are unchanged, and families (understood as groups of parents and their children) remain in the same position generation after generation. Cell 2 depicts a society in which the structure has changed and families have simply been transposed from one position in the older system of inequality to a comparable position in the new one, as might occur if change was imposed by the more powerful groups. Cell 3 represents what can be called an open class system, in which the structure of positions is relatively unchanged but families and family members interchange positions from generation to generation. Cell 4 represents rapid social change and the total upheaval of the social structure, as in a socialist revolution or the transition from a traditional to a so-called modern society.

The foregoing crude scheme merely illustrates the fundamental complementarity of the concepts of social structure and social mobility. Marxists may emphasize structure because they believe modern industrial mixed economies are oppressive, exploitative and impede progress. They see few if any prospects for

151

improvement short of a fundamental alteration of the system whereby people and rewards are allocated to unequal positions. Students of mobility processes tend more often towards a gradualist stance about social change, perhaps because of the time perspective that is inherent in mobility research, or because an alternative structure along Marxist lines seems to offer no clear prospect for improvement, or because they do not perceive a single factor (such as the ownership of the means of production) as the obstacle to a more just society.

While status attainment research initially focused on the analysis of mobility processes, it is increasingly applied to measuring the extent of and trends in inequality, and to assessing how different kinds of inequities reinforce or counter one another. To be sure, most mobility studies take structures of inequality as given and focus on the allocative processes within those structures; but adequate theories of social change must account for process as well as structure.

Data sources and variable construction

The 1973 survey sampled Australian men and women aged between 30 and 69 years of age. Partly because the lower age limit was truncated at age 30, respondents were asked about their children's education and jobs so that data on the experience of younger persons could be obtained. Some findings from those data and related methodological issues are reported elsewhere (Broom *et al.*, 1977a, b; 1978a, b). This chapter identifies for analysis pairs of respondents and fathers, as well as pairs of respondents and children where the child had started work and was 21 years of age or older at time of interview. For present purposes the grandfather (father of the respondent) must be the 'real' or adoptive father, and not a father-substitute such as some other relative or an unrelated individual. All 3,166 male respondents were screened, and cases were excluded if a father-substitute was recorded as caring for the respondent when he was 14 years old, or if there was no child aged 21 or over who had started work by 1973.

The selection procedure was carried out in two steps. In the first step only respondents with eligible sons were selected, yielding a sample of 677 respondents, their fathers and their sons. The second step identified respondents with eligible daughters resulting in a sample of 678 respondents, their fathers and their daughters. In the first sample, the 677 respondents had a total of 1,061 eligible sons; 392 had one eligible son, 184 had two, 65 had three, 20 had four and 6 had five. In the second sample, 394 respondents had one eligible daughter, 201 had two, 43 had three, 22 had four, 6 had five and 1 had six (totalling 1,049). Forty-three per cent of these respondents had at least one eligible son and one eligible daughter and therefore appear in both samples, while the remainder had only a son or a daughter eligible, and therefore appear in one of the samples.

Because a main objective here is to compare the process of status attainment in two different pairs of generations (respondents and their fathers, compared with respondents and their children), one son or daughter was selected at random in cases where more than one eligible child was available. Thus, 677 cases remain for analysis in the sample of sons, and 678 cases in the sample of daughters. One child is taken at random rather than by some arbitrary selection (say, the oldest eligible child), because the respondents themselves are a random sample of the population and therefore a random sample of 'children' is also required.

Variables included as causes or outcomes of the status transmission process in each generation must be confined to those common to parents of respondents, and respondents and children. For children only sex, age, age at completing full-time education (EDUC), first job (JOB1) and industry, 1973 job (JOBN) and industry, and country of residence were sought. For (grand)father's generation, the variables available are job held when the respondent was 14 years old (DADJOB), the number of years of schooling completed by the respondent's father (DADED) and mother (MOMED), the economic status of the family of orientation (WLTH, indexed by a composite of five consumer durables) and size of the family of orientation (FAMSZ). These five family background variables, together with the respondent's years of schooling (EDUC), first job (JOB1) and present job (JOBN) comprise the basic model examined here. More detailed analyses also include community size when the respondent was growing up, country of birth, period when the respondent entered the work-force, and position in the occupational hierarchy. These measures are explained below.

Since interviews had to be kept to a reasonable length it was not possible to secure equally detailed and exact measures of some variables for all generations. Respondent's country of birth was directly ascertained. For children, country of birth is inferred from father's birthplace, the year of his arrival in Australia and the child's age. If a child was born before the father arrived in Australia, the child's birthplace was assumed to be that of the father. Job when the respondent was aged 14 (DADJOB) is available directly from the questionnaire, as are DADED, MOMED and WLTH. FAMSZ is calculated as the number of brothers and sisters plus the respondent. However, in comparing respondents and their children, two variables have to be constructed. The job the respondent had when

153

his child was an adolescent is approximated from information on the occupational career of the respondent. The index of family possessions can be constructed only from data relating to possessions at time of interview, not to possessions when the child was growing up. WLTH is therefore measured with more error in analyses involving respondents and children. All the children were at least 21 in 1973, their average age was 28 years, and about 10 per cent were 35 or older. The difference in the WLTH measures needs to be remembered in interpreting the analysis presented.

The choice of the respondent's job when his son or daughter was growing up was selected to take into account changes in school-leaving age. Respondents on average left school at about 14. This was the age when they and their parents were faced with deciding whether they should stay on in school or start work. For respondents' sons and daughters, however, this decision arose when the child was about 16, the average (and modal) age at which the younger generation left school. The selection of a functionally equivalent DADJOB for pairs of respondents and children was therefore made as follows: from the child's age in 1973, find the year in which he or she was 16 years old. Examine the years when the respondent held his first job, his job 10, 20, 30 or 40 years later, and his 1973 job (last job, if retired). Select the job nearest to the year when the child was 16 years old, provided the child was not over 18 years old at that time. If he or she was over 18 years old, select an earlier job. Illustrative figures from the sons' sample show that for respondent and son pairs about half the jobs selected by this procedure were 30 years after first job. About one-third were 20 years after first job (34 per cent). The remainder came from job 40 years after workforce entry (12 per cent) and job 10 years after first job (1 per cent). In only one case was the first job selected.

A similar task of reconstruction is necessary to select the respondent's JOBN, the comparison point with his father analogous to the son's or daughter's job in 1973. Recall that for children information was collected only on first job and job in 1973. Because children in this analysis varied in age from 21 to their mid-40s, they were at different stages of their socioeconomic life-cycles. Three out of four were in their 20s, and therefore only in the first or second decade of their working lives.

To accommodate this variability in life-cycle stage among children, the JOBN selected for respondents had to be at a comparable stage of their life-cycles. The respondent's JOBN was selected as follows: calculate the number of years since his child left school. Add this number to the year in which the respondent took his first job and find the job in his career nearest to this year. Such a selection procedure can be only approximate since the respondent's career is measured at ten-year intervals from first job. However, the approximation is reasonably good. The average number of years elapsed since first job was 11·9 years for JOBN among respondents, compared with 11·2 for sons.

These selection procedures result in six analytic samples. Two samples consist of respondents and fathers, one based on eligible sons, the other on eligible daughters. These two samples are partly independent, replicating internal samples. There should be no significant differences in the pattern of status attainment for them, since there is no reason to suppose that the sex of a child has any selective, let alone causal, effect on the status attainment of the father. Two other samples are formed by respondents and their sons, and respondents and their daughters. For these two samples we do expect to find significant differences. For example, Australian men and women have different expectations about how much education boys and girls should get, and men and women participate in a highly segregated labour market (Broom and Jones, 1976, pp. 14–15, 38–9). Finally, there are two samples spanning three generations: (grand)parents, respondents and sons; and (grand)parents, respondents and daughters. These six analytic samples provide the basis for the subsequent discussion.

Figures 6.1 and 6.2, together with Tables 6.1 and 6.2, describe the basic characteristics of these samples, again with illustrative data from the sons' sample. Figure 6.1 shows stages in life-cycle for fathers, respondents and sons when they held different jobs. In each case the interquartile range is shown, together with the mean age. For example, 50 per cent of fathers were aged between 40 and 50 when the respondent was 14 years old, and the median age of fathers in the sons' sample was 46. For respondents in the second panel, DADJOB refers to the time when the son was about 16; 50 per cent of respondents were aged between 36 and 45, with a mean age of 43. The difference of three years between generations results from declining family size and earlier completion of families. Fathers averaged 32 years of age when the respondent was born, whereas respondents averaged 29 years when their selected son was born. As we see from Tables 6.3 and 6.5 below, family size was a little over five in the generation of fathers but declined to between three and four in the respondents' generation. It should be remembered that couples with no children are of course excluded from this analysis.

For first job the interquartile range is predictably very narrow because school-leaving ages are highly clustered. As Table 6.1 shows, 46 per cent of respondents left school at 14 years with eight years of education. Sons received one or two years more schooling than their fathers, with about equal numbers leaving school at 15

155

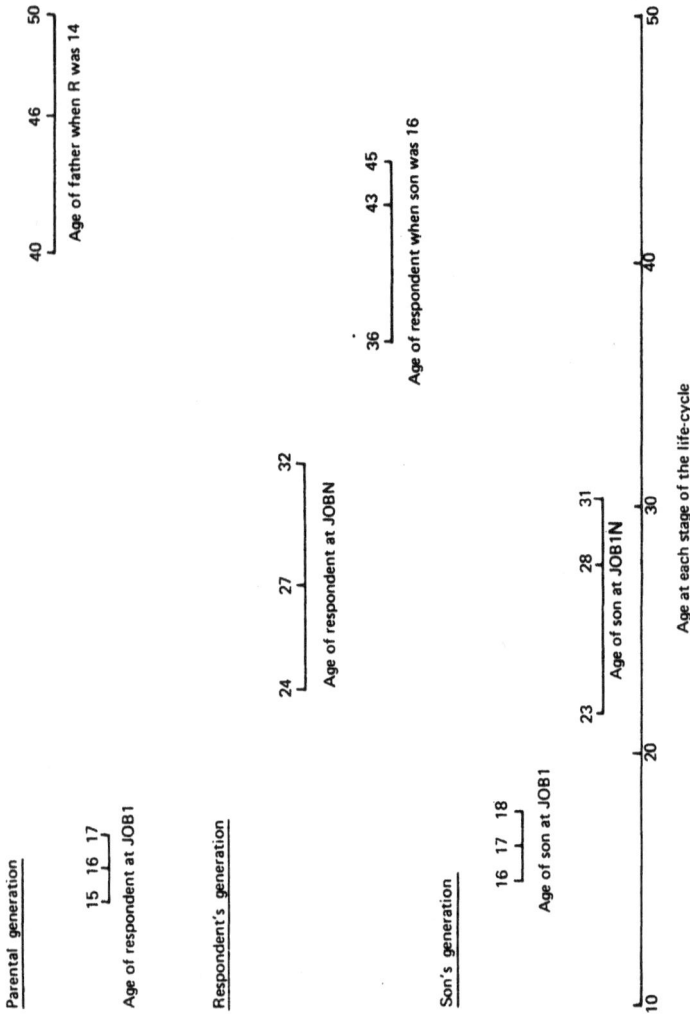

Figure 6.1 Life-cycle stages for fathers, respondents and sons in a three-generational model. Interquartile ranges and medians are shown.

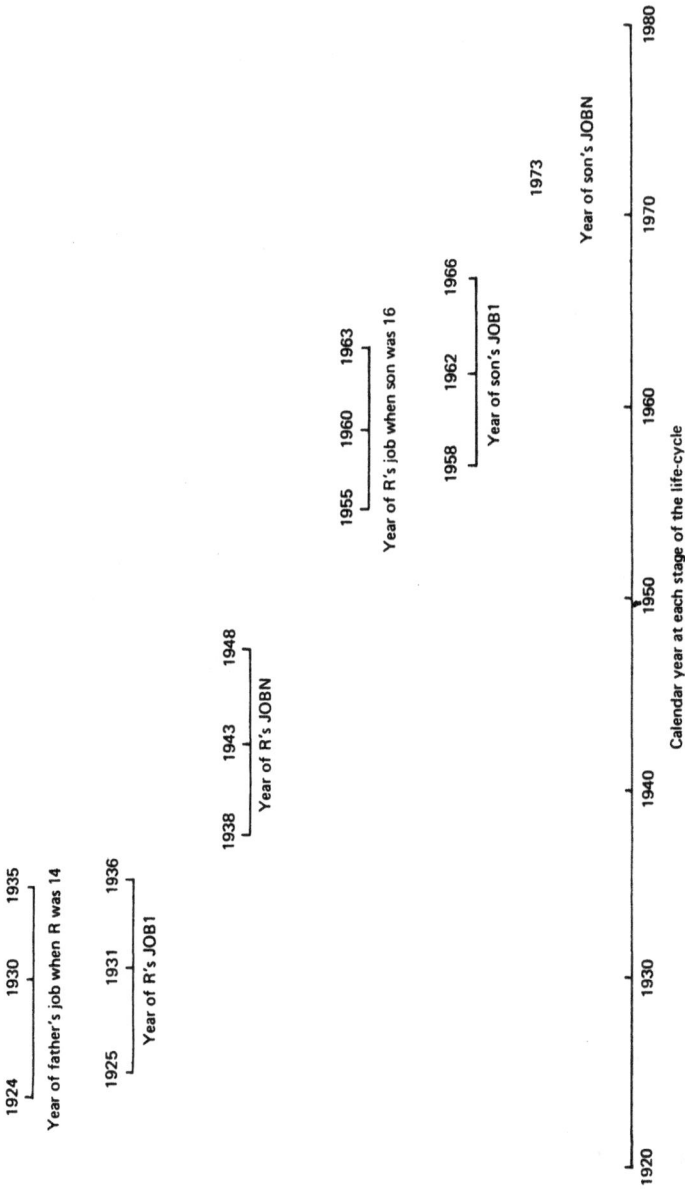

Figure 6.2 Historical period. Interquartile ranges and medians are shown.

TABLE 6.1   *Years of education for family members across three generations*

Years of education	R and parents			Parents and son		
	DADED	MOMED	R's EDUC	DADED (R's EDUC)	R's wife's EDUC	Son's EDUC
−5	2·7	1·3	0·8	0·8	1·0	—
5	2·7	1·5	—	—	0·7	—
6	16·3	13·2	3·4	3·4	2·5	0·5
7	14·2	13·1	8·2	8·2	5·8	0·8
8	42·5	54·8	45·8	45·8	42·9	10·9
9	8·9	8·3	17·3	17·3	20·1	25·6
10	4·6	3·4	10·6	10·6	14·7	26·9
11	2·0	2·2	5·2	5·2	4·9	16·1
12	2·2	0·7	2·5	2·5	2·7	7·4
13	0·9	0·4	0·8	0·8	1·4	1·7
14	0·5	0·2	0·6	0·6	0·1	2·1
15	0·4	0·1	0·4	0·4	0·7	2·2
16	0·4	0·2	0·8	0·8	0·4	1·8
17	0·4	0·2	1·0	1·0	—	1·2
18	0·2	—	0·1	0·1	0·5	2·0
19+	1·1	0·4	2·5	2·5	1·6	0·6
N (100%)	539	533	634	634	619	633
N missing	104	110	9	9	24	10

TABLE 6.2   *Occupations of family members across three generations*

Occupation group	R and father			Father (R) and son		
	DADJOB	R's JOB1	R's JOBN	DADJOB (R's job)	Son's JOB1	Son's JOBN
Professional	5·0	4·6	4·7	6·6	14·3	15·9
Managerial	8·8	0·8	3·7	11·0	1·4	8·7
White collar	6·0	16·1	23·8	11·3	20·0	15·4
Total nonmanual	19·8	21·5	32·2	28·9	35·7	40·0
Skilled	13·2	18·7	17·4	18·7	28·8	24·1
Semiskilled	22·6	23·9	22·5	27·6	18·1	21·5
Unskilled	19·1	6·6	9·3	12·8	5·3	7·4
Total manual	54·9	49·2	49·2	59·1	52·2	53·0
Farmers	18·9	3·7	7·9	8·0	1·6	3·1
Farm workers	6·3	25·5	10·7	4·1	10·4	3·8
Total farm	25·2	29·2	18·6	12·1	12·0	6·9
N (100%)	639	642	620	631	643	643
N missing	4	1	22	12	0	0

and 16. Sizeable proportions left school at older ages. The lumping of the respondents' educational distribution means that many of the career points chosen for estimating DADJOB in the second panel are either 34 or 44 (twenty or thirty years after leaving school at age 14). About one-third of the jobs selected were those held when respondents were at one of these two ages.

The spread of ages for JOBN is comparable in the two samples. Half of the respondents were aged between 24 and 32 when they held JOBN, averaging 27 years. For sons the interquartile range is 23 to 31 years, with an average of 28 years. These figures show how closely we were able to match stage of life-cycle. Since respondents on average left school two years earlier than their sons, an exact comparison would have been an average JOBN age of 26 years, rather than the observed 27 years.

In interpreting differences in the educational and occupational experience of men and women in these analytic samples, it is important to relate their experience to the historical context surrounding their careers. Figure 6.2 provides the relevant information. For both generation sets, the historical contexts of DADJOB and JOB1 obviously overlap, since the time selected for DADJOB was chosen to match the son's age at leaving school and taking his first job. For approximately half the fathers, DADJOB relates to the years from 1924 to 1935, averaging 1930; and about half the respondents took their first job between 1925 and 1936, averaging 1931. Thus a sizeable proportion of jobs held by the older generation relate to the unsettled economic period immediately after World War I, and extend into the even more unsettled years of the great depression. Moreover, about half the respondents held JOBN during World War II, and presumably their civilian careers were affected for better or worse by military service or the exigencies of a wartime economy.

In contrast, the younger generation started work in the period of economic expansion after World War II. DADJOB covers the period between 1955 and 1963 for about half the respondents, and JOB1, the years 1958 to 1966 for a similar proportion of sons. JOBN relates to 1973 before the rapid increase in inflation and unemployment. These sharp differences in economic conditions clearly affect the careers of men and women in the samples.

The main features of Table 6.1 have already been described. Table 6.2 shows the broad shifts in job distribution for the two samples. Given the special selection procedures used to construct these samples, the trends can not be generalized in detail to the whole workforce. Nevertheless they mirror broader changes in the occupational structure: the sharp decline in the farm sector, unusually high proportions of fathers in unskilled work and respondents in farm labour (JOB1) during the depression years, and their movement later (JOBN) into the lower echelons of nonmanual work. Among respondents and their sons, the continued decline of the farm sector is evident (JOBN), with a compensating rise in the proportion of professionals and a generally higher skill level among those in manual work. While the following analysis uses the status scale rather than occupational groupings, these broad changes need to be kept in mind in interpreting differences in status attainment processes.

Analytic models

The model of status attainment adopted here is much the same as the basic model of chapter 2, except that further education and income cannot be included as possible causes or effects of job status. Nor is information available on the earnings of children or on the earnings of respondents when they were at the same career stage as their children. Status outcomes are therefore confined to basic education, first job and current job. We are mainly concerned to compare the same model across generations for the six sub-samples defined above and to identify differences by generation, gender and other factors influencing educational and work experience.

Table 6.3 presents simple correlations and descriptive distributional measures for the eight variables in the basic model. The averages for the education variables show the expected trend. The amount of education obtained by fathers (DADED) increases by one year from the oldest to the middle generation, and the variation around the average, expressed in the coefficient of variation, also increases, mainly because there is more variation at higher years of schooling (see Table 6.1). Years of mother's education (MOMED) shows similar increases for the same reasons. There is also a slight narrowing of the gap in years of education obtained by fathers and mothers. The difference in years of education between respondents and sons (EDUC) is somewhat greater, averaging one and a half years.

Compensating for missing data

At this point a comment on the problem of missing data is indicated. To test whether the way variables affect education and jobs is related to differences in generational level, historical period, sex, ethnicity and the like, we use dummy variables and interaction terms in which different variables can have different effects from one sub-group to another. In such analyses pairwise deletion of missing variables is unsatisfactory because cases with missing data enter some analyses, but not others, and flaw the estimation procedure. Listwise deletion of missing cases must be used, and individuals with missing data on *any* of the eight variables in the basic model must be omitted. In small analytic samples like the ones in this chapter, listwise deletion is wasteful of data, especially since about one in six respondents did not know how old his father or

TABLE 6.3 *Measures of association and distribution of status attainment for parents, respondents and sons*[a]

Status characteristic	DADED	DADJOB	MOMED	WLTH	FAMSZ	EDUC	JOB1	JOBN	Mean	Standard deviation	Coefficient of variation
DADED		0·27	0·61	0·25	−0·16	0·46	0·26	0·31	8·03	2·17	0·27
DADJOB	0·46		0·19	0·32	−0·02	0·20	0·29	0·34	510·75	102·94	0·20
MOMED	0·32	0·29		0·30	−0·14	0·39	0·16	0·23	7·90	1·50	0·19
WLTH	0·26	0·38	0·23		−0·14	0·28	0·20	0·25	−0·09	1·78	n.a.
FAMSZ	−0·05	−0·05	0·01	−0·10		−0·24	−0·09	−0·14	5·13	2·74	0·53
EDUC	0·41	0·41	0·30	0·24	−0·18		0·39	0·38	9·04	2·37	0·26
JOB1	0·34	0·39	0·30	0·20	−0·15	0·71		0·53	476·84	80·29	0·17
JOBN	0·22	0·38	0·19	0·22	−0·15	0·57	0·67		494·92	92·16	0·19
Mean	8·95	509·34	8·89	0·04	3·57	10·50	508·95	531·61			
Standard deviation	2·40	109·89	1·93	1·60	1·94	2·31	98·12	113·61			
Coefficient of variation	0·27	0·22	0·22	n.a.	0·54	0·22	0·19	0·21			

[a] Above-diagonal figures are for respondents and their parents (*N* = 549). Below-diagonal figures are for respondents (fathers), their wives and their sons (*N* = 571). See text for definition of variables.

161

mother was when he or she left school. In preliminary analyses, listwise selection for the respondent-father samples reduced (weighted) sample size from between 600 and 700 persons to between 400 and 500 persons.

Because the main sources of missing data are DADED and MOMED, these variables were estimated in respondent and parent samples from their overall relationship with other social background variables (DADJOB, WLTH, FAMSZ, and either DADED or MOMED depending on which of these two measures was being estimated). A missing value was not estimated unless there was complete information on the remaining background variables. In this way about half the missing cases were recovered and the usable sample was raised from about 450 to 550, with the advantage that estimates become more stable, particularly for small groups such as persons born in a non-English-speaking country. Detailed comparisons of results suggest that this procedure has no significant impact on the analysis except to increase the sample size and reliability. The regression analysis that follows is based on listwise deletion of missing values, with estimates of DADED and MOMED for about 100 respondents. It should be mentioned that other background variables explain between 30 and 35 per cent of the variance in DADED and MOMED. To avoid introducing correlation among the error terms for the dependent variables, outcome variables were not used to estimate these background variables.

Comparing the generations

A comparison of the two generational sets indicates, as expected, that family size (FAMSZ) declined from just over five children in the respondents' families of orientation to between three and four children in their own families of procreation. A small part of this difference may be attributed to the fact that some respondents may not have completed their families by the time they were interviewed. However, that can not be an important influence because only 3 per cent of respondents in this analysis are under 45 years of age.

Since the average status of men's jobs has increased over recent decades it is surprising that father's job status (DADJOB) is about the same for the older and the middle generation, especially as the job statuses for fathers (respondents) of the sons in this analysis almost all refer to the period after 1945, whereas many of the jobs reported by respondents for their fathers relate to the depression. There probably is some tendency for respondents to report the best job their father held during their adolescence. As already noted, the index of family possessions (WLTH) is measured more validly for the older than for the middle generation. For the latter it pertains to the time when the respondent was interviewed (1973) and not to the time when the son was actually 16 years old. Because this measure has been standarized, its coefficient of variation is not calculated.

The measures so far described constitute a set of family resources and characteristics that influence the course of a person's educational and occupational career. One aim of the following analysis is to assess how far these resources and characteristics work to the advantage or disadvantage of individual careers. As already mentioned, about half the respondents in the middle generation started work during, and about half before, the depression of the 1930s. The first group experienced occupational handicaps in their career beginnings (JOB1) and the others in their early career, the period covered by their 'current job' (JOBN). As Table 6.3 shows, son's JOB1 and JOBN are about 30 status points higher than those for respondents because almost all the sons began work in the period of postwar expansion and were able to enter better, and more varied, jobs than their fathers at comparable stages of their careers. These observations are confirmed in Table 6.4, which reports the process of status attainment in each generational set.

Intergenerational differences in status attainment

According to Table 6.4, the extent to which family background influenced educational attainment was almost exactly the same in the interwar and postwar periods: family background explains a little over a quarter of the variance in years of education obtained by both groups of men. However, the regression technique described in chapter 2 reveals two significant differences in the relative impact of the indicators of family background. For respondents DADJOB has no significant effect on EDUC, but for sons it has a large, indeed equal largest, impact on educational attainment. However, as already noted, DADJOB and WLTH are measured with different validity for parents and respondents so that some of the error in each indicator is compensated for by the other. Because of this complication, differences that probably result from differential measurement error are not worth interpreting. We simply note that the social background factors have the same total effect on educational attainment, and that over the last half-century there has been no appreciable shift in the degree to which education depends on family background.

People from large families also come from families where parents have less education, lower occupational status and fewer possessions. They also leave school earlier because of competition for

TABLE 6.4 *Standardized and unstandardized coefficients in two models of status attainment for parents, respondents and sons[a]*

Dependent variables	Independent variables							Rsq. (Intercept)
	DADED	DADJOB	MOMED	WLTH	FAMSZ	EDUC	JOB1	
Respondents and their parents								
EDUC	0·31	0·04	0·13	0·13	−0·15	—	—	0·27
	(0·34)	(0·00)	(0·21)	(0·17)	(−0·13)			(4·84)
JOB1	0·09	0·20	−0·07	0·04	−0·01	0·33	—	0·20
	(3·19)	(0·16)	(−3·79)	(2·00)	(−0·17)	(11·03)		(300·68)
JOBN	0·08	0·16	0·01	0·05	−0·05	0·13	0·40	0·36
	(3·31)	(0·14)	(0·80)	(2·61)	(−1·70)	(5·12)	(0·46)	(134·54)
Respondents and their sons								
EDUC	0·24	0·24	0·15	0·04	−0·16	—	—	0·28
	(0·23)	(0·01)	(0·18)	(0·05)	(−0·19)			(4·99)
JOB1	0·00	0·11	0·07	−0·01	−0·03	0·64	—	0·52
	(−0·04)	(0·10)	(3·79)	(−0·48)	(−1·29)	(27·08)		(144·71)
JOBN	−0·10	0·14	−0·04	0·05	−0·03	0·19	0·52	0·49
	(−4·60)	(0·14)	(−2·12)	(3·34)	(−1·82)	(9·15)	(0·60)	(102·71)

[a] Underlined coefficients do not exceed twice their standard error. Unstandardized coefficients are shown in brackets.

scarce resources. The unstandardized coefficients of Table 6.4 indicate that every additional child in the family reduced a respondent's, or a son's, educational attainment by between one-tenth and two-tenths of a year, after the effects of other social background factors are taken into account. By contrast, every additional year of education his father and mother had obtained was converted into about half a year more education for their son. Broadly speaking, how long a man stays in school is determined by how long his parents stayed in school and how many brothers and sisters he had.

A comparison of the determinants of first job in each gener-ational pair using the technique described in chapter 2 reveals one minor and two major differences. Whereas the net effect of mother's education on first job is not significant for respondents, it does have a small but significant positive effect for sons. However, the difference is slight both in substantive terms and in causal impact. The more important differences relate to the range in status of first jobs available to school-leavers in each period, the increased impact of education on career beginnings, and consequently the much greater explanatory power of the model for the youngest generation. As noted in Table 6.3, the average status of sons' first job was higher than the first job of respondents, and the sons entered a wider variety of jobs. Thus, about one son in ten started work as a professional, technical or higher managerial worker compared with only one in twenty respondents. At the other end of the occupational scale, rather more respondents than sons began work as labourers or low-status service workers: 10 and 7 per cent respectively.

Both respondents and their sons began work most often as shop assistants (6 and 5 per cent respectively), farm workers (14 and 5 per cent), and clerical workers (8 and 11 per cent), but 81 per cent of respondents began work in jobs with less than average status, that is, a status score of less than 500. Career beginnings were uncertain in the interwar period, but more determinate after World War II because of increased credentialism in the job market. Years of education (EDUC) is a significantly more important determinant of career beginnings among sons than among respondents. Whereas an additional year of education (net of social background) raised the status of a respondent's first job by an estimated 11 status points, for a son the gain was two to three times greater. For both generations the other substantial determinant of first job status was father's job status. As the regression coefficients indicate, a difference of 100 points in father's status converted to an average gain of 16 points for a respondent and 10 points for a son. Increasingly years of education emerge as the main influence of social background on JOB1 and subsequent occupational careers. It is hardly surprising that a society which between 1948 and 1966 more than doubled the share of its national product devoted to educational expenditure (Karmel, 1976, p. 150) should rely increasingly on educational credentials in the workplace.

In the case of 'current' job (that is, 1973 job for sons, and an equivalent career point for respondents), more of the variability in status attainment can be accounted for among sons than respondents because of the significantly greater impact of career beginnings on current job. The net impact of first job on current job is about one-third greater in the case of sons for two reasons. Younger men experienced a more favourable job market. Their careers did not suffer the disruption of a depression and a war but took place in an expanding, stable, peacetime economy. Also, more sons than respondents began work in professional occupations, which have the lowest rate of career mobility of any broadly defined occupational group (Broom and Jones, 1976, p. 93).

There is a fairly consistent ordering of effects on early careers for both respondents and sons. For first job the most important determinants are years of education and father's job. For current job they are first job, education and father's job, although for respondents the ordering of the last two is reversed. Except for father's job (and in the case of sons perhaps mother's education), the main effects of social background are transmitted through educational attainment, which is then converted into occupational status. The persistence of a direct and significant effect of father's job independent of education indicates that while educational credentials are the main path to occupational status, there are alternative routes through the inheritance of family businesses (including farms) and through family sponsorship into high-status positions.

The latter processes cannot be investigated directly with our data, but indirect evidence of variation in status attainment processes by sub-groups can be obtained through comparisons such as those carried out in chapter 2. This task is eased because there is no basis for taking seriously observed differences in the upper panels of Tables 6.4 and 6.6: a man's career cannot be retroactively affected by the gender of his child. The group comparisons discussed below focus on differences that emerge for respondents and their parents in both Tables 6.4 and 6.6, for both the sons' and the daughters' analytic samples, and on relatively large differences for respondents and sons versus respondents and daughters, for whom it is reasonable to expect differences.

Community size

How far does the size of the community in which the respondent grew up modify the process of status attainment? Community size is defined as a dummy variable in which the respondent is scored zero if he lived on a farm, in a village or in a country town, and 1 if he lived in a middle-sized or large city. This variable reflects differences in educational and occupational opportunities, since the variety of educational institutions, educational aspirations and job opportunities is usually greater in large cities. To identify significant differences involves testing a model in which the explanatory variables can have different effects depending on the size of the community in which the respondent grew up. The following discussion does not present the many tabulations summarizing these analyses but simply reports the chief differences found. We again caution the reader (and ourselves) that because this is an explanatory rather than an hypothesis-testing analysis there is a risk of over-interpreting results. When many tests for interactions are made, some significant results will be found merely by chance.

No significant effects for community size emerge in both the sons' and the daughters' samples for respondents and their fathers. The sons' sample (upper panel of Table 6.4) shows a tendency for men reared in small communities to have less schooling (about half a year less on average) but in the daughters' sample it is only about one-third of a year and is not significantly different. Similarly, in small communities DADED is a more important influence on years of education in the son's sample, but this difference does not replicate in the daughters' sample. The failure to find significant differences cannot be because of small sample sizes: 48 per cent of respondents were reared in cities and 52 per cent in farms, villages or country towns. The absence of stable and significant effects implies that the breakdown by community size does not capture general and systematic differences in processes of status attainment. Whatever differences may exist do not aggregate into a significantly different pattern but are probably idiosyncratic and specific to particular kinds of small communities.

Ethnicity

To explore problems of immigrant disadvantage, respondents born in Australia or another English-speaking country were distinguished from those born in other countries. For the non-English-speaking group (9 per cent of the sample) there is little point in discussing the determinants of EDUC and JOB1 because the amount of education a respondent received and the status of his first job pertain more to conditions in the country of birth than to conditions in Australia. However, we can note again the finding from chapter 2 that years of education has less effect on JOB1 for men born in non-English-speaking countries. This finding may result from discrimination in the job market, but other factors such as disruptions to careers caused by migration, language difficulties and inability to win recognition for educational credentials gained in a foreign country may also be involved.

In the case of current job, JOB1 is less important in the non-English-speaking group. One hundred status points of JOB1 convert to only 30 points for JOBN in the non-English-speaking group, but to 50 points for men born in English-speaking countries. Non-English-speakers have more discontinuous careers and experience less upward mobility than others.

Impact of the depression

Many respondents in this survey faced especially difficult economic conditions when they entered the labour market. Throughout the 1920s male unemployment in Australia ran at about 5 per cent. In the 1930s it rose to double figures and peaked at 31 per cent. To explore the impact of the depression on status attainment, respondents were divided into two groups: those who started work between 1929 and 1939 (49 per cent of respondents) when unemployment ran at above 10 per cent, and those who started work before 1929 (37 per cent of respondents). Men who started work during World War II (12 per cent) are excluded from this analysis, in order to focus attention on the impact of the depression.

There is no evidence of large differences in the effects of family background on EDUC. During the depression there was a slight tendency for people to stay longer at school: average years of education rose from just under nine to just over nine years for the two groups. When job prospects are poor, the opportunity cost of staying in school is less than when job prospects for school-leavers are good.

For first and current jobs the only stable differences are direct period effects. Men who started work in the depression entered lower-status jobs and were still in lower-status jobs at JOBN than men who started work before the depression. Starting off in the depression cost respondents about 20 status points for both JOB1 and JOBN, or an effect equivalent to two years' less education at first job and four years less at JOBN. Analyses not reported here suggest that starting work in the depression retarded career mobility by about five years.

Privilege and disadvantage

An analysis of status attainment in the sample as a whole is a statement about average tendencies. The value of such an average statement depends on how much or how little variation exists within the population in underlying causal processes. By comparing particular groups such as men reared in cities with men reared on farms or in villages and country towns, we can gain some idea whether the same processes are probably involved. It is commonly suggested that the world behaves differently for the haves and have-nots, that a cycle of self-perpetuating privilege exists at the top, and a cycle of self-perpetuating disadvantage at the bottom. The possibility of testing such ideas with a sample of only 1 in 800 private dwellings is limited because the small minority of very rich and powerful families are not likely to appear in such a sample. Similarly, if the cycle of poverty applies to only 1 or 2 per cent of workers, our data cannot detect it.

However, if wider definitions of privilege and disadvantage are used, some evidence can be marshalled. Dummy variables were defined identifying the bottom and top 10 per cent of fathers in terms of their occupational status when their sons (respondents) were growing up. In other words, the experience of persons at the extremes of the status distribution were contrasted separately against the remaining 90 per cent. For respondents from high-status backgrounds (mainly professionals, higher managers and graziers), the only major difference that emerges in both samples (upper panels of Table 6.4 and 6.6 respectively) is the influence of MOMED on JOB1. In the sample overall MOMED has no significant influence on first job status. In the high-status group, however, there is a small positive effect on career beginnings. MOMED also has a larger positive effect on respondent's education for the high-status group in the sons' sample (upper panel of Table 6.4) but this effect does not appear in the daughters' sample (upper panel of Table 6.6). The importance of MOMED in the high-status group results from a more marked tendency of like to marry like: the correlation between MOMED and DADED is 0·66 in this group, but 0·58 for the rest of the sample.

For the low-status group (the bottom 10 per cent in terms of father's job), no significant differences could be established for either sample. It is worth noting, however, that in the sons' sample large family size significantly depresses EDUC net of other background factors. This finding fits with other evidence that large families are associated with poverty.

No other major effects can be identified and there is little evidence of a cycle of disadvantage or a cycle of privilege, at least among respondents and their parents. This does not imply that persons from high- and low-status backgrounds have similar experiences of the educational system or the labour market. It simply means that there was no *additional* gain or penalty from having originated from in the top or bottom 10 per cent of the status hierarchy. As we shall see in the next section, this generalization does not apply to status attainment among children in the postwar period.

Community size, ethnicity and cohort effects among sons

We now turn to a parallel analysis of respondents and sons. Father's education tends to be a more important determinant of EDUC for sons who grew up in small communities (40 per cent of this sample) rather than cities, where father's job status has a larger effect (lower panel, Table 6.4). This reversal of relative importance between DADED and DADJOB may result from the more restricted educational experience of men raised in small communities. The correlation between DADED and EDUC is 0·45 in small communities and 0·39 in cities. Sons reared in cities enjoyed about half a year's advantage in years of schooling compared with their rural counterparts, and education exerted a stronger influence on their first job status. An additional year of education added about 30 points to first job status for city youth, but only about 20 for rural youth. Family size also had a more marked (but in absolute terms small) negative effect in cities but was insignificant in small communities. First job status is more predictable in cities: the model explains 61 per cent of the variance in first job status for sons reared in cities but only 35 per cent for sons reared in other kinds of communities. There are no significant differences among the determinants of current job status by community size.

In the case of mother-tongue, no differences were found in the relative importance of social background, education or first job on the status of son's job in 1973. Many sons who started work in the economic upswing of the postwar period of sustained economic growth up to 1973 were born during the depression of the 1930s and because of the low birthrate in those years belong to a relatively small birth cohort. They later enjoyed advantages in school and at work because they had fewer native-born competitors. In the postwar period their competitors for schooling and jobs were often immigrants, many of whom were not native speakers of English.

A variable was constructed to distinguish sons born in years when the birth cohort was small from sons who were born into larger birth cohorts. In practice this division is between those aged 28 or older in 1973, and those between 21 and 27 years of age (the postwar 'baby boom' cohort). Because this age division affects length of working career, the two groups cannot be compared on JOBN. However, the pattern of effects for EDUC and JOB1 can be compared. The only significant educational difference between the two groups is that younger men had more education. That is, the time trend for people to stay on longer at school swamps any other differences. Sons born before 1946 averaged 10·3 years of EDUC, compared with 10·6 years for those born after 1945. There are no other significant differences in the equations for EDUC, but the hypothesized effects for JOB1 are found. In the smaller birth cohort there is a direct effect of the cohort dummy variable on JOB1 status, and their status gains from education were significantly greater. Belonging to the smaller birth cohort confers a direct advantage of 30 status points, and the effect of EDUC is about 25 per cent greater (32 versus 25 status points). The basic model explains 57 per cent of the variance in first job status for the pre-1946 cohort but only 47 per cent for the younger group.

High- and low-status effects

Coming from a family in which the father's job was in the top 10 per cent of the status hierarchy seems to have conferred a considerably greater advantage in the expansionary period after 1945 than in the interwar period. Father's job, mother's education and family possessions have different effects in the two groups. Belonging to the high-status group has a significant direct effect on EDUC, even after the other variables are included. Most sons in this sample left school at 16 or younger, but sons from high-status families on average remained in full-time education until they were 18 years old. As a consequence, their first and current jobs were 70 to 100 status points higher than for sons from other families. Upper-middle-class families, mainly professionals and managers, were able to capitalize on postwar economic opportunities for their sons, primarily by keeping them at school longer. It is important to note that the relative importance of education *per se* as a determinant of first and later jobs was no greater for sons from the top of the status hierarchy: they simply stayed in school longer than would otherwise be expected from the simpler (additive) model.

At the other end of the status scale, the bottom 10 per cent of the father's (respondent's) status distribution, there is some evidence of a 'cycle of poverty'. Status returns to EDUC were less for sons from low-status backgrounds. Each additional year of EDUC adds only 13 points to JOB1 status compared with 28 points for the rest of the sample. In the more meritocratic postwar period, young men with less education fared poorly in the competition for first jobs. This difference does not persist to current job status, where no significant differences in the pattern of effects were found.

The main conclusion from this analysis can be briefly summarized. In the postwar period education had a stronger influence on career beginnings in cities than in smaller communities because labour markets in cities are more impersonal and rely more on credentialism than employers' personal knowledge of employees or job applicants. Being born in a non-English-speaking country did not in itself modify the process of status attainment, at least so far as current job status is concerned. That does not mean that persons of non-English-speaking origins were necessarily similar to the English-speaking majority in terms of social origins, schooling or career beginnings. It means only that, other things being equal, there is no *additional* penalty deriving from ethnic origin. This finding is consistent with ethnic differences in other areas of social life, such as residential segregation and limited social participation with native English-speakers. Moreover, there are almost certainly differences within the non-English-speaking population which would be detected in a larger sample.

Size of birth cohort did modify the process of status attainment among sons. While almost all the sons participated in an expanding labour market, those who were born before 1946 and belonged to a smaller birth cohort started work in higher-status jobs. They also enjoyed greater status returns from their education, even though on average they had slightly less education than men born in later years. The educational and occupational worlds behave much more predictably for men from high-status families than for others, but we have no evidence that high social status directly influenced careers. It seems rather that families in which the father had a high-status job used the educational system to keep their children longer in school and thereby to secure higher-status jobs. At the other end of the scale, there is a hint of a cumultative cycle of disadvantage, in that coming from a low-status family further depresses educational attainment. Sons from poor families got less education and even the little they did get secured lower returns when they first started work.

Status attainment among daughters

The relevant information for daughters is contained in Tables 6.5 and 6.6. For reasons already mentioned, we expect no significant differences for respondents and fathers, and a casual comparison of Tables 6.3 and 6.5 and the upper panels of Tables 6.4 and 6.6 supports that impression. The largest single difference is the coefficient for the effect of DADJOB on JOBN, which is somewhat stronger in the sons' than the daughters' sample. But the difference between the two samples is small and insignificant.

The more interesting comparisons are between the lower panels of Tables 6.4 and 6.6 because they throw light on the way family background influences the education and careers of sons and daughters. In fact, there are surprisingly few differences. Family background influences years of education to about the same degree, and the pattern of relative effects is much the same for sons and daughters. The only significant difference is that boys remained longer at school: only one in seven girls stayed on in school after the age of 16, compared with one in three boys.

Sons enter higher-status first jobs than daughters and have a wider choice of first jobs. The five most common career beginnings for girls (stenographers and typists, shop assistants, clerks in private employment, office machine operators and nurses) account for 54 per cent of the daughters' first jobs; but the five most common first jobs for boys (clerks in private industry, shop assistants, motor mechanics, mixed farm workers and clerks in government) account for only 25 per cent. DADJOB is a significant influence on sons' careers but is irrelevant to daughters' occupations, whether JOB1 or JOBN. Because the workforce is segregated by sex, and because the jobs that most women enter have lower status (cf. Tables 6.3 and 6.6), the kind of work a father does has no significant direct effect on his daughter's occupation.

We also related the educational and occupational experience of daughters to the size of the community in which they grew up, their ethnic origin, birth cohort and social background. Girls reared in cities tended to get slightly more schooling than those reared on farms or in villages or country towns. However, the economic status of the family (WLTH) had more influence on education in small than in large communities.

For current job status (JOBN) the relative importance of education and career beginnings were reversed, with EDUC being the main influence on JOBN in small communities and JOB1 the main influence in cities. This last finding is probably related to age differences in the two groups. Daughters still at work in cities in 1973 were generally younger than those in small communities. This may result from sampling variation or from differences in age at marriage. Marriage and childbearing are the main selective processes influencing the chances of a woman remaining in the paid workforce. As the last row of Table 6.5 indicates, fewer than half the daughters had a job outside the home in 1973, a proportion which is lower in cities than in smaller communities.

Coming from a non-English-speaking background had no measurable effect on the current job status of daughters, As among

TABLE 6.5 *Measures of association and distribution of status attainment for parents, respondents and daughters*[a]

Status characteristic	DADED	DADJOB	MOMED	WLTH	FAMSZ	EDUC	JOB1	JOBN	Mean	Standard deviation	Coefficient of variation
DADED		0·31	0·57	0·20	−0·21	0·41	0·17	0·26	7·97	2·29	0·29
DADJOB	0·45		0·18	0·33	−0·11	0·22	0·24	0·24	511·97	106·69	0·21
MOMED	0·31	0·33		0·26	−0·20	0·31	0·10	0·23	7·82	1·55	0·20
WLTH	0·21	0·32	0·21		−0·16	0·20	0·12	0·20	0·20	1·84	n.a.
FAMSZ	−0·07	−0·05	−0·01	−0·10		−0·23	−0·12	−0·17	5·29	2·72	0·51
EDUC	0·38	0·39	0·32	0·28	−0·12		0·39	0·39	9·06	2·40	0·26
JOB1	0·31	0·28	0·24	0·24	−0·17	0·68		0·54	473·88	80·87	0·17
JOBN	0·27	0·27	0·26	0·25	−0·04	0·67	0·70		494·14	95·76	0·19
Mean	8·89	509·50	8·82	0·05	3·60	10·15	495·94	528·62			
Standard deviation	2·26	107·53	1·87	1·64	1·98	1·80	73·57	92·15			
Coefficient of variation	0·25	0·21	0·21	n.a.	0·55	0·18	0·15	0·17			

[a] Above-diagonal figures are for respondents and their parents ($N = 550$). Below-diagonal figures are for respondents (fathers). their wives and their daughters ($N = 249$), where $N = 598$ except for JOBN. where $N = 249$). See text.

sons, daughters born after 1945 stayed at school longer, but even so the older and smaller cohort gained larger returns in first job status, although this advantage did not persist to their job in 1973. Each additional year of education obtained by the older cohort increased the status of their first job by 30 points compared with 22 points among the younger cohort.

Daughters from high-status families were not especially advantaged in their schooling or first job status. Among high-status women EDUC emerges as a more important influence on JOBN than on JOB1, but because women from high-status backgrounds were on average younger, this discrepancy probably results from age differences between the two groups. Coming from a low-status background did not alter the basic pattern of effects shown in Table 6.6.

In general, among the daughters there are few important departures from the overall picture given in the bottom panel of Table 6.6. Parental resources significantly influence schooling but have small direct effects on occupational careers. Most of the effect of unequal family backgrounds is mediated through schooling, and schooling has a greater effect on the careers of daughters than sons, among whom father's job has a significant direct effect.

A three-generational model

At the outset of this chapter we noted Bottomore's view that inequality is largely transmitted from generation to generation. The evidence examined so far provides some support for that view but not to the extent implied by his statement. Family background explains about a quarter of the variation in years of schooling of Australian men and women, and not even the most generous allowance for measurement error or omission of relevant family background characteristics would increase this estimate to more than half. Moreover, even if family background did determine schooling to this greater extent, it has less direct effects on occupational careers. The weight of evidence for Australia falls at least as heavily on the side of openness in the process of status transmission across generations as it does on rigidity.

It is possible, however, that the social mobility experienced in one generation may be reversed in the next, that, as the saying has it, many families go from shirtsleeves to shirtsleeves in three generations. If such countermobility is frequent, grandparental characteristics should account for differences in the status attainment of grandchildren at least as well as those of the middle generation. This folk hypothesis can be tested by extending the

TABLE 6.6 *Standardized and unstandardized coefficients in two models of status attainment for parents, respondents and daughters*[a]

Dependent variables	Independent variables							R sq. (Intercept)
	DADED	DADJOB	MOMED	WLTH	FAMSZ	EDUC	JOB1	
Respondents and their parents								
EDUC	0·29 (0·31)	0·07 (0·00)	0·08 (0·13)	0·08 (0·18)	−0·12 (−0·11)			0·20 (5·34)
JOB1	−0·01 (−0·17)	0·17 (0·13)	−0·05 (−2·59)	−0·00 (−0·01)	−0·03 (−0·98)	0·36 (12·24)		0·18 (323·74)
JOBN	0·04 (1·69)	0·05 (0·04)	0·09 (5·39)	0·07 (3·47)	−0·04 (−1·46)	0·14 (5·44)	0·45 (0·53)	0·36 (121·32)
Respondents and their daughters								
EDUC	0·21 (0·17)	0·20 (0·00)	0·16 (0·15)	0·12 (0·14)	−0·09 (−0·08)			0·25 (5·88)
JOB1	0·05 (1·70)	−0·01 (−0·01)	0·02 (0·75)	0·04 (1·98)	−0·08 (−2·99)	0·63 (25·88)		0·47 (226·35)
JOBN	−0·00 (−0·08)	0·02 (0·02)	0·03 (1·49)	0·05 (2·77)	−0·01 (−0·36)	0·32 (14·01)	0·46 (0·51)	0·56 (95·65)

[a] Underlined coefficients do not exceed twice their standard error. Unstandardized coefficients are shown in brackets.

analyses of the lower panels of Tables 6.4 and 6.6 with information from the upper panels. .

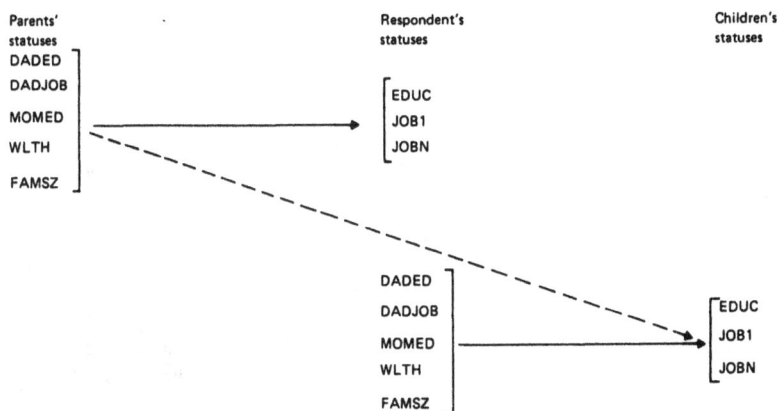

Figure 6.3   A scheme of status attainment.

Figure 6.3 expresses the idea in diagrammatic form. It hypothesises that the attainment of children is influenced by their fathers' family of orientation as well as by their own family of orientation. In addition to the five variables shown in Figure 6.3, dummy variables were used to represent the extremes of the grandfather's status distribution (top and bottom 10 per cent of DADJOB).

The results are unequivocal: there are no paternal 'grandparental' effects. Adding seven indicators of the respondent's social background has no discernible impact on the amount of variance explained in the years of education a son received, and only an insignificant influence on the years of education that a daughter received (an increment in R sq. of 1·4 per cent). For first job and current job no increase exceeds 1 per cent. No grandparental status has any significant direct effect on the statuses of their grandchildren. Just as the process of status transmission within individual careers is largely step-by-step, so the consequences of unequal social background are transmitted in one step from each generation to the next.

In a class society where inequalities were rigidly transmitted from one generation to the next, no additional explanation would be gained by extending the generational span. But in such a hypothetical society grandparental statuses ought to tell as much about the status of grandchildren as do parental statuses. This theory can be evaluated by seeing whether grandparental statuses perform as well as parental statuses in predicting the status attainment of children.

Again the result is unequivocal: the five variables listed in Figure 6.3 explain only 6·6 per cent of the variation in the sons' years of education, a figure which is increased to only 7·8 per cent when dummy variables for high- and low-status origins are added. Only FAMSZ is statistically significant. This overall figure of 7 to 8 per cent can be compared with the figure of 28 per cent when parental (middle generation) statuses are used to predict the level of schooling obtained by sons. Results for daughters are almost identical with only 6·5 per cent of the variance in education explained with the same seven grandparental statuses, compared with 25 per cent using five parental statuses (Table 6.6). Clearly, the evidence points to a progressive weakening of unequal origins with the passage of time. Only the most quixotic allowances for measurement and specification errors could bridge these gaps.[1]

Inheritance, achievement and public policy

We have demonstrated that a significant degree of inequality is transmitted from generation to generation and have examined the mechanisms through which that transmission occurs. Furthermore, it has been shown that the extent to which family background influences schooling has remained largely unchanged over the last half-century. In a society where the choice of whether a child continues schooling beyond the legal minimum is largely a private decision conditioned by existing inequalities in resources and opportunities, there is no avoiding the conclusion that many inequalities will be perpetuated.

In order to distil our findings and highlight their implications for public policy, we use the preceding analysis to devise a summary measure of inheritance across generations. The three-generational model was designed partly to compare processes of status attainment during the last half century by contrasting the experience of respondents and their parents on the one hand, with respondents and their children on the other. The data for such a comparison were selected so that the life-cycle stages being compared were as similar as possible. The five background variables for the parents of respondents were all chosen to characterize the socioeconomic climate of the home when most respondents were about 14 years old and were deciding whether to continue their schooling or enter the workforce. Similarly, the same five variables for respondents were selected to characterize the socioeconomic climate of the home when their son or daughter was making the same decision around age 16.

An estimate of the total effect of social inheritance across generations can be made simply by establishing the degree of similarity in the socioeconomic positions of parents and respondents at these comparable stages in their life-cycle. Both parents and respondents were in mid-career, married and had at least one teenage child. How similar are their relative socioeconomic positions after the passage of thirty years?

Of the various ways to make such an assessment the principal components method and canonical correlation are used. In the former the common or shared elements in socioeconomic position are extracted (the first principal component for each set of five variables), and these two summary measures can then be correlated. Canonical correlation is a method that calculates the maximum possible correlation between two sets of variables, in this case five indicators of the relative socioeconomic positions of a respondent when he was about 40 years old and of his parents thirty years before when they were at a similar stage of their life-cycle.

The two methods give virtually identical results. The correlation between the composite measures summarizing the socioeconomic statuses of families after a thirty-year interval is 0·598; the canonical correlation between the two sets of family background variables is 0·602. Allowing for measurement error, we assume that parental characteristics are measured with a reliability of 0·825 and that the respondent's own characteristics are measured somewhat more reliably, at 0·875. We can then calculate the upper limit of the correlation for the intergenerational transmission of inequality as $(0·602)\sqrt{(0·825)^*(0·875)}$, or 0·709, a figure somewhat higher than those reported in other studies. To put the matter more succinctly, we can explain half the variance in the socioeconomic positions of families in 1973 by knowing the positions of their families of orientation thirty years before.

Inheritance, achievement or luck?

It would be tempting to interpret such a summary statement to mean that contemporary Australian society represents an almost equal mix of inheritance and achievement. But such a facile identification of similarity in socioeconomic position with inheritance and of family dissimilarity with achievement is not warranted. There is no simple way to distinguish inheritance from achievement in an overall measure of similarity in socioeconomic position. Doubtless there is some element, perhaps even a large element, of inheritance which contributes to family similarities across generations, but as we have already seen part of this total effect is indirect through schooling and, presumably, through motivations towards schooling and achievement. Similarly, what is left unexplained by family origins represents all other possible factors, including chance or luck, and not simply achievement.

The summary analysis only gives an upper limit to the *total* effect of family origins. It does not differentiate processes of direct inheritance (whether property, influence and income) and indirect influences through schooling and socialization, which involve personal effort as well as inheritance. Moreover, since we include wife's education, we also have included a measure of the tendency of like to marry like, which in contemporary Australian society has little to do with family inheritance in any strict sense.

What general policy implications can be drawn from these findings? We do not suppose that governments will introduce policies to prevent parents inculcating values and attitudes in their children, to force people into particular kinds of marriages designed to balance social differences, or issue vouchers according to social or genetic criteria allowing them to have a specific number of children. Such policies are not of course inconceivable, and in some circumstances they have been advocated and even put into limited practice. The treatment of minority groups has sometimes involved such policies,[2] but in more enlightened moments we regard them as barbarous anomalies.

The dilemma for a liberal democracy characterized by major social inequalities is that some proportion of intergenerational family similarity reflects an unequal start and not differences in personal effort. In liberal democracies redistributional policies vary from taxes on accumulated wealth to programs of compensatory education, the setting of minimum income levels, and different kinds of transfer payments. Some have so despaired at the tentative, indeed timid, style of such efforts and the meagre results from then that they have instead urged a direct policy of equalizing outcomes (Jencks *et al.*, 1972), a policy which may penalize effort as well as inheritance.

In an unequal society, how can groups with little control over social resources bring the existing distribution into balance? We do not pretend to answer this stubborn political issue, but if it is to be intelligently confronted and fairly resolved, a knowledge of how inequality is transmitted across generations is required. The analyses presented above have attempted to contribute to that understanding. Uninformed action will achieve little and may create the impression that little can be achieved, encouraging defeatism.

What is an acceptable level of family inheritance in contemporary Australia? It might be argued that if as much as half the variation in the socioeconomic position of a man's family can be explained by knowing the socioeconomic position of his parents thirty years before, that itself is *prima facie* evidence of too much family inheritance. If one were to say that one-third is a more acceptable fraction than one-half, the implication is that processes of social change should be accelerated so that the shifts in socioeconomic position that occur over three generations would be compressed to the span of two generations. The reasoning is based on the interpretation that our highest estimate of the intergenerational correlation of inheritance (0.71) has to be multiplied three times to reduce the dependence of a man's social position on that of his parents from one-half to about one-third. If a more radical criterion of one-quarter were taken as an acceptable figure for family inheritance (using inheritance in the broadest possible sense), we would in effect recommend an acceleration of social change so that changes which would otherwise take four generations (over a century) would occur in one generation. The reader can carry out other calculations embodying more or less radical preferences.

We have tried to make it clear that public policies dealing with finite lives within continuing family groups take time to produce stable effects. Although compensatory social programs in the school and in the marketplace can moderate the effects of an unequal start, they do not provide blanket solutions. The independence of family groups and the high value placed on individual choice in liberal democracies imply that such programs need to be reinforced by policies designed to equalize resources before and not merely after a person's socioeconomic career has begun. In other words, it is not enough to increase equality of opportunity in schooling and jobs. It is also necessary to moderate the economic inequalities associated with the job market and family inheritance. However, balancing the demands of equity, efficiency and opportunity requires a different calculus from one that merely accelerates the movement of family members from much the same set of unequal positions from one generation to the next.

In a liberal democracy, striking a balance between competing claims is the task of policy-makers responsible to an electorate. The most rigorously grounded evaluation must wait upon the working out of personal careers in changing economic and social circumstances. Nevertheless we believe that important steps have been made towards specifying what needs to be taken into account and how to take it into account, including the identification of those aspects of society that are amenable to quantification and those that are not (cf. Fairley and Mosteller, 1977). It is reasonable to hope that the sorts of analytic procedures used here to weigh and interpret the effects of past circumstances and policies will become increasingly sensitive guides to the probable results of alternative policy proposals. We do not of course believe that such methods in and of themselves will resolve major differences and conflicts in society, but they may help to clarify them and point to more constructive resolutions.

Notes

Chapter 1 Introduction

1 Related projects were initiated in 1975 by John Higley on contemporary elites and in 1976 by William Rubinstein on the social characteristics of the wealthy in nineteenth- and twentieth-century Australia.

2 We first proposed the term 'event analysis' in a paper presented at the International Sociological Conference convened by the Polish Academy of Sciences at Jablonna near Warsaw in 1974, published later in revised form in Broom *et al.*, (1977a, pp. 7–8).

3 For a recent overview of this literature see Sahota (1978, pp. 11–19).

Chapter 2 The socioeconomic career: a basic model

1 At this point we note that for the sake of brevity and convenience computer acronyms are often used to designate variables. These are given in capital letters. Although they are sometimes less than felicitous, we shall not apologize further for their use.

2 Goldberger and Duncan (1973) represents a recent attempt to bring together work in this field.

3 See Featherman and Hauser (1976a, b) for a bibliography and their report of a replication of the Blau–Duncan study.

4 The small standard deviations for JOB1 and the low explanatory power of the JOB1 equations for both rural groups support this interpretation.

Chapter 3 Education and career beginnings

1 Men who entered secondary school on or before their twelfth birthday at a time when five years of secondary schooling was the norm for matriculation in some Australian States could have matriculated while they were still aged fifteen.

2 An attempt to include both SED and SED sq. in the same model produced a singular matrix and the coefficient could not be estimated. The correlation between the two terms was 0·99.

Chapter 4   Careers and career contingencies

1 An experimental analysis treating their job at time of interview as if it were the job ten years after their first job had no measurable effect on the general results.

2 The decline in farm jobs does not counterbalance the increase in professional jobs because most job entrants in the rural sector were coded as farm workers rather than farmers. Ten years later most farm entrants were either employed as farmers or had left farming altogether, and so are coded as mobile in either case (see Figure 4.9).

3 This is the only instance where both a father and his son were respondents in the survey; they lived in separate houses, but in a sample block where every dwelling was included.

4 The ratio of observed percentages in a particular cell of a given row to the percentage in the comparable cell for the total sample.

Chapter 5   Status and income

1 To retain maximum information, Tables 5.2–5.9 include all economically active males who reported data on the relevant variables.

Chapter 6   Status attainment over three generations

1 The price of assuming greater measurement error in paternal grandparental statuses is the concession that education depends less on family background now than a generation ago. So far as specification error is concerned, it is true that maternal grandparental statuses probably also have some additional effects, but because like tend to marry like their inclusion would not even double the explanatory power of such variables because of analytic redundancy. Dynastic marriages may still occur among the very wealthy, but if such marriages were at all frequent in the rest of the population, the dummy variable representing high status origins should come into play. It does not.

2 For the example of Australian Aborigines, see Broom and Jones (1973, pp. 4–7).

Bibliography

ALEXANDER, KARL L., and ECKLAND, BRUCE K. (1975), 'Basic attainment processes: a replication and extension', *Sociology of Education*, 48 (Fall): 457–95.

ALEXANDER, KARL L., ECKLAND, BRUCE K., and GRIFFIN, LARRY J. (1975), 'The Wisconsin model of socioeconomic attainment: a replication', *American Journal of Sociology*, 81 (September): 324–42.

ALLISON, PAUL D. (1977), 'Testing for interaction in multiple regression', *American Journal of Sociology*, 83 (July): 144–53.

ALTHAUSER, ROBERT P. (1971), 'Multicollinearity and non-additive regression models', in Blalock, Hubert M., Jr (ed.), *Causal Models in the Social Sciences*, Aldine Atherton, Chicago, pp. 453–72.

ALWIN, DUANE F., and HAUSER, ROBERT M. (1975), 'The decomposition of effects in path analysis', *American Sociological Review*, 40 (February): 37–47.

ARROW, K. J. (1973), 'Higher education as a filter', *Journal of Public Economics*, 2: 193–216.

AUSTRALIA, BUREAU OF CENSUS AND STATISTICS (1971a), *Classification and Classified List of Occupations, 1971*, Government Printer, Canberra.

—— (1971b), *Industry Classification: Division, Sub-Division, Group and Class Titles*, Commonwealth Bureau of Census and Statistics, Canberra.

AUSTRALIAN BUREAU OF STATISTICS (1976), *Income Distribution 1973–1974*, Australian Bureau of Statistics, Canberra (Ref. no. 17.6).

AUSTRALIAN GOVERNMENT COMMISSION OF INQUIRY INTO POVERTY (1975), *Poverty in Australia* (First Main Report), 2 vols, AGPS, Canberra.

AUSTRALIAN POPULATION AND IMMIGRATION COUNCIL (1976), *A Decade of Migrant Settlement: Report on the 1973 Immigration Survey* (prepared by the Social Studies Committee, Chairman J. I. Martin), AGPS, Canberra.

BECKER, G. S. (1964), *Human Capital*, National Bureau of Economic Research, Columbia University Press.

185

BIBLIOGRAPHY

—— (1972), 'Schooling and inequality from generation to generation: comment', *Journal of Political Economy*, 80 (May–June): S252–5.

BERG, IVAR (1970), *Education and Jobs: the Great Training Robbery*, Penguin Education, London.

BIELBY, WILLIAM T., HAUSER, ROBERT M., and FEATHERMAN, DAVID L. (1977), 'Response errors of black and nonblack males in models of the inter-generational transmission of socioeconomic status', *American Journal of Sociology*, 82 (May): 1242–88.

BLAU, PETER M., and DUNCAN, OTIS D. (1967), *The American Occupational Structure*, Wiley, New York.

BOTTENBERG, ROBERT A., and WARD, JOE H., JR (1963), Applied Multiple Linear Regression (Technical Documentary Report PRL–TDR–63–6, Lackland Air Force Base, Texas, Air Force Systems Command).

BOTTOMORE, T. B. (1965), *Classes in Modern Society*, Allen & Unwin, London.

BOWLES, SAMUEL (1972), 'Schooling and inequality from generation to generation', *Journal of Political Economy*, 80 (May–June): S219–51.

BOWLES, S., and GINTIS, H. (1976), *Schooling in Capitalist America: Educational Reform and the Contradictions of Economic Life*, Basic Books, New York; Routledge & Kegan Paul, London.

BRITTAIN, J. A. (1977), *The Inheritance of Economic Status*, Brookings Institution, Washington.

BROOM, LEONARD, and CUSHING, R. G. (1977), 'A modest test of an immodest theory: the functional theory of stratification', *American Sociological Review*, 42 (February): 147–69.

07BROOM, LEONARD, and JONES, F. LANCASTER (1969a), 'Father-to-son mobility: Australia in comparative perspective', *American Journal of Sociology*, 74 (January): 333–42.

—— (1969b), 'Career mobility in three societies: Australia, Italy, and the United States', *American Sociological Review*, 34 (October): 650–8.

—— (1973), *A Blanket a Year*, ANU Press, Canberra.

—— (1976), *Opportunity and Attainment in Australia*, ANU Press; Stanford University Press.

BROOM, LEONARD, and McDONNELL, PATRICK (1974/7), 'Current research on social mobility: an inventory', *Current Sociology*, 22: 353–91.

BROOM, LEONARD, DUNCAN-JONES, PAUL, JONES, F. LANCASTER, and McDONNELL, PATRICK (1977a), *Investigating Social Mobility*, Department of Sociology, RSSS, Australian National University, Canberra (Departmental Monograph no. 1).

—— (1977b), 'The social standing of jobs: scores for all Australian occupations', *Social Science Research*, 6 (September): 211–24.

—— (1977c), 'Worker traits and worker functions in DOT', *Journal of Vocational Behavior*, 11 (October): 129–52.

—— (1978a), 'Two perspectives on social mobility', in Wesolowski, W. (ed.), *Social Mobility in Comparative Perspective*, Polish Academy of Sciences, Warsaw, pp. 131–58.

—— (1978b), 'Is it true what they say about daddy?' *American Journal of Sociology*, 84 (September): 417–26.

CAIN, G. G. (1976), 'The challenge of segmented labor market theories to orthodox theory: a survey', *Journal of Economic Literature*, 14: (December): 1215-57.

CARLSSON. GOSTA (1958), *Social Mobility and Class Structure*, Gleerup, Lund.

CARNOY. MARTIN (1974), *Education as Cultural Imperialism*, David McKay, New York.

CONNELL. R. W. (1977), *Ruling Class, Ruling Culture: Studies of Conflict, Power and Hegemony in Australian Life*, Cambridge University Press.

CONNELL. W. F., STROOBANT. R. E., SINCLAIR. K. W., CONNELL. R. W., and ROGERS. K. W. (1975), *12 to 20: Studies of Youth*, Hicks Smith, Sydney.

COOLEY. CHARLES HORTON (1918), *Social Process*, Scribner's, New York.

DIGMAN. J. M. (1966), 'Interaction and non-linearity in multivariate experiment', in Cattell, R. B. (ed.), *Handbook of Multivariate Experimental Psychology*, Rand McNally, Chicago, pp. 459-75.

DOERINGER. P. B., and PIORE. M. J. 09(1971). *Internal Labor Markets and Manpower Analysis*, Heath, Lexington, Mass.

DUNCAN. OTIS DUDLEY (1961), 'A socioeconomic index for all occupations', in Reiss, Albert J., Jr (ed.), *Occupations and Social Status*, Free Press, New York, pp. 109-38.

—— (1968), 'Ability and achievement', *Eugenics Quarterly*, 15 (March): 1-11.

DUNCAN. O. D., FEATHERMAN. DAVID L., and DUNCAN. BEVERLEY (1972), *Socioeconomic Background and Achievement*, Seminar Press: New York.

ECKLAND. BRUCE K. (1967), 'Genetics and sociology: a reconsideration', *American Sociological Review*, 32 (April): 173-94.

EMERY. F. E., and PHILLIPS. C. (1976), *Living at Work: a 1973 Study for the Australian Minister for Labor and Immigration of the Urban Workforce, Its Attitudes to Work and Matters Influencing these Attitudes*, AGPS, Canberra.

EZEKIEL. M., and FOX. K. A. (1967), *Methods of Correlation and Regression Analysis*, Wiley, New York.

FÄGERLIND. INGEMAR (1975), *Formal Education and Adult Earnings*, Almqvist & Wiksell, Stockholm.

FAIRLEY. WILLIAM B., and MOSTELLER. FREDERICK (eds) (1977), *Statistics and Public Policy*, Addison-Wesley, Reading, Mass.

FEATHERMAN. DAVID L. (1971), 'A research note: a social structural model for the socioeconomic career', *American Journal of Sociology*, 77 (September): 293-304.

FEATHERMAN. DAVID L., and HAUSER. ROBERT M. (1973), 'On the measurement of occupations in social surveys', *Sociological Methods and Research*, 2 (November): 239-51.

—— (1975), 'Design for a replicate study of social mobility in the United States', in Land, Kenneth C., and Spilerman, Seymour (eds), *Social Indicator Models*, Russell Sage Foundation, New York, pp. 219-51.

—— (1976a), 'Sexual inequalities and socioeconomic achievement in the U.S., 1962-1973', *American Sociological Review*, 41 (June): 462-83.

—— (1976b), 'Changes in the socioeconomic stratification of the races, 1962-1973', *American Journal of Sociology*, 82 (November): 621-51.

BIBLIOGRAPHY

—— (1978), *Opportunity and Change*, Academic Press, New York.

FORD, G. W. (1970), 'Work', in Davies, A. F., and Encel, S. (eds), *Australian Society: an Introduction*, Cheshire, Melbourne, 2nd ed., pp. 84–145.

GIROD, ROBERT, PRILE, GIANNI, 09and WEISS, PIERRE (1977), 'The other road: the role of vocational training in the process of achievement', paper presented at ISA Stratification Research Committee meeting, Dublin (April).

GLASS, D. V. (ed.) (1954), *Social Mobility in Britain*, Routledge & Kegan Paul, London.

GOLDBERGER, ARTHUR S., 09and DUNCAN, OTIS DUDLEY (eds) (1973), *Structural Equation Models in the Social Sciences*, Seminar Press, New York.

GOLDTHORPE, J. H., and 07HOPE, K. (1972), 'Occupational grading and occupational prestige', in Hope, K. (ed.), *The Analysis of Social Mobility: Methods and Approaches* (Oxford Studies in Social Mobility), Clarendon Press, pp. 19–79.

GRANOVETTER, MARK S. (1974), *Getting a Job*, Harvard University Press.

GRIFFIN, LARRY (1976), 'Specification biases in estimates of socioeconomic returns to schooling', *Sociology of Education*, 49 (April): 121–39.

GRILICHES, ZVI, and MASON, WILLIAM M. (1973), 'Education, income and ability', in Goldberger, Arthur S., and Duncan, Otis Dudley (eds), *Structural Equation Models in the Social Sciences*, pp. 285–316.

GUJARATI, DAMODAR (1970), 'Use of dummy variables in testing for equality between sets of coefficients in linear regressions: a generalization', *American Statistician*, 24 (December): 18–22.

HALLER, A. O. (1970), 'Changes in the structure of status systems', *Rural Sociology*, 35 (December): 469–87.

HALLER, A. O., and PORTES, A. (1973), 'Status attainment processes', *Sociology of Education*, 46 (winter): 51–91.

HECKMAN, J., and POLACHEK, S. (1974), 'Empirical evidence on the functional form of the earnings-schooling relationship', *Journal of the American Statistical Association*, 69 (June): 350–4.

HEYNS, BARBARA (1978), Review essay of Bowles and Gintis, *Schooling in Capitalist America*, *American Journal of Sociology*, 83 (January): 999–1006.

HIGLEY, J., DEACON, D. and SMART, D. (1979), *Elites in Australia*, Routledge & Kegan Paul, London.

HILL, T. P. (1959), 'An analysis of wages and salaries in Great Britain', *Econometrica*, 27: 355–76.

JACKSON, ELTON F., and BURKE, PETER J. (1965), 'Status and symptoms of stress: additive and interactive effects', *American Sociological Review*, 30 (August): 556–64.

JENCKS, CHRISTOPHER, et al. (1972), *Inequality: a Reassessment of the Effect of Family and Schooling in America*, Basic Books, New York; Penguin Books, London.

JONES, F. LANCASTER (1975), 'Measures of father-to-son mobility: a liberal or radical criterion of evaluation?', *Quality and Quantity*, 9: 361–9.

KARMEL, PETER H. (1976), 'Some arithmetic of education', in Harman,

G. S., and Selby Smith, C. (eds), *Readings in the Economics and Politics of Australian Education*, Pergamon Press, Sydney, pp. 148–61.

KATZ, MICHAEL B. (1971), *Class, Bureaucracy, and Schools*, Praeger, New York.

KELLEY, JONATHAN (1973a), 'Causal chain models for the socioeconomic career', *American Sociological Review*, 38 (August): 481–93.

—— (1973b), 'History, causal chains and careers: a reply', *American Sociological Review*, 38 (December): 791–6.

LAKATOS, IMRE (1970), 'Falsification and the methodology of scientific research programmes', in Lakatos, Imre, and Musgrave, Alan (eds), *Criticism and the Growth of Knowledge*, Cambridge University Press, pp. 91–195.

LANE, ANGELA (1968), 'Occupational mobility in six cities', *American Sociological Review*, 33 (October): 740–9.

—— (1975), 'The occupational achievement process, 1940–1949: a cohort analysis', *American Sociological Review*, 40 (August): 472–82.

LEIBOWITZ, ARLEEN (1977), 'Family background and economic success: a review of the evidence', in Taubman, Paul (ed.), *Kinometrics: Determinants of Socioeconomic Success Within and Between Families*, North-Holland, Amsterdam, pp. 9–33.

LEWIS, OSCAR (1968), 'The culture of poverty', in Moynihan, Daniel P. (ed.), *On Understanding Poverty*, Basic Books, New York, pp. 187–200.

LOPREATO, JOSEPH, and HAZELRIGG, LAWRENCE E. (1972), *Class, Conflict, and Mobility*, Chandler, San Francisco.

MCLAREN, JOHN (1968), *Our Troubled Schools*, Cheshire, Melbourne.

MARTIN, JEAN I. (1972), Migrants: Equality and Ideology, Meredith Memorial Lecture, La Trobe University, Melbourne.

MEADE, J. E. (1973), 'The inheritance of inequalities: some biological, demographic, social, and economic factors', *Proceedings of the British Academy*, 49: 355–81.

MINCER, JACOB (1974), *Schooling, Experience, and Earnings*, National Bureau of Economic Research, New York.

MUKHERJEE, RAMKRISHNA (1954), 'A study of social mobility between three generations', in Glass, D. V. (ed.), *Social Mobility in Britain*, pp. 266–87.

MÜLLER, WALTER (1973), 'Family background, education, and career mobility', in Müller, Walter, and Mayer, Karl U. (eds), *Social Stratification and Career Mobility*, Mouton, The Hague, pp. 223–55.

—— (1977), 'Further education, division of labour and equality of opportunity', *Social Science Information*, 16: 527–56.

NUTTALL, DESMOND L. (1975), 'Examinations in education', in Cox, Peter R., Miles, H. B., and Peel, John (eds), *Equalities and Inequalities in Education*, Academic Press, London, pp. 67–77.

OLNECK, MICHAEL R. (1976), 'The effects of education on occupational status and earnings', Discussion Paper 358–76. University of Michigan Institute for Research on Poverty, Madison.

ORNSTEIN, MICHAEL D. (1976), *Entry into the American Labor Force*, Academic Press, New York.

189

BIBLIOGRAPHY

PONTINEN, SEPPO, and UUSITALO, HANNU (1975), 'Socioeconomic background and income', *Acta Sociologica*, 18: 322–9.

RIST, RAY C. (1973), *The Urban School: a Factory for Failure*, MIT Press.

ROBINSON, ROBERT V., and KELLEY, JONATHAN (1979), 'Class as conceived by Marx and Dahrendorf', *American Sociological Review*, 44 (February): 38–58.

ROGOFF, NATALIE (1953), *Recent Trends in Occupational Mobility*, Free Press, Chicago.

ROONEY, C. B. (1966), *Choosing Your Career: Advice to School-leavers and Their Parents*, Ure Smith, Sydney.

RUBINSTEIN, W. D. (1979), 'The distribution of personal wealth in Victoria, 1860–1974', *Australian Economic History Review*, 19 (in press).

SAHOTA, GIAN SINGH (1978), 'Theories of personal income distribution: a survey', *Journal of Economic Literature*, 16 (March): 1–55.

SAMUELSON, PAUL A., HANCOCK, KEITH, and WALLACE, ROBERT (1973), *Economics*, McGraw Hill, Sydney (2nd Australian ed.).

SCHULTZ, T. W. (1961), 'Investment in human capital', *American Economic Review*, 51 (March): 1–17.

SEWELL, WILLIAM H., HALLER, ARCHIBALD O., and PORTES, ALEJANDRO (1969), 'The educational and early occupational attainment process', *American Sociological Review*, 34 (February): 82–92.

SEWELL, WILLIAM H., HALLER, ARCHIBALD O., and OHLENDORF, GEORGE W. (1970), 'The educational and early occupational status attainment process: replication and revision', *American Sociological Review*, 35 (December): 1014–27.

SEWELL, WILLIAM H., and HAUSER, ROBERT M. (1972), 'Causes and consequences of higher education: models of the status attainment process', *American Journal of Agricultural Economics*, 54 (December): 851–61.

—— (1975), *Education, Occupation, and Earnings*, Academic Press, New York.

SMITH, CYRIL, CARSWELL, R. W., ELTHAM, E. P., BEST, KATHLEEN, MILLS, R. C., and WILSON, R. C. (n.d.), *Repatriation and Rehabilitation*, Australasian Publishing Co., Sydney.

SORENSEN, AAGE, B. (1974), 'A model for occupational careers', *American Journal of Sociology*, 80 (July): 44–57.

—— (1975) 'Growth in occupational achievement: social mobility or investment in human capital', in Land, Kenneth C., and Spilerman, Seymour (eds), *Social Indicator Models*, Russell Sage Foundation, New York, pp. 335–65.

—— (1976) 'Models and strategies in research on attainment and opportunity', *Social Science Information*, 15: 71–91.

SOROKIN, PITIRIM A. (1927), *Social Mobility*, Harper, New York.

SPAETH, J. L. (1977), 'Differences in the occupational achievement process between male and female college graduates', *Sociology of Education*, 50 (July): 206–17.

SPECHT, DAVID A., and WARREN, RICHARD D. (1976), 'Comparing causal models', in Heise, David R. (ed.), *Sociological Methodology 1976*, Jossey Bass, San Francisco, pp. 46–82.

STOLZENBERG. ROSS M. (1974), 'Estimating an equation with multiplicative and additive terms, with an application to analysis of wage differentials between men and women in 1960', *Sociological Methods and Research*, 2 (February): 313–31.

—— (1975a), 'Education, occupation, and wage differences between white and black men', *American Journal of Sociology*, 81 (September): 299–323.

—— (1975b), 'Occupations, labor markets and the process of wage attainment', *American Sociological Review*, 40 (October): 645–65.

SVALASTOGA. KAARE (1959), *Prestige, Class and Mobility*, Glydendal, Copenhagen.

—— (1973), 'Measurement of responsibility', in Müller, W., and Mayer, K. U. (eds), *Social Stratification and Career Mobility*, Mouton, The Hague, pp. 75–85.

SWEETSER. DORRIAN APPLE. and MCDONNELL. PATRICK (1978), 'Social origins, education and fraternal mobility', *American Journal of Sociology*, 83 (January): 975–82.

THUROW. LESTER C. (1975), *Generating Inequality: Mechanisms of Distribution in the U.S. Economy*, Basic Books, New York.

THUROW. LESTER C., and LUCAS. ROBERT E. B. (1972), *The American Distribution of Income: a Structural Problem*, Government Printer (Joint Economic Committee, 92nd Congress), Washington.

TREIMAN. DONALD J. (1977), *Occupational Prestige in Comparative Perspective*, Academic Press, New York.

WELCH. F. (1973), 'Black-white differences in returns to schooling', *American Economic Review*, 63 (December): 893–907.

WESOLOWSKI. W. (1979), *Classes, Strata and Power*, Routledge & Kegan Paul, London (first published in Warsaw in 1966).

WILLIAMS. T., MCDONNELL. P., JONES. F. L., (09and BROOM. L. (1977), 'Public and private: school system effects on social and economic attainments in Australia', paper presented to annual conference of Australian Association for Research in Education, Canberra (November).

WINSBOROUGH. H. H. (1975), 'Age, period, cohort, and education effects on earnings by race', in Land, Kenneth C., and Spilerman, Seymour (eds), *Social Indicator Models*, Russell Sage Foundation, New York, pp. 201–17.

WRIGHT. ERIK OLIN. and PERRONE. LUCA (1977), 'Marxist class categories and income inequality', *American Sociological Review*, 42 (February): 32–55.

Index

For Product Safety Concerns and Information please contact our EU
representative GPSR@taylorandfrancis.com
Taylor & Francis Verlag GmbH, Kaufingerstraße 24, 80331 München, Germany

www.ingramcontent.com/pod-product-compliance
Lightning Source LLC
Chambersburg PA
CBHW050439280326
41932CB00013BA/2179